WRITERS, EDITORS AND REFORMERS

Social and Political Transformations of Maharashtra, 1830-1930

SOUTH ASIA INSTITUTE, NEW DELHI BRANCH
HEIDELBERG UNIVERSITY
SOUTH ASIAN STUDIES NO. XXXIV

WRITERS, EDITORS AND REFORMERS

Social and Political Transformations of Maharashtra, 1830-1930

Edited by

N. K. WAGLE

MANOHAR
1999

First published 1999

ISBN 81-7304-214-4

Published by
Ajay Kumar Jain for
Manohar Publishers & Distributors
2/6, Ansari Road, Daryaganj
New Delhi 110002

Typeset by
A J Software Publishing Co. Pvt. Ltd.
305, Durga Chambers,
1333, D.B. Gupta Road,
Karol Bagh, New Delhi 110005

Printed at
Rajkamal Electric Press
B 35/9 G T Karnal Road Indl Area
Delhi 110033

FOR

GÜNTHER-DEITZ SONTHEIMER

(1934–92)

Contents

Introduction

The chapters in the book emphasize the political and social transformations in Maharashtrian society brought about by the efforts of reformers, editors and writers of Maharashtra roughly from 1830 to 1930. The chapters of Jayant Lele, Rajendra Vora, Uttam Bhoite and Enrico Fasana deal with the transformations of political ideologies and practices from the late nineteenth to the mid twentieth centuries. Jayant Lele focuses on the growth of the non-Brahman movement in western Maharashtra from the effective control of the Brahman Peshwas to the emergence of Congress as a ruling party in Maharashtra, dominated by the Maratha elite. Lele suggests that the anti-Brahmanism of the Maratha elite leaders prevented radical movements from taking roots among dispossessed Maratha Kunbi labourers, artisans and dalit workers. Rajendra Vora describes the history of *Maharashtra Dharma*, a political concept linked with regional and national unity, from its beginning in the seventeenth to the early twentieth centuries. *Maharashtra Dharma* in the twentieth century, according to Vora, was appropriated by leaders with different political ideologies such as Lokamanya Tilak, a Hindu nationalist, Vinoba Bhave, a disciple of Mahatma Gandhi, and Maharaja Shahu of Kolhapur, a political conservative and a social reformer. Uttam Bhoite analyses the roots of untouchable liberation movement in Vidharba region of Maharashtra. He contends that Babasaheb Ambedkar built on the earlier efforts of leaders like G.K. Walunkar, S.J. Kamble and V.R. Moon Pande who had successfully launched their campaign against the 'touchable' Hindus of Maharashtra. In his seminal contribution, E. Fasana examines the influence of *Resorgimento*, the Italian nationalist movement as led by Mazzini, Garibaldi and Cavour, on the nationalist ideology of *Hindutva* and *Hindupadpadshahi* of Maharashtrian leaders like N.C. Kelkar and V.D. Savarkar.

It seems that the mid-nineteenth century Marathi periodicals and English newspapers had undertaken a mission to transform ideas and thoughts of their Indian and Maharashtrian readers. J.V. Naik, Milton Israel and Aroon Tikekar examine the impact of editors in analysing the changing nature of Indian society under British rule. Bhau Mahajan, the subject of J.V. Naik's study, while appreciating the British rule, at times offered stinging criticism of the British policies in India. As Naik puts it, Bhau published radical reformist articles by Lokahitvadi and others, and endorsed the reforms himself by writing caustic editorials in his *Prabhakar*. Milton Israel closely studies the Indian daily, the *Bombay Chronicle*, owned by Indians, that articulated the complexities of Indian nationalists viewpoints from 1920-30. According to Israel, B.G. Horniman,

Marmaduke Pickthall and S.A. Brelvi, the editors of *Bombay Chronicle* from 1920-30, brought with them their sympathetic understanding of Indian nationalism. Aroon Tikekar analyses the controversial career of George Buist, the editor of *Bombay Times* from 1840-57, who championed the civil rights of Indians and endorsed India's economic and industrial growth. However, Buist virtually turned a racist, condemning and ridiculing Indians in his editorials with the outbreak of the 1857 rebellion, which led to his removal from the job.

The influence of Western medicine, science, history and literature on Maharashtrian intellectuals is analysed in the essays of J. Masselos, R.N. Dandekar and Philip Engblom. Masselos clarifies the early nineteenth century efforts of the British administrators to transform Indian traditional views of science and medicine to Western ones. He demonstrates that there was a sufficient intellectual curiosity found among Indians who were prone to accept Western science, and could in fact excel in it. But the discourse between the Indians who received Western scientific knowledge and the British who gave access to it, was unequal according to Masselos. In his biographical sketch of R.G. Bhandarkar, R.N. Dandekar credits the former with 'academic renaissance' for introducing the study of Indology and history of India on a late nineteenth century European model. Unlike the European Orientalists, Dandekar states, Bhadarkar genuinely took pride in India's contribution to world knowledge in Sanskrit literature and language. Philip Engblom surveys the nineteenth century Marathi poetry, which, he says, was heavily influenced by classical Sanskrit tradition. Engblom argues that pioneering efforts of Vishnu Moreshwar Mahajani's lyric poems, specially the sonnet, were explicit adaptations of the English poems. Engblom argues that, although such adaptations were devoid of originality and flair, they laid the foundation of original modern poetry in Marathi.

The essays by I.M.P. Raeside, Pratibha Bhattacharya, H. Kotani, Meera Kosambi and N.K. Wagle deal with the social reformers of late nineteenth and early twentieth centuries Maharashtra. On reformers' agenda were: women's education, women's welfare, widow remarriages, eradication of the shortcomings of the *jati* institution, and general reform of Hindu law and customs. Gopal Ganesh Agarkar is regarded as the Dean of Maharashtrian reformers and the ideas of Hari Narayan Apte and Lokahitvadi are measured in relation to the standards set by Agarkar. For Baba Padmanji and Pundita Ramabai the reform of Hindu society necessitated conversion to Christianity. Govind Babaji Joshi pursued his reformist convictions by marrying his daughters outside his caste.

I.M.P. Raeside investigates the reformist impulses found in the novels of Hari Narayan Apte. Raeside calls Apte a 'closet reformer' and substantiates his arguments through Apte's correspondence with the husband-wife team of Kanitkars, who were his personal friends and associates in a Marathi magazine *Manoranjan*. Pratibha Bhattacharya's essay praises Agarkar's bold and up front views advocating reforms in Maharashtra. However, Bhattacharya charges Lokahitvadi with duplicity concerning the criticism he leveled against Hindu customs and institutional mores. H. Kotani discusses the options available to the new intellectuals of Maharashtra who responded to the Western ideas. Kotani notes the inner struggles of Baba Padmanji which ultimately led him to reject Hinduism and accept Christianity. Meera Kosambi's chapter deals with Pandita Ramabai, a Christian convert from Hinduism, whose lifetime mission was to improve the lot of women and widows of Maharashtra. Despite the tirade of criticism from the likes of Lokamanya Tilak, Ramabai's advocacy of woman's rights and eradication of prejudices of Hindu society were backed up by her practical efforts at establishing schools and sanctuaries for women. N.K. Wagle examines the views of the late nineteenth century Maharashtrian Brahman, Govind Babaji Joshi, who married his daughter to a man outside his Chitpavan *jati*. His convictions, and the personal, social and political context within which he promoted inter-caste marriage, reveal the struggles of the Maharashtrian intellectuals wanting change in their *jati* institution.

I gratefully acknowledge the help given by late Ms Stephanie Zingel-Ave Lallemant, in-charge of publications, South Asia Institute, University of Heidelberg in editing this volume. I am thankful to the Publication Committee of the South Asia Institute who accepted the manuscript of this book for publication in their New Delhi series. My thanks are due to Mr Ramesh Jain of Manohar who took personal interest in making editorial recommendations and expediting the publication. Most of the chapters which appear in this book were originally presented at the International Conference on Maharashtrian Culture and Society held at the University of Heidelberg in 1989. The chapters were subsequently revised by the authors. Professor Günther-Deitz Sontheimer (1934-92) had handed over the chapters to me for editing it as a book. His passing away meant a great personal loss to me and to his friends. This book is dedicated to him for his uncompromising scholarship.

Toronto N.K. WAGLE
August 1998

From Reformism to Interest Group Pluralism: The Relevance of the Non-Brahman Movement for an Understanding of Contemporary Maharashtra

JAYANT K. LELE

Much literature exists on the non-Brahman movement in Maharashtra, but attempts to locate its dynamics and its transitions in the changing political economy of colonial India do not seem to have been particularly productive. I wish to explore that relationship, the relationship between ideas and the changing material conditions of Maharashtra, in a preliminary way.

A hundred and fifty years of colonial rule brought about major changes in Maharashtrian society. The response of the indigenous society to the inroads of a capitalist economy was a complex mixture of resilience, continuity and change. In many ways the transition was slow. It gave the old order an opportunity to adapt gradually to the new world. In the rural areas, despite cataclysmic changes for some, the ruling classes were able to retain the *fiction* of the community, while at the same time the *jat-vatan-gaon* social relations of production were yielding to the new administrative arrangements. The rise of cash crop farming, mainly cotton for the world market, had its impact on the production of most other crops, and on the social structure of rural India (Banaji 1978). So did the new land revenue systems, the rise of administrative and marketing towns, and the introduction of administrative-judicial institutions. The entire colonial experience can be divided into three periods: Company Rule, Colonial Parliamentary Raj, and (for want of a better label), the period of the emergence of the Congress Party as 'the Government in waiting'. In this paper I propose to focus primarily on the second of these periods.

The arrival of Company Raj in Maharashtra was preceded by the rule of the Peshwas, during which a Chitpavan Brahman family, having usurped actual power from the house of Shivaji, had established the Maratha confederacy. Despite dramatic military and diplomatic successes, the centre of the confederacy operated with minimal legitimacy. The feudatories of the regime, old and new, Maratha and Brahman, collected revenue and took part in the wars of contending Muslim nobles as paid partisans, often on their own initiative and without any reference to the centre. The Brahman Peshwas were treated with well-deserved suspicion by the older Maratha chiefs and the newly created Brahman feudatories, mostly Chitpavans, do not seem to have had a tradition of caste or state loyalty. The major contribution of this period seems to have been, in fact, the unfolding of a nascent national consciousness, *Maharashtra Dharma*, which had been strenuously nurtured by Shivaji, from its authentic and popular roots dating back to the days of early Varkari *sants* (Lele 1980).

The regime of the Peshwas prepared Maharashtra for a relatively smooth British takeover. It brought into the open the often hidden conception that the legitimacy of the state is primarily dependent on the efficient delivery of a modicum of well-being to its citizens. The norms arising from shared world-views, which Shivaji had tried to cultivate during his short but effective rule, were replaced by a predisposition to bargaining and competitive power play between the rulers and the dominant elites, something that the representatives of 'the nation of shopkeepers' were to find much easier to live with. It is not surprising, therefore, that the Peshwas were paid in their own currency by their Chitpavan and Maratha *sardars*, once the cement of power and patronage dissolved during the incompetent reign of Bajirao II.

While the Peshwa interlude, and the special advantage it conferred on the members of their caste, are generally known, scholars describing subsequent attempts at political mobilization of non-Brahmans have not fully explored their significance. There has been a tendency to exaggerate the extent of the Brahman domination of rural Maharashtra, and to misunderstand their traditional place in the socio-polity of the region in rigid *varnashrama* terms. The *peshwai* contributed significantly to the later tension between Chitpavans and the local Maratha-Kunbi elites. It also placed the *deshastha*-Brahmans in a dilemma by trying to gain their loyalty through grants and privileges for the display of Brahman erudition. On the whole, it led to the widening of the gap between Brahmans on the one hand and all the others, summarily lumped together as Shudras in the elite *peshwai* conception. A gulf separating the idols of worship and the forms of entertainment of the Brahman elite from those of the local masses became blatantly apparent when massive state patronage was channeled to those in charge of the former. Chitpavans had failed to create for themselves a place and a sense of belonging with the people over whom they ruled as administrators, diplomats and feudal lords.

By far the most damaging legacy of the Peshwas, and the one that contributed the most to the resentment of the local and regional Maratha elites towards Brahmans (primarily Chitpavans), was the decay of a cultural tradition that had been shared by the masses across caste boundaries. During the Peshwa regime the leadership of the Varkari tradition was taken over by Brahman organizers, and its message was reinterpreted and delivered by Brahman mendicants and storytellers (*katha* and *keertan* performers). It was employed to encourage fatalism and to justify the *varnashrama* hierarchy. Even earlier Ramdas' (1608-81) militant political nationalism had become a vehicle for the glorification of Maratha-Brahman dominance. Through the exercise of state power this was also nurtured effectively by Shivaji. Ramdas declared the *varnashrama* order divine and hence eternally valid. The prospect of equating *Maharashtra Dharma* with *varnashramadharma* was first visualized in this period. The authenticity and robustness of the Marathi *sant* literature, characteristic even of Ramdas, declined and was replaced under the official encouragement by the Peshwas of an artificially Sanskritized idiom and by the hollow acrobatics of *pandit* poetry. A wide gulf came to separate genuine folk literature from the literary atavisms of elite Brahmans. This cultural decay was accompanied by the hypocrisy of rituals and orthodoxy.

Like the preceding *Peshwai* period, Company Rule was a period of transition, towards full incorporation into the world capitalist system. The Peshwas' territory was not a major hinterland for the Company's exports out of Surat and Mumbai. Not much was to change in that respect during the first phase of colonial expansion. As Stokes (1978: 28) points out, the purpose of the Company's regime 'remained mercantilist, to using surplus from the Indian revenue sufficient to purchase its annual investment of Indian goods and . . . supply the silver required by the Canton treasury for the China tea trade'. In Maharashtra, except for some streamlining of the revenue administration, and the consequent enhancement of the efficiency of tax collection, nothing substantial was attempted in terms of capitalist development.

In the city of Mumbai, however, it was a different story. The decline of demand in Europe for goods out of Surat led to the eventual fall of that port. A purely trading centre, Mumbai began to thrive. The shift to raw cotton and the end of the Company's trade monopoly brought more and more traders to town. The annexation of Peshwa territory allowed its wealth to be directed to the rapid promotion of this commercial centre into the political capital of western India. Its administrative, maritime and mercantile establishments were quickly and visibly spruced up after 1818. With its new role as the administrative centre of Bombay Presidency, its need for an 'educated' and disciplined cadre of men to work at the lower and middle levels of the state apparatus was immediately felt. Both the state and the Christian missionaries (who were permitted to be openly active in the city after 1814) responded. Several educational institutions emerged between 1815 and 1850 (e.g. the Bombay Native Education Society), leading in 1857 to the establishment of the University (Masselos 1974; Kosambi 1980).

Unlike other British factory towns, Mumbai had been forced to attract merchants and workers from Surat, on their own terms, during the early period of its growth. The open and relatively egalitarian interaction between the English, the merchants of various castes and faiths and the new professionals was perhaps responsible for the type of enlightened reformism that first arose in this city. The most significant feature of this reformism was a strong reflexive-hermeneutic orientation to religion. Along with this surfaced a new fusion of ideas about a new normative and political order. The reformists refused to merely accept or reject the old, or the new, order out of expediency or emotion. They tried to develop a critical understanding of the past, out of which emerged the dream of an all-encompassing, humane religion and a just society. These universalistic tendencies, which guided the early Marathi intellectual enlightenment, were later misrepresented and misunderstood (Bedekar 1977).

As a poor Chitpavan, without a place in the traditional *jati* hierarchy, M.G. Ranade (1842-1902) symbolized the new breed of Brahman intellectuals. The 'new Brahmans' had the difficult task of explaining the benefits of colonial rule to the people and to themselves, as agents of alien forces that had begun (by 1850) to restructure the economic and political order. In that coming restructuring the early intellectuals expected to play an active role. With English higher education restricted to a small group, they saw themselves as interpreters and transmitters of the best in the European and Indian traditions. With training in a variety of disciplines, such as literature, law, medicine, and civil engineering, they hoped to be able to occupy most of the crucial positions in the state, thus setting the direction for the modernization of the entire nation.

British racism and the compulsions of the crisis of British capitalism had yet to hit the political economy with their full force. Ranade's universalistic interpretations of the past were the outcome of the optimism natural to a Chitpavan alienated from the society which men of his caste had once ruled with impudence. A counter to that interpretation, equally universalistic in its intentions but with an authentic appeal to those at the receiving end of Brahman oppression, was provided by Jyotiba Phule (1827-90). During the second phase of colonialism both these critical impulses were reappropriated by the rising urban petit bourgeoisie and the established Maratha-Kunbi peasantry for their own ends.

The first phase of colonialism died with the Company Raj. The second phase began with the Government of India becoming directly responsible to the Crown. This, in a sense, marked the triumph of industrial capital in England. During the first half of the nineteenth century, as Britain gained unmatched supremacy in capitalist industrialization and commercial growth, her empire underwent substantial territorial expansion. The conquest of the Peshwa and allied territories was but an insignificant piece in that overall development. In terms of the economic demands of England's capitalism raw cotton, instead of manufactured textiles, had become one of the major items of import by the beginning of the century. The growing English textile industry depended on American raw cotton and until 1846, when the failure of the American crop alerted it to the instability of that source, there had been little interest in systematically organizing the widely scattered cotton production and trade of Maharashtra.

During these years the general expansion of educational institutions had taken place largely due to the efforts of the Brahman elite. More and more young men, mostly Brahmans, were now seeking employment with the government, and in industry, where some additional employment (white collar) opportunities had emerged. With the growth in textile industries, many impoverished Kunbis began migrating to the urban centres. In agriculture, this period was marked by a sustained rise in the area under cultivation and by the relative increase in the area under cash crops. This pattern of growth remained steady until the mid-1880s when a crisis occurred. Before the crisis, with the rising tempo of economic growth and opportunity, new aspirations had emerged among the growing class of educated Indians, but by 1890 the prospects of their fulfilment had substantially receded. Only the lower and middle ranks of the civil service were open to Indians at this stage. The benign view of the role of the state now became more and more difficult to sustain. Earlier, sustained economic growth had brought with it greater differentiation of interests. The impossibility of their fulfilment by the colonial state was becoming increasingly obvious to the proponents. The view of the colonial state held by an earlier generation of intellectuals had prompted them to advocate major social reforms under government auspices. They had also spoken in favour of the state's promoting the interests of the rising entrepreneurial classes and had expected this to happen without the infliction of undue hardship on the working population. This all-inclusive view of the state and society conflicted with the facts of life. Without massive state intervention, accompanied by the rapid and planned expansion of economic opportunities, even a semblance of an acceptable, pluralist state-society could not have been created. The colonial state and its metropolitan masters had both become particularly unsuitable for such a project by 1890.

The crisis that hit Maharashtra in the 1880s was part of the Depression in Europe. Although Britain still continued to lead in the production of coal and steel, her relative decline *vis-a-vis* Germany and the United States had already begun. Britain, from this point of view, became more and more dependent on specific political arrangements (such as preferential tariffs), with its old and new colonies in order to sustain its outdated and declining industrial system. According to Hobsbawm (1978) Britain escaped the Great Depression of 1873-96 by exploiting the empire. It continued to practice that strategy even after the crisis had passed, using the empire as a cushion in the increasingly harsh world of competitive, nationalist capitalism. In India, this meant, according to Seal (in Gallagher, *et al.* 1973), that the administrative grid was pressed down more firmly by the intervention of the Raj in local matters. A search for new collaborators was on. Rothermund (1970) suggests that a corresponding official ideology of interest group pluralism was already in the making.

Tilak's Hindu revivalism was the same as, and at times closely linked with, the nation-wide Hindu revivalist tendencies. Its consequences were also the same. Identical movements were also developing simultaneously in Indian Islam. These movements contributed to the unification of privilege and deprivation in either community, and to the widening gulf between the two. Hindu revivalism helped to camouflage the emerging cleavages between the privileged and the disadvantaged sections of urban Hindu society, while the Islamic reaction bridged the economic, linguistic, sectarian and regional differences between individual Muslim communities. In both cases this form of aggregation and articulation of interest effectively blunted the edge of the working class movement in urban Maharashtra.

Just as critical interpretations of Ranade's ideas on tradition and the past helped the aggregation of the diverse interests of the Hindu petit bourgeoisie, and to some extent the working classes, and just as the Muslim reaction consolidated, another reinterpretation of an earlier, universalistic, view of the past led to the consolidation of the Maratha hegemony over the differentiated peasant and rural labouring classes. Jyotiba Phule, in language reminiscent of Tukaram, had announced his mission of saving 'the lower castes from hypocritical Brahmans and their opportunistic scriptures' (Heimsath 1964: 103). The focus of his critique was Brahmanism and the all-pervasive stranglehold of Brahman administrative and political power. As with Ranade and Tilak, Phule's impulse was appropriated and put to use by his Maratha successors. They began to speak of a generalized 'peasant' interest at a time when the peasantry was becoming increasingly fragmented along class lines. This mode of aggregating potentially conflicting interests and presenting them in a garb that made them appear to be shared, was an antagonistic reaction to the nationalism of the petit bourgeoisie represented by Tilak's Congress. It came fully into its own in the third phase of colonialism.

It is important to remember that the non-Brahman movement gathered momentum in Maharashtra during the ascendance of the Maratha elite trying to reassert its former dominance, and not as a consequence of the rise of consciousness among oppressed groups. Phule had attempted to mobilize all the backward classes with a view to establishing a society based on *sarvajanik dharma*. That goal now shrank to the reassertion of Maratha hegemony and the fulfilment of elite interests. Some of Phule's principal goals were now rejected. His attack on inequality and casteism, his battles against untouchability, his active promotion of women's equality and his opposition to such restrictive social practices as child marriage, were largely forgotten.

The best way to sum up the transition from Phule to Shahu is perhaps to say that it was a change from universalistic humanism and anti-Brahmanism to anti-Brahman Brahmanism. Elite Maratha leaders of the non-Brahman movement systematically avoided any association with the urban petit bourgeois nationalists and devoted their attention to nurturing links with the state. Given the continuity of their hegemony, in spite of the growing differentiation of the peasantry under colonial rule, anti-Brahman Brahmanism effectively prevented radical movements from taking roots among dispossessed Maratha-Kunbi labourers, artisans and *dalit* workers. The effectiveness of the patriarchal ideology was symbolized by their widespread rejection of the Kunbi designation in western Maharashtra between the Censuses of 1921 and 1931.

The non-Marathi (English, Gujrati, Marwari, Parsi and Muslim) bourgeoisie, strong in the textile industry and in overseas commerce, the petit bourgeoisie, the primarily Marathi urban working class, the peasantry, the landless proletariat and tribal groups were the major social divisions of Maharashtra during the second phase of colonialism. In concrete terms their interests were often in competition—if not in direct conflict—with each other. The most interesting fact is that political mobilization in this period did not lead to the articulation of these differences in such objective terms.

There seems no better way to describe the political scene than by the familiar idiom of 'interest group pluralism'. The essentials of such a political practice were in place in India by the end of the nineteenth century. British policy, despite differences between the core and the periphery, bears witness to the emergence of such interest group politics. The Indian Councils Act of 1909 introduced the principle of elections, gave greater scope for discussing the budget to elected members, and fostered the representation of diverse interests such as those of the 'professional classes, the landholders, the Mohammedans, European commerce and Indian commerce'. In recognizing these interests, and not others, in introducing differential income qualifications for Hindus and Muslims and in ensuring that 'government servants, pensioners and landlords' had access to the political arena prior to the radicalized professionals, the state was also fostering certain modes of political mobilization over others. The interaction between imperial interests and the emerging interests of the privileged indigenous classes became clearer in the third phase, where the latter eventually prevailed over the internally weakened imperial power.

India became politically independent in 1947, but the state of Maharashtra was not created until 1960, and then only in response to prolonged agitation against the central government, led by a Congress Party committed to re-organization of states along linguistic lines (Kamat 1983). The agitation itself demonstrated dramatically the workings of elite pluralism. It was based on selective mass mobilization. An alliance of all the dominant regional interests successfully exploited the national consciousness of Maharashtrians. Parties and leaders more concerned with socio-economic deprivation had to choose between joining the agitation or being marginalized. The enthusiasm with which all the classes responded to the fight against 'internal colonialism' seemed to pose enough of a threat to the privileged group for the nation-state to resist the demand at that stage. Success came only after the agitation was transformed into a negotiated coalition of leading interests, susceptible to management within and through the established institutions of parliamentary democracy. This could not have been accomplished without the participation of the Congress elite, consisting primarily of Marathas. The projection of Y.B. Chavan as the *avatar* of Shivaji was not only clever management of a hollow myth, but a clear indication of the continuity and resilience of the hegemonic alliance of Brahmans and Marathas (Lele 1982). Under Chavan's leadership, stability and order, necessary for the protection of existing privileges and for rapid capitalist development in both town and country, were ensured.

The transition from Phule's universalistic *sarvajanik dharma* to the interest group pluralism of the non-Brahman movement and the takeover of Ranade's universalism by Tilak's militant nationalism, were followed by the subsequent hegemonic appropriation and manipulation of the political apparatus by the Maratha elite under Chavan. This process may be termed the re-Brahmanization of tradition. It required an overt acceptance by Brahmans and other so-called upper castes of a position of subaltern elites. Today they are joined by a smaller group from other castes at various levels of the occupational hierarchy. Many of the latter are from land controlling, hegemonic Maratha families while others are from the middle and even from the scheduled castes.

Both in politics and in the professional world the entry of members of the scheduled castes seems to be resisted by an ideologically sustained and widely disseminated prejudice about their inadequacy for responsible roles in public life. Even a limited increase in their visibility in the spheres of their previous exclusion has produced a backlash out of all proportion. Anti-*dalit* and anti-Muslim agitations have thus acquired a persistent and vicious character (Seth 1987), as part of the revival of Hindu fundamentalism. In Maharashtra this has once again exposed the oppressive face of the Maratha-Brahman alliance, manifested in such organizations as the Patit Pawan Sanghatana, Hindu Ekata Andolan, Maratha Mahasangh and Shiv Sena which now also seek to incorporate large segments of the urban underclass of *savarna* middle and lower caste origin. The recently renewed convergence of *Maharashtra Dharma* and *varnashramadharma* in the ideology of these organizations indicates a dramatic change in the political economy of Maharashtra, as well as the resilience of the Maratha-Brahman alliance (Vora and Palshikar 1989). As expected, the most malignant face of that alliance comes in focus under conditions of severe crisis.

Men like Ranade, Phule and Ambedkar, who spoke in universalistic terms about tradition, had been exposed to Western thought and came to appreciate its liberating origins in the Enlightenment. They developed their interpretations of India in that context. Those who inherited and transformed their ideals were also exposed to Western currents, though their daily life was still deeply-rooted in the traditional world-view that they tried to reform. This duality in their lives was often expressed in the contrast between their public stance and private behaviour. At the same time, because of the overt and at times malevolent racism of the state, there was always a strong resistance to the total encompassing of the past as a strategy of myth management and symbol manipulation for the sole purpose of legitimating the state. The gradual erosion of this resistance under the pressures of elite pluralism was further accelerated with the spread of 'modern' schools and colleges into smaller towns and villages during and after the colonial period.

The possibility of a new integration of indigenous and Western knowledge, on terms set by the life practice of ordinary people and transcending the particularities of elite-dominated ideological distortions, was aborted early in the colonial era. Under the economic pressure exerted by the industrializing metropolis and with the collusion of its allies, the older institutions of appropriating and investing creative thinking surplus of the producing classes had been systematically starved (Dharampal 1983). In the agricultural sector the replacement of traditional cropping patterns by export-oriented monoculture was accompanied by an education and research strategy that ignored traditional know-how to the detriment of the producers (Innis 1980). The lasting impact of such modernization was perceived by Gandhians at an earlier stage, but the post-Independence thrust of capitalist agriculture, promoted by the Maratha elite, successfully marginalized their concerns. Thus, in rural Maharashtra, the increasing alienation of the ruling classes from their disadvantaged kin is now firmly rooted in the appropriation of both material and intellectual surpluses.

The reduction of independent producers to wage labourers thus involves even their intellectual subordination.

The beginnings of this process can be seen in Hindu chauvinism, as well as in the non-Brahman movement of the colonial period. The intelligentsia has grown rapidly in size since Independence, thanks to the educational system which the colonial comprador elites had helped to develop. The discrepancy between the public pronouncements of the latter and their private lives shows that their disjunction from the past was slow and painful. Such a dual existence, without a successful transcendence of either East or West, would have been impossible without the Anglo-Saxon mode of thought characterized by a tragic 'dissociation of sensibility' (Eliot 1932: 286). Separation of knowledge and know-how, of theory and information, of reflexion and implementation has now become a way of life and thought for Indian intellectuals. The consequent separation of instrumental activity at work from life outside is now accepted without misgiving. It is, indeed, necessary for a free movement between the Anglicized 'rationalism' of the workplace and Hindu 'familism' at home. Some see this flexibility as a commuting between two cultures, between tradition and modernity, but its culmination is now seen in the mindless fascination with new information technology and the slogans of rapid movement into the twenty-first century (Lele and Singh 1989).

The newly ascendant techno-elite in both the public and private sectors *and* the populist legitimizers of the regime who theorize for, encourage and support the new 'Sergeants at Arms' of ethnic fundamentalism (Vora and Palshikar 1989) require the appropriation of popular thought. This can be done, both technologically and ideologically, through homogenization and through marginalization as well as victimization of dissent (Kothari 1988). Early indications of this strategy were noticeable in the slogan of *bahujanasamaj* propagated by elite Marathas as part of the non-Brahman movement. Without an understanding of this dimension of historical continuity in elite strategies of hegemonic appropriation, our understanding of the current malaise is likely to remain incomplete.

REFERENCES

Banaji, J., 1978, 'Capitalist domination and the small peasantry: Deccan districts in the late nineteenth century', in *Studies in the Development of Capitalism in India*, Ashok Rudra *et al.* (eds.) Lahore: Vanguard Books.

Bedekar, D.K., 1977, *Dharma cintan,* Pune: Samaj Prabodhan Samstha.

Dharampal, 1983, *The Beautiful Tree: Indigenous Indian Education in the Late 18th Century*, Delhi: Biblia Impex.

Eliot, T.S., 1932. *Selected Essays*, London: Faber and Faber.

Gallagher, J. *et al.*, 1973, *Locality, Province, and Nation: Essays on Indian Politics*, Cambridge: Cambridge University Press.

Heimsath, C. H., 1964, *Indian Nationalism and Hindu Social Reform*, Princeton: Princeton University Press.

Hobsbawm, E., 1978, *Industry and Empire: from 1750 to the Present Day*, Harmondsworth: Penguin Books.

Innis, D.Q., 1980, 'Traditional deshi agriculture in Maharashtra', in *Images of Maharashtra: a Regional Profile of India,* N.K. Wagle (ed.), London: Curzon Press.

Kamat, A.R., 1983, *Essays on Social Change in India. Pune: Indian Institute of Education. Study of Two Indian Cities: 1650-1900,* Stockholm: Universitat Stockholms.

Kothari, R., 1988, 'Integration and exclusion in Indian politics', in *Economic and Political Weekly,* XXIII. 43: 2223-7.

Lele, J., 1980, 'The two faces of nationalism', in *National and Ethnic Movements*, J. Dofni, and A. Akiwoo (eds.), London: Sage Publications.

———, 1982, 'Chavan and the political integration of Maharashtra', in *Contemporary India: Socio-economic and Political Processes*, N.R. Inamdar *et al.* (eds.), Pune: Continental Prakashan.

Lele, J. and R. Singh, 1989, 'Modernizing intellectuals or commuters between cultures: a reexamination of tradition and modernity', in *Sociology of Development and Change.* C. Bhat (ed.), Delhi: Orient Longman.

Masselos, J., 1974, *Towards Nationalism: Public Institutions and Urban Politics in the Nineteenth Century*, Mumbai: Popular Prakashan.

Rothermund, D., 1970, *The Phases of Indian Nationalism and Other Essays*, Mumbai: Nachiketa Publications.

Set, D.L., 1987, 'Reservations policy revisited', *Economic and Political Weekly,* XXII.46: 1957-62.

Stokes, E., 1978, *The Peasant and the Raj: Studies in Agrarian Society and Peasant Rebellion in Colonial India.* Delhi: Vikas.

Vora, R. and S. Palshikar, 1989, 'Neo-Hinduism: case of distorted consciousness', in *State and Society in India: Change and Continuity in the Social Bases of Indian Politics*, J. Lele and R. Vora (eds.), Leiden: E.J. Brill.

Maharashtra Dharma and the Nationalist Movement in Maharashtra

RAJENDRA VORA

The nationalist movement as a response to colonialism began in Maharashtra in the middle of the nineteenth century, and from a number of studies, autobiographies and accounts of it available in Marathi and English, it is clear that it went through several phases. It began as a liberal-nationalist organization, which believed in taking up reforms simultaneously in social, political and economic fields. Lokahitvadi (Gopal Hari Deshmukh 1823-92), M.G. Ranade (1842-1901), G.G. Agarkar (1856-95) and G.K. Gokhale (1866-1915) held that the social institutions should be reformed on the principle of individual liberty, and that representative institutions should be introduced only gradually. They were therefore known as moderates. The extremists in contrast opposed reforms in the Hindu social system, but demanded immediate reforms in political institutions. Such views appeared in the 1870s in the form of V. S. Chiplunkar's (1850-82) *Nibandhamala* and developed into B.G. Tilak's (1856-1920) politics. Also, while the moderates communicated in English, believed in the liberalism of the colonial rulers and could appeal only to the English-educated class, the extremists communicated the message of Hindu nationalism in Marathi by using religious symbols, exposed the darker side of colonialism, and could mobilize to a large extent the lower middle class, as well as, occasionally, farmers and workers.

The extremism of Tilak's party never went beyond organizing mass movements. Those who did not believe in parliamentary politics took recourse to violence. In particular, V.B. Phadke (1845-83), Damodar Chaphekar (1870-97) and V.D. Savarkar (1893-1966) organized underground terrorist activities to overthrow the colonial regime.

When Gandhi appeared on the political scene, the nationalist movement in Maharashtra had become divided into two camps, the Gandhians and the Tilakites. The Tilakites, led by N.C. Kelkar (1872-1947), opposed Gandhi's programme of non-cooperation and Hindu-Muslim unity, and eventually founded the Hindu Mahasabha. The Gandhians, including Shankarrao Dev (1895-1974), Acharya Vinoba Bhave (1895-1982) and Acharya Javadekar (1894-1955), mobilized political support for the Satyagraha movement and prepared the philosophical justification of Gandhism in Maharashtra. However, as all these groups were said to be interested primarily in mobilizing Brahman support as an avenue to political power, a non-Brahman party was also founded in 1920 to fight Brahman dominance. This movement, led by Shahu Maharaj (1874-1922), is considered radical since it was inspired by Mahatma Phule's (1827-90) idea of overthrowing the caste-system (Omvedt 1976: 2).

Studies of the nationalist movement in Maharashtra have attempted to discern differences in approach. In particular, biographers and students of political thought have emphasized the distinctive nature of the groups to which their subjects belonged, and their rivalries. Much has been written, for example, on the radicalism of the non-Brahman movement which separated it from Brahman nationalism. These debates have also been reproduced amongst the scholars themselves. Indeed, this tendency has been carried to such an extent that significant areas of agreement between all these movements have been overlooked, and it is the purpose of this paper to find the common ground of the nationalist movement of Maharashtra. It is argued, in particular, that all schools of nationalism share a fundamental belief in *Maharashtra Dharma*. A close analysis of the ideas and actions of the leaders and ideologues reveals that, despite the diverse trends, all wanted to establish a link between themselves and the *dharma* of the saint movement and in the Maratha empire of the seventeenth and eighteenth centuries. This *Maharashtra Dharma* could be tentatively defined as *varnashramdharma*, wherein the Brahmans and the Kshatriyas are supposed to observe their own *dharmas* as well as provide leadership to the other two varnas, thereby defending Hindu culture and the Hindu nation (Agnihotri 1977: 193).

Each school of nationalism had tried to relate to *Maharashtra Dharma* or appropriate and interpret this pre-colonial form of national consciousness. Lokahitvadi, an eminent liberal nationalist of the pre-Ranade period, for instance, thought that revolution only occurred once in India, under the leadership of Shivaji, a disciple of Ramdas (1608-81), who liberated Maharashtra from the Mughals (Priyolkar 1967: 29). The same Lokahitvadi, who was founder-president of the Arya Samaj in Bombay, believed that the *chaturvarna* system of the Vedic period, based on function and merit, should be revived to take the place of the caste system. Lokahitvadi had a long association with the founder of the Arya Samaj, Swami Dayananda Saraswati (1824-83), and wrote a book on him in 1884 (Parikh and Parikh 1988: 13-14).

The first attempt to revive the term *Maharashtra Dharma* in the new context of nineteenth century nationalism, however, was made by M.G. Ranade in his classic *Rise of the Maratha Power* (1881). Ranade, the chief architect of moderate nationalism, interpreted the saint movement and the Maratha Empire as efforts to arouse the feeling of patriotism among the people, and establish a Hindu state in Maharashtra in the seventeenth and eighteenth centuries. According to him, the rise of Maratha power was not an accident but a genuine attempt by Hindu nationality to form a 'state animated by a common patriotism'. The history of the Marathas was particularly relevant then because it was the history of the formation of a true Indian nationality. Indians could think of establishing a Hindu Padshahi in Delhi due to the efforts of the Marathas. Like Lokahitvadi, Ranade also identified Shivaji's endeavour as a political revolution (Ghurye *et al.* 1960: 4-5), preceded and to some extent caused by the religious upheaval of saints like Ramdas and Tukaram. Ranade gave special attention to Ramdas as he was Shivaji's spiritual advisor and believed in the use of political means; it were his ideas, combined with the actions of Shivaji that led to the formation of Swaraj in seventeenth-century Maharashtra. Ramdas, indeed, was the ideologue of *Maharashtra Dharma*, which he distinguished from Hindu *dharma*; he wanted Sambhaji, son of Shivaji, to unite all Marathas in its realization. His *Dasbodh* (1659) was, according to Ranade, an encyclopaedia of political theory, which was essential to an understanding of *Maharashtra Dharma* (Ranade 1902: 321-9). Ranade also argued that the spirit of Maharashtra nationalist movement was not born as late as the nineteenth century, since the Marathas regarded themselves as a distinct community since the days of Shivaji.

The liberal nationalist venture to revive *Maharashtra Dharma* nevertheless remained at the theoretical level of interpreting Maratha history. It is true that Ranade had convened a meeting in Pune in 1885 to petition the government for funds to restore the mausoleum of Shivaji. But nothing could be done in that connection afterwards, and it was left to the extremists to carry the torch. Tilak's (1976: 955-62) assessment of Ramdas and Shivaji is not much different from Ranade's; he also felt that Ramdas had all the qualities that were essential for preparing Maharashtra for Swaraj under Shivaji. He saw the relationship between these two men as parallel to that between Krishna and Arjun. Tilak considered Shivaji the incarnation of God (*avatari purush*), who created a sense of unity among people of diverse castes, so that all could take pride in the Swaraj established by him. Tilak put forward this interpretation because he, too, wanted to build a nation out of a heterogeneous, caste-ridden society. Thus there is little difference between his and Ranade's interpretations. The latter had argued, for example, that the religious revival of the saints was non-Brahman in character and following, the joint work of all the castes. Shivaji too had followed the policy of giving due place to all the castes in his administration. Thus the unity of the Marathas was a goal stressed by both schools of nationalist thought.

More significant than Tilak's writings were his efforts at establishing *Maharashtra Dharma*. Since the publication of Grant Duff's *History of the Marathas* (1826) the life and times of Shivaji had been an important topic of discussion in Maharashtra. But only Tilak grasped the importance of this hero as the symbol of extremist Hindu nationalism. He began to mobilize public opinion through the *Kesari* for a Shivaji memorial in April 1895. He called a public meeting in Pune on 30 May of the same year to discuss the issue. At the time of the Pune Congress Session in December 1895, he organized another meeting to explore the possibility of celebrating a Shivaji festival (Ahluwalia and Ahluwalia 1984: 60-80). The latter's birth anniversary was eventually celebrated on 15 and 16 April 1896 at Raigad, his capital. From then on, the Shivaji festival, along with the Ganapati festival, became a part of the extremist nationalist movement, and functioned as a medium of mobilization for the cause of Swaraj, by evoking the glorious memories of the Maratha empire.

These interpretations of Maratha history were substantiated and supported by V.K. Rajvade (1863-1926), an eminent historian of Maharashtra. Rajvade pointed out that at the beginning of the seventeenth century the minds of the elites of Maharashtra were preoccupied with the idea of establishing *Maharashtra Dharma* (Joshi 1967: 168-265). The difficult task of realizing this idea fell to Shivaji: it was not merely Hindu *dharma*, as its scope exceeded that of religion. The Hindus of Maharashtra were unlike their counterparts elsewhere who had tamely submitted to Muslim rule. In Maharashtra the overthrow of the Muslims became a part of the Hinduism of the people, so that *dharma* could be established, cows and Brahmans protected. But even the overthrow of Muslims was not sufficient: Swaraj was necessary. Rajvade thus believed that *Maharashtra Dharma*—a term first mentioned in the seventeenth-century *Mahikavatichi bakhar* (and subsequently popularized by Ramdas)—consisted of Hindu *dharma*, the protection of cows and Brahmans, the establishment of Swaraj and the integration of the people and the leadership. Shivaji and his followers sacrificed their lives in the cause of *Maharashtra Dharma*, and the concept was central to the activities of the Marathas for almost a century and a half. In the eighteenth century Swaraj had been converted into the *Hindupadpadshahi* by the Peshwas, and the Marathas were attempting to carry *Maharashtra Dharma* into the rest of India, sometimes under the leadership of the Maratha caste and sometimes under that of the Brahmans. While the Sikhs and the Bundelas had the same aim, they lacked the unity, determination and leadership that was required, and found only among the Marathas. The latter not only had the personal qualities of bravery but were also united and inspired by the precepts of Ramdas. Like Ranade and Tilak, Rajvade viewed Ramdas as the ideologue of Shivaji, and the inspiration behind Maharashtrian nationalism and patriotism, which enabled the Marathas to carry on their struggle even after Shivaji's death. Ramdas performed the invaluable task of restoring the *chaturvarna* system, and reestablishing morality, *dharma* and Swaraj, which had all degenerated under Muslim domination.

Rajvade was also of the opinion that the other saints, Tukaram and Eknath, were inclined towards morality and *bhakti*, neglecting nationalistic and political matters. Although these saints pointed out the shortcomings of the Brahman leaders of the *chaturvarna* system, they were incapable of showing the right path. Indeed, by exposing only the dark side of Hinduism, they merely demoralized and split up the community. Ramdas had shown the right path. Once again, these views differ little from those held by Ranade and Tilak. Later, nationalists were also much influenced by Rajvade's analysis of Maratha history.

Terrorist nationalism also found its parallels in Maratha history. Vasudev Balwant Phadke, the first terrorist nationalist of Maharashtra was inspired by Shivaji's deeds (Phadke 1989: 25). Chaphekar and his friends were likewise inspired by the Shivaji festivals organized by Tilak, and formed an organization to remove the obstacles in the path of Hinduism (Ahluwalia and Ahluwalia 1984: 70). V.D. Savarkar, the principal philosopher of terrorism, published his *Hindupadpadshahi* in 1925, in which he also attributed the rising political fortunes of Hindus to the concept of *Maharashtra Dharma* as realized by Shivaji and Ramdas. In his words, *Maharashtra Dharma* was a new force 'animating the dying spirit of the national life of the Hindu race' during Shivaji's time. He (1947:

4-5) visualized a similar effort to establish *Hindupadpadshahi* under the leadership of Maharashtra in his time.

After the death of Tilak in 1920, N.C. Kelkar emerged as one of the most important Tilakite leaders. His early reluctance to follow Gandhi—whose entrance led to the emerging all-India character of the nationalist movement—and his subsequent independent stand could also be interpreted from the standpoint of *Maharashtra Dharma*. Apart from the need of Maharashtra to find its own leader, militant Hindu nationalism, which was a reaction to the Muslim breakaway and to Gandhi's attempts at fostering communal unity, was also a contributing factor. Hence the Hindu Mahasabha leaders, Kelkar and Savarkar, projected Shivaji as a symbol of pan-Hindu unity, and attempted to break away from Gandhi's secular all-India movement.

Kelkar (1938: 923-6), defines the religion of Maharashtra as pragmatic; it does not believe in extreme other worldliness. The saints of Maharashtra were pragmatic and, therefore, could arouse national consciousness. Marathas created a tide of freedom which at one time touched Delhi. It was from the Marathas that the English army had to conquer India.

Gandhism and these Mahasabhists were thus political rivals. However, belief in the former did not mean the abandonment of *Maharashtra Dharma* by its proponents. The appeal of the leaders of the Mulshi Satyagraha (1921-4) was thus based on the idea that the lands about to be submerged by the Mulshi dam belonged to the Mavalas, followers of Shivaji, and the area was where Shivaji had made his earliest attempts to establish Swaraj. That volunteers from even remote corners of Maharashtra came to join the Mavalas in their struggle indicates that this appeal to *Maharashtra Dharma* on the part of Congress leaders had the desired mobilizing effect (Bhuskute 1968: 20-42). In a similar vein, Acharya Vinoba Bhave, a leading Gandhian, edited a monthly named *Maharashtra Dharma* in 1923, the publication of which was suspended because of the Satyagraha movement, to be resumed in 1927. The choice of title was due to the deep impact of the concept on the Acharya and his friends during their school and college days (Bhave 1984: 260). The purpose of the periodical was to emphasize that it was wrong to separate politics and religion, since religion was at the core of individual, social and political life. In his article on V.K. Rajvade's critique of such saints as Eknath and Tukaram, Vinoba Bhave (1958: 143-9) observed that such criticism, coming out of a sincere concern for the nation, was understandable. He also published a lengthy article on Tilak. Tilak by now had become a symbol to whom Gandhians had to relate at a philosophical level, and Vinoba's article (1958: 9-16) was an effort in this direction.

Acharya S.D. Javadekar was another important exponent of Gandhism in Maharashtra, as well as an ideologue of the socialist movement which began in the 1930s within the fold of nationalism. He performed the theoretical exercise of reconciling Gandhism and socialism and, more than anyone else, could establish a link between Tilak's nationalism and the Gandhian movement in Maharashtra. He wrote a number of articles in the 1920s and 1930s in Marathi periodicals, attempting to appropriate the heritage of Tilak, the man who became known as the Ramdas of the twentieth century (Tilak 1976: 961). According to Javadekar, there were three political parties in Maharashtra, the moderate (following Ranade and Gokhale), the extremist (following Tilak) and the terrorist (following Savarkar), and Gandhi represented a continuation of the second trend. Tilak had advocated non-violent revolutionary politics, and since Gandhi took over from him, Javadekar regarded Tilak the true father of Indian nationalism. Tilak's *Gitarahasya* (a commentary on the Gita) explained the true nature of Hindu *dharma*, and his studies in English convinced the world of the antiquity of Indian civilization. He also democratized Indian politics and developed the spirit of nationalism by creating self-respect among the masses. He fought the colonial bureaucracy at the head of a popular movement. By starting the Shivaji and Ganapati festivals, he also gave religious and historical support to nationalism and captured the minds of the people. The logical culmination to all these trends was to be found, in Javadekar's view, in Gandhi's movement (Javadekar 1946: 10-19).

Non-Brahmans likewise tried to relate to *Maharashtra Dharma* from their point of view. The first to so utilize the Shivaji tradition was Mahatma Phule. His ballad published in 1869, painted Shivaji as a Shudra king, and undermined the role of the Brahman saint Ramdas (Keer and Malshe 1969: 15). This assessment of the Maratha empire was followed by other non-Brahman leaders. The differences between Shivaji's rule, which laid the foundations of Maratha power, and that of the Brahman Peshwas was also emphasized, though these later studies maintained that Shivaji belonged to the Kshatriya and not the Shudra varna.

Shahu Maharaj (1874-1922), a Maratha ruler of Kolhapur state, and the most important leader of the non-Brahman movement, also tried to assert his right as a Kshatriya, especially after he came to know that the religious ceremonies of his palace were performed according to Puranic rather than Vedic rites. However, Brahmans refused to regard him a Kshatriya king, and treated him as a Shudra. These initiated a controversy about *vedokta* (rites prescribed in the Vedas) which lasted from 1901 to 1905 (Phadke 1986: 62-100). Unlike Phule, who rejected the Vedas, the Puranas and the *chaturvarna* system itself, Shahu believed in the Vedas and in the pre-eminence of Kshatriyas. He rejected Phule's more radical principles which were followed by the Satya Shodhak Samaj founded in 1873, and followed instead the ideals of the Arya Samaj. He started a branch of this organization in Kolhapur in 1916. He also brought educational institutions in his state under the management of the Arya Pratinidhi Sabha and used Dayanand Saraswati's *Satyartha Prakash* as a textbook in some of the schools. Shahu presided over conferences on the Arya Dharma in 1918 and 1920, and the All-India Kshatriya conference held at Kanpur in 1919. While Phule totally rejected priesthood, Shahu appointed Sadashiv Patil Benadikar as *kshatrajagatguru* (high priest) in 1920 and instituted a Kshatriya Vedic Patshala in Kolhapur in 1921. In his article on the founder of the Arya Samaj he argued that the ideal Vedic varna system should replace the caste system (Shahu 1922: 122).

Non-Brahman periodicals throw more than sufficient light on the fact that the non-Brahmans, especially the Marathas, believed in a *Maharashtra Dharma* which gave the leading role to the Kshatriyas. *Rashtraveer*, a Maratha paper published in Belgaum expressed its concern over the status of non-Brahmans in the Hindu Dharmashastras (26 February 1922), which relegated all of them to the status of Shudras in the *Kaliyuga*. In the same article the Marathas demanded religious rituals appropriate to their status as Kshatriyas. When a statue of Shivaji was erected in Pune (in 1921), the non-Brahman papers took care to remind people of the Peshwas' betrayal of the Chhatrapati and of the ability of the Maratha community to produce great leaders like Shivaji. In 1932, the *Rashtraveer* supported the cause of separate electorates for Hindus, and observed that the Hindu Mahasabha could have represented all the Hindus, were it not for the domination of that organization by Brahmans (4 October 1932).

Marathas also celebrated their Kshatriyahood by observing the *Shravani* (reaffirmation of twice-born status by the ceremony of the sacred thread), annually. A book entitled *Kshatriyanche Vedokta Shravani Puran* (Phadke 1986: 281) had acquired fame in the 1920s, and several others emphasizing Kshatriyahood emerged in the same period, their announcements and advertisements being carried in the non-Brahman papers of the day.

Some of the followers of the Satya Shodhak Samaj made a feeble attempt at distinguishing between their radicalism and contemporary non-Brahmanism. However, this argument did not appeal to the non-Brahman leaders, who maintained that Phule himself had been a strong supporter of Hinduism, and could not tolerate the criticisms of the latter by missionaries. He had believed that the Hindus became spineless due to the slavery imposed on them by the Brahmans; anti-national Brahmanism was in fact the ruin of Hinduism. Phule was thus, according to this school of thought, devoted to regenerating rather than abolishing the Hindu religion, and the Satya Shodhak Samaj was not a distinct sect but an organization devoted to this aim. Indeed, according to Dinkarrao Jawalkar (1898-1932), Phule fought for all Hindus, while Tilak represented only the Brahmans. He also felt that Ramdas had tried to take over Shivaji's state as *bhiksha* that was due to him; just as in ancient times King Bali was deceived by Waman; as in the middle ages Ramdas tried to deceive Shivaji, so in recent times Tilak played against the interests of King Shahu (Phadke 1984: 110-13).

Another non-Brahman leader, Keshav Sitaram Thakare, published a weekly, *Prabodhan*, which carried articles on Hinduism and on the activities of Hindu organizations and conferences. He was a Chandraseniya Kayastha Prabhu, particularly interested in the role of his own caste through history, (though, like Shahu and Jawalkar, he also tried to establish a spirit of Kshatriyahood within the fold of *varnashramadharma*, instead of criticizing the whole setup of Hinduism). If we compare the speeches of these leaders to their non-Brahman audiences with the speeches of Savarkar to the Brahmans, the common ground regarding Hindu society and politics in Maharashtra becomes immediately apparent.

Maharashtra Dharma was thus another name for Maharashtrian nationalism, and was rooted in the historical experience and cultural traditions of the people of Maharashtra. *Maharashtra Dharma* enabled the newly emerging middle class

Brahman and non-Brahman to assert his place in society, as it preserved the ancient and medieval social system, and through it regulated the relationship of this class to the masses on the one hand and to the colonial overlords on the other. This class could not forget its regional roots even during its participation in the nationwide nationalist movement. However, cosmopolitan Mumbai could not accept such an ideology, and the more embracing form of nationalism was strongly supported by Parsi and Gujarati businessmen. Gokhale, dependent upon the city's support, could never project himself as a viable representative of Maharashtrian nationalism. Gandhi, likewise, found his support in Mumbai, rather than in the followers of *Maharashtra Dharma*, which included most of the Maharashtrian middle class, who particularly objected to Gandhi's policy towards Muslims. Even those who joined Gandhi did not wish to lose the identity of *Maharashtra Dharma* in the all-India movement. It is not, therefore, surprising, that after the transfer of power this ideology re-emerged in the form of demands for a Marathi-speaking state, and also sought to continually protect the interests of the emerging dominant class composed of Marathas and Brahmans.

REFERENCES

Agnihotri, D.H., 1977, *Maharashtra sanskritiche tatvik adhisthan*, Nagpur: Suvichar Prakashan.

Ahluwalia A.K. and S. Ahluwalia (eds.), 1984, *Shivaji and Indian Nationalism*, Delhi: Cultural Publishing House.

Bhave, S.N., 1984, *Vinboba jeevan darshan*, Mumbai: Maharashtra Rajya Sahitya ani Sanskriti Mandal.

Bhave, Vinoba, 1958, *Madhukar*, Pavnar: Gram Seva Mandal.

Bhuskute, V.M., 1968, *Mulshi satyagraha*, Pune: Dastane Ramchandra.

Ghurye, G.S. *et al.* (eds.), 1960, *Rise of Maratha Power and Other Essays by M.G. Ranade, and Gleanings from Maratha Chronicles by K.T. Telang*, Mumbai: University of Bombay.

Javadekar, S.D., 1946, *Lokamanya Tilak va Mahatma Gandhi*, Pune: Rajhansa Prakashan.

Joshi, L.S. (ed.), 1967, *Rajvade lekhasangraha*, Mumbai: Popular Prakashan.

Keer, D and S. Malshe (eds.), 1969, *Mahatma Phule samagra vangmaya*, Mumbai: Maharashtra Rajya Sahitya Sanskriti Mandal.

Omvedt, G., 1976, *Cultural Revolt in a Colonial Society: The Non-Brahmin Movement in Western India: 1873-1930*, Mumbai: Scientific Socialist Education Trust.

Parikh, G. and I. Parikh (eds.), 1988, *Lokahitwadi samagra vangmaya*, Mumbai: Maharashtra Rajya Sahitya ani Sanskriti Mandal.

Phadke, Y.D., 1984, *Dinkarrao Javalkar samagra vangmaya*, Pune: Shrividya Prakashan.

———, 1986, *Shahu Chhatrapati ani Lokamanya*, Pune: Shrividya Prakashan.

———, 1989, *Visavya shatakatil Maharashtra*, Pune: Shrividya Prakashan.

Priyolkar, A.K. (ed.), 1967, *Lokahitavadikrit nibandhasangraha*, Mumbai: Popular Prakashan.

Ranade, R. (ed.), 1902, *Nyaymurti Ranade yanchi dharmapar vyakhyane*, Lonavala: Ramabai Ranade.

Savarkar, V.D., 1942, *Hindupadpadshahi*, Mumbai: Manohar Granth Mala.

Shahu Maharaj, 1922, 'Bahiskritoddharak Rishi Dayananda', *Prabodhan* 1: 122-3.

Tilak, B.G., 1976, *Samagra Lokamanya Tilak*, vol. 6, Pune: Kesari Prakashan.

Pre-Ambedkar Untouchable Liberation Movement in Maharashtra

UTTAM BHOITE

Every kind of social inequality involving the domination of one group over another requires ideological sustenance. Often the sway of the legitimizing ideology is so comprehensive and powerful that the emergence of any counter-ideology becomes impossible. The ideology itself becomes sacrosanct and the critical impulse of the oppressed finds it extremely difficult to express itself. Under the hegemony of the ruling classes, the contradictions in the life-situations of the oppressed remain hidden. In such a situation, what is required for the redemption of the oppressed is either a charismatic leader who would inject a revolutionary spirit in them, or an extraneous factor that would change radically the existing power structure, or both.

The more or less undisturbed continuity of the caste system for centuries, and its suppression and exploitation of untouchables, can be explained by its well-entrenched ideological basis. This is not to say that the legitimacy of the system was never questioned. Critiques came in the forms of Buddhism, Sikhism, the Warkari cult, and the like. Despite that, the plight of untouchables remained more or less unchanged.

Babasaheb Ambedkar emerged as a leader of the (ex)untouchables around 1925, and gave them leadership for the next three decades. Voluminous analytical accounts of his role as an emancipator of the untouchables are now available. However, regrettably, in the glow of glory of his leadership, researchers have almost lost sight of the pioneering work done by a few leaders of the untouchables who were the forerunners of Ambedkar and who paved the way for him.

This paper discusses the liberation efforts made by the leaders of the Mahar caste (to which Ambedkar himself belonged), mainly between 1890 and 1925. This effort assumed the dimensions of a movement, which may be aptly called the Mahar movement. During the pre-British period, for centuries, the untouchables were not only hampered by their social and ritual status, they were also the most economically deprived and exploited group, lacking also in any political power. Under the hegemony of upper caste Hindus, their critical impulse remained largely suppressed.

With the advent of British rule, great changes took place in the traditional social, economic, and political structure of India. Although initially the British Government adopted the policy of recognizing and accommodating the traditional social order, profound changes took place in society with the collapse of the traditional power elites, with changes in political economy, with the introduction of a universalistic legal system and administrative order, and with a new education system. There appeared new opportunities for gain and self-development, including a variety of administrative positions. Similarly, with the expansion of the market economy and industries, there also emerged new occupations. With this expansion a few new avenues of mobility thus became available.

These changes stirred the impulse of self-government and advancement of the traditionally deprived sections of society, including untouchables. The British established, for the first time in India, the rule of law, and shattered the traditional power structures. In the changed situation the untouchables began to visualize the strong possibility of social emancipation. The alien government had no tradition to fall back on for legitimation. After the traumatic experience of 1857, it decided to adopt the strategy of appeasement in order to win over the support of different sections of the Indian population. It began to project an image of a government with legal and moral obligations towards all its subjects. This is evidenced in Queen Victoria's Proclamation of 1858 which said that any person having the required education, abilities and efficiency would be recruited to any position of power and responsibility in the service of the government, irrespective of caste or creed.

Like other sections of the population, the untouchables understood well the character of the new government, particularly its amenability to pressure and anxiety for support. They realized that the time was now opportune for concerted efforts for social emancipation and economic development. Among those who began to mobilize for this purpose were the Mahars in Bombay Presidency and in the adjoining Marathi-speaking regions of the Central Provinces and Berar (the Vidarbha region).

The Mahars are the largest among the untouchable castes. Their proportion of the state population is estimated to have been around nine per cent at the turn of the century, with a particularly heavy concentration in the Vidarbha region.[1]

Although they had no traditional caste occupation, the Mahar was part of traditional village administration, along with the Patil (village headman) and the Kulkarni (village revenue officer). It was his prerogative to be consulted in disputes over village boundaries, land demarcations, and the like. Although his judgements were honoured, his social and ritual status in the village hierarchy was very low. Mahars had no access to public places and several social, cultural and religious rights were denied them. It is true that the practice of untouchability in Maharashtra was not as degraded as in many other regions of India, for example, the Madras Presidency (Gupta 1985: 85), but historical evidence indicates that during the Peshwa regime untouchability was certainly practised in an atrocious manner (Gavali 1981).

As a unit in the village *baluta* system, Mahars were entitled to a share in the produce of their farmer-masters for services rendered during the year. This was an important source of livelihood to people who did not have a traditional occupation and whose services to others were residual and largely undefined. Those Mahars who were part of the village administration were called *gawaki mahars*. Their duties included attending to visiting government officials, carrying messages, maintaining vigilance, and the like. The *rabata mahars* owed various kinds of personal service to farmers, whose *baluta* clients they were, and would work almost as bonded labourers. Some Mahar families also had *vatan*[2] lands. Mahars were also granted the right to collect charges for certain services which they could render to other castes. There are two charters available, one given by Muhammed Shah of Bedar (1463-82), and another dated 1615, given by a Nizam Shahi ruler, specifying fifty-two such rights (Gavali 1981: 49-58).

The Mahars, with fifty-two subcastes, were not a homogeneous community (Khairmode 1978: 215). Many subcastes were endogamous, observed strict rules of commensality, and had their caste councils, which supervised social and religious affairs.

During the pre-British period, the Mahars lived a miserable life, both socially and economically. British rule, as an extraneous factor, brought about a great deal of social change, some of which was designed to ensure the stability of imperial rule and colonial economy. There was also the outcome of innovations like railways and industries. The social order which then started emerging was secular, competitive and civic in nature. This was viewed as propitious for the liberation struggle of the Mahars.

The task of pinpointing the origin of any social movement is as difficult as tracing the source of a river. The situation conducive to a movement already prevails, and then some major event occurs which marks the beginning of the movement. In the present case we may consider the year 1894 as the beginning of the Mahar movement, since it was then that Gopal Baba Walunkar, a retired Mahar serviceman, started mobilizing the support of his people for a petition to the government to lift a ban on the recruitment of Mahars into the army.

Although the movement originated in western Maharashtra, it gained more vigour in the Vidarbha region, as a fairly large number of its early leaders came from there. Although the Mahar leaders from different parts of Maharashtra were interlinked, it must be said that a unified leadership was lacking until Ambedkar appeared on the scene around 1925. In western Maharashtra, the leadership was provided mainly by persons retired from the British army. Gopal Baba Walunkar, Raghoram Sajjan Ghatge and Subhedar Bahaddar Gangaram Krishnaji Bhatankar were, to name a few, prominent among them. Not only Mahar servicemen, but also their children were given compulsory education (Ramtake 1983: 83), and this created awareness in their minds about their plight as untouchables. A strong urge which emerged in them for self-reform and social emancipation was evident in the speeches and writings of these leaders. However, it is not true, as is sometimes suggested, that only retired servicemen provided leadership to the movement (Zelliot 1970: 401).

In Vidarbha some Mahar families belonged to the group of traditionally rich agriculturalists. Some were even *malgujars*, important revenue functionaries. Within the framework of the political economy of the British regime, a small group of Mahars flourished as cotton-traders and railway construction contractors. Hence, leadership in this region came from both traditionally wealthy as well as *nouveau riches* families, as also from teachers, clerks and government officials, who represented a nascent middle class (Moon 1987).

With the advent of the British regime, waves of change encompassed the traditional social structure and economic relations in India. The British introduced a new administrative and revenue system, and different sections of the population were increasingly drawn into the nexus of a cash economy. In the process quite a few groups were uprooted from their traditional moorings, the Mahars among them. In the new administrative setup the Mahar lost his job and his significance as a village functionary. The spread of a cash economy in the countryside also changed the pattern of economic ties between the farmer and his *baluta* clients: under the heavy burden of land-tax the farmer began to find it difficult to fulfil his obligations to the various service castes, Mahars included. Moreover, the village economy could no longer accommodate increasing numbers of Mahars within its fold, thus pushing them out of their villages.

In the meantime, the American Civil War had begun, giving a small boost to the Indian economy. A few textile mills were established in Mumbai, Nagpur and elsewhere—by 1879, there were 56 cotton mills employing 43,000 persons, 75 per cent of them in the Bombay Presidency. These provided jobs to large numbers of Mahars who migrated to Mumbai and Nagpur.[3] Others accepted jobs in the army, while job opportunities in urban areas also expanded considerably with the expansion of the administrative machinery.

Mahars who migrated to the cities became change-oriented as their perception of society and their place in it changed. They could visualize the possibility of further uplift, and they gave a positive response to the call of their leaders and made themselves available for mobilization from time to time.

The pre-Ambedkar movement was not neatly organized. It lacked a unified leadership. It had yet to evolve a common programme. A few of its programmes were closely connected with individual leaders, however; by giving an account of the latter, the nature of the entire movement will be better understood.

GOPAL BABA KRISHNA WALUNKAR

Walunkar had served in the British army for a number of years, before retiring in 1894. While in the army, he had an opportunity to learn to read and write. He read the Hindu scriptures meticulously, and formulated his own views regarding untouchability and related matters. By using the traditional medium of mass-communication, *kirtan*, he tried to convince his people that the caste system and untouchability were not created by God, and that untocuhables had a natural right to live, like others, as free human beings. With a view to providing an institutional base for his activities for the eradication of untouchability, Walunkar instituted the Anarya Dosh Parihar Samaj (Association for the Eradication of the Shortcomings of Non-Aryans). The organization was so named because Walunkar believed and argued that the upper caste Hindus were Aryans, while the untouchables belonged to the non-Aryan stock.

Walunkar was a prolific writer. His articles on untouchables and untouchability were published in various renowned periodicals of his time. In 1888, he published *Vital Vidwansan*, exposing the fraud committed by caste Hindus[4] on the untouchables. Walunkar was greatly influenced by the work and ideas of contemporary reformers like Phule and Ranade. As mentioned earlier, he submitted a petition to request the government to resume the recruitment of Mahars in the army. In one of his memoranda (1897) he reminded the Indian National Congress that it would be morally justifiable for them to ask for independence only after bringing about certain fundamental social reforms.

SHIVARAM JANABA KAMBLE

Inspired by the writings of Walunkar, Phule, Baba Padmanji, Rajaramshastri Bhagwat and others, Kamble joined the liberation movement around 1902. His father worked as a servant in a British family, where Kamble had the opportunity to learn English and to read books and newspapers. That created in him a new consciousness and helped him enlarge his cognitive world.

For the propagation of his ideas among his caste-fellows, Kamble adopted the modern technique of organizing conferences. During his career as an activist, he organized two conferences of Mahars, the first at Sasvad (District Pune) in 1904, which several hundred Mahars from 51 villages attended. Its major achievement was a charter of demands signed by 1,558 participants, perhaps the first written petition ever made to the British Government. The fact that Kamble mailed copies of it to important persons and major English dailies in both India and England speaks volumes for his ingenuity. The second conference was held at Jejuri (District Pune) in 1910.

Kamble also established an association, the Shri Shankar Prasadik Somvanshiya Hitchintak Mitra Samaj, so named because *Somvanshi* was probably the largest among the 52 Mahar subcastes. Kamble felt deeply concerned about certain evil social practices and customs among his people. He wrote extensively about them in his own periodical, *Somvanshiya Mitra*, which he edited for about three years. He also realized the significance of schools and libraries in social awakening, and so established a few for his own people. Finally, Kamble was militant; he often criticized the British Government for neglecting the interests of untouchables and once had a confrontation with B.G. Tilak.

VITOBHA RAOJI MOON PANDE

Moon Pande can be considered the father of the Mahar movement in Vidarbha. As a tradesman he had to travel a lot. His wide contacts with people of his own caste made him aware of their degraded state. He used the medium of religious discourse to create a new awakening in them. He tried to bring about internal social reforms by persuading his people to refrain from eating beef and carcasses, and from consuming alcohol.

Moon Pande took a leading part in building up the organizations of Mahars in Vidarbha. He was instrumental in establishing two major associations, the Antyaja Samaj Committee in 1906 and Mahar Sabha in 1912. Mahar leaders of the nineteenth century in general did not make a secret of their loyalty to British rule, which Moon Pande, for example, considered a boon for untouchables. This is why he encouraged his people to join the army during World War I.

KISAN BHAGOJI BANSODE

Bansode was one of the most active, enterprising and influential leaders in Vidarbha. He created a network of associations to carry out his activities. Bansode realized the significance of education in the emancipation of the untouchables, and he opened a school for girls in 1907. Wishing to reduce the number of drop-outs, and also to enable rural students to enrol, he encouraged the establishment of hostels for untouchable students. He even started a small industrial school for untouchables and trained them for industrial jobs.

Like other Mahar leaders, Bansode was aware of the potential of the printed page in bringing about social change. He started and edited *Nirasrit Hind Nagarik*, *Vital Vidwansan* and a few other periodicals. His writings were also published in such reputed newspapers as *Dnyanprakash, Deenbandhu* and *Mumbai Vaibhav*. He was an architect of the *Tarun Mahar Sangh*, a militant organization of young Mahars, whose members were required to take oaths not to perform the traditional duty of removing carcasses, not to eat beef, not to spend extravagantly on weddings, and so on. Bansode thus often took militant postures and had quite a few serious encounters with caste Hindus. He was opposed to religious conversion, however, and thus was to develop a serious rift with Ambedkar.

GANESH AKKAJI GAWAI

Gawai was an associate of Bansode. They together started a branch of the Depressed India Association in Nagpur in 1922, and edited a periodical, *Bahiskrit Bharat*, for a number of years. Gawai was called upon to give evidence before the Southborough Committee[5] along with Ambedkar. His tenure as a nominated member of the Legislative Council of the Central Provinces and Berar from 1921 to 1923 and later, from 1924 to 1930, was effective, since he raised a number of issues concerning untouchables.

KALICHARAN NANDGAVALI

The Mahar movement in Vidarbha carried the imprint of Nandgavali's leadership. From a traditionally rich *malgujar* family, he was intimately connected with a number of associations. It was because of his generous grant that a school for girls of the untouchable castes could be started in Gondia in 1911. Nandgavali, like Gawai, was a member of the Legislative Council of the Central Provinces and Berar from 1919 to 1923; he was instrumental in having a committee of the House appointed to go into the problems of the untouchables.

Besides these six leading persons there were numerous others who contributed significantly to the movement between 1890 and 1925. They included Jairam Shetya Gaekwad, Yenku Sakharam Saokar, Fathuji Shende, Pandurang Bhatkar, Janoji Khandare, Bhatankar and others.

During the period under review numerous conferences and conventions of the Mahars were organized in different parts of Maharashtra, with a view to generating a collective consciousness and giving the movement a populist image. Traditionally, Mahars had used religious congregations to discuss caste affairs; now the same idiom was utilized to generate public support for the movement. It is through these meetings that a new collective identity began to take shape.

A reference was made earlier to two major conferences organized by Shivaram Kamble. In the first, public expression was given to a number of grievances and the intervention of the government was sought through a petition. At the second, several resolutions outlining the untouchables' expectations from the government were carried. Copies of a memorandum containing these resolutions were sent to the Provincial and Central Governments. Despite the latter's cold response, Kamble submitted a similar memorandum in 1910 to the Earl of Crewe, Secretary of State for India. Copies of this petition were also sent to eminent members of the British Parliament and to the editors of newspapers.

The petition said that although a good deal of improvement had taken place in the condition of untouchables, things could have still been better. Kamble alleged that British officers were not very positively disposed towards the untouchables because they feared that caste Hindus would be displeased. A major demand of the petition was that Mahar candidates be given preference in appointments to the lower-grade positions of the revenue and police departments, and in the army. This was probably the first ever articulation of the now familiar demand for reservation of a proportion of jobs for untouchables in government service. Since there were few educated untouchables at the time, Kamble showed practical wisdom in asking for reservations only in the lower-grade jobs. In the same petition, he also pleaded for compulsory, free education for untouchables.

Both Walunkar and Kamble submitted a number of other petitions and memoranda to the government, making appeals to its sense of justice, moral commitment and humanism. This shows how quickly the leaders mastered the art of using constitutional means for pressuring the government (Zelliot 1973: 20-69).

Since 1915, there had been much political awakening among the untouchables. With a view to giving public expression to their political aspirations, a national conference, the Bharatiya Bahiskrit Parishad was organized in Nagpur in 1920. The initiative was taken by Gawai, Bansode and other Mahar leaders. Although it was a conference of all the untouchable castes, it was dominated by Mahars, and gave a strong boost to their collective identity.

At the Conference, Nandgavali criticized the government for its half-hearted efforts to protect the interests of the untouchables. He also urged his people to dissociate themselves from the Indian National Congress. A strong plea to adopt strict measures for the abolition of untouchability, and for the adequate representation of untouchables in legislative councils was also made, and it was urged that only untouchables be nominated to represent their own interests. A demand for a separate department for protecting untouchable interests was also voiced. Interestingly, it was also demanded that Brahmans should not be appointed as education ministers, and that there should be a legal ban on eating carcasses.

Another national conference was held in December 1922 to coincide with the visit of the Prince of Wales. In the presence of 60,000 untouchables, Gawai urged the Crown Prince not to leave the untouchables to the mercy of caste Hindus. Numerous other meetings, large and small, were also organized in different parts of Maharashtra, facilitating the participation of the masses in the movement.

Formal organization was an alien phenomenon in India, arriving with the British, but within a short span of time the Mahar leaders started using such organizations skilfully. During the period under review numerous formal associations and institutions, which were functionally differentiated, were started, among them some for the purpose of articulation and propagation of the new liberating ideology. Internal social reforms were on the agenda of others. A few remedial institutions, like schools and boarding houses were also established.

As mentioned earlier, the Anarya Dosh Parihar Samaj established by Walunkar in 1893 was probably the first formal organization of untouchables in Maharashtra. It aimed at bringing about internal social reforms among members. It subsequently became so renowned that its members were called for consultation by Risley while he was documenting Hindu customs and traditions.

In the Vidarbha region Moon Pande formed the Arya Samaj Committee in 1906, and used it to bring about religious reforms among Mahars. The Mahar Sabha, established also by Moon Pande in 1913, constructed a drinking-water well and a caravan-serai for Mahars. Among its other activities were providing financial aid to needy students, and bringing about reconciliations between separated husbands and wives! The sabha also made efforts to foster unity among the various Mahar subcastes.

A number of educational institutions and other organizations, named after the Mahar Chokha Mela, a renowned fifteenth-century Marathi poet-saint, were established in different places. One such organization was the Shri Chokha Mela Samaj, established in Vidarbha in 1920. It was primarily involved in educational activities, though a resolution passed at one of its meetings also signifies its political orientation. It was resolved that the non-cooperation movement was harmful to the interests of the untouchables, who were advised thus to stay away from it. Yet another organization named after Chokha Mela was established at Nagpur in 1922. In one of its resolutions, passed in 1923, it thanked the caste Hindus of Nagpur for allowing Mahars to participate in their religious functions. The resolution further said that since the untouchables themselves were Hindus, they should enjoy the same religious rights as the members of the higher castes.

Finally, the Depressed Indian Association, started by Bansode and Gawai around 1915, soon became a leading organization of untouchables. Its officials were invited to give evidence before the Southborough Committee in 1918. Besides education, the Association also showed interest in moral, social and economic uplift and the protection and promotion of the interests of farm labourers and mill workers.

With the introduction of printing technology the printed page became an important medium of mass communication and mobilization. The first Marathi periodical, *Darpan*, appeared in 1832. Subsequently, newspapers and periodicals were used by political reformists for mobilizing public support for the independence movement, and by social reformists for creating a critical awareness of social and religious issues among the people, and to develop in them new sensitivities.

The first periodical owned and edited by a Mahar was published in 1908, the *Somvanshiya Mitra* edited by Shivaram Kamble. It was published for about three years; most of its contents were of the nature of discourses on issues concerning untouchables. Kamble declared that his main goal was to make people aware of their basic human rights, and to provoke some introspection (Nirmale 1987). Kishan Bansode also published four periodicals—*Nirashriya Hind Nagarik, Vital Vidwansan, Majoor Patrika* and *Chokha Mela*. Bansode owned a printing press and had trained his wife in the art of composing. His press was destroyed by Hindu fundamentalists who disapproved of his views on Hinduism. Similarly, Gawai started his own periodical, *Bahiskrit Bharat*; but its publication stopped after a few issues.

This brief survey reveals how perceptive Mahars were in sensing the possibility of their social emancipation and economic uplift under British rule. One factor that played a crucial role in raising their self-awareness was service in the British army. In fact, in pre-British times they had served in the armies of both Muslim and Maratha rulers. However, despite their commendable record of valour, their position in the social-ritual hierarchy remained unchanged (Khairmode 1978: 146-53). In the more secular environment of the British army, valour could win more laurels (ibid: 224), and strengthen their belief in their own potential. More importantly, a Mahar non-commissioned officer could lord it over his caste Hindu subordinates. This experience brought about some change in the traditionally subservient psyche. Also, the education received in the army, and elsewhere, developed their thinking and reflexive abilities. There emerged in them new aspirations, a new world-view, and a sense of a new identity which fostered a spirit of rebellion. In the Vidarbha region, rich Mahars joined in the movement, with the hope of enhancing their status. They could muster the support of their compatriots by promising them a better future.

In retrospect, it can be said that the early leaders were right in recognizing the significance of education and of government jobs in the process of the emancipation and economic uplift of the untouchables. They repeatedly voiced their demand for free, compulsory education, and for the reservation of jobs in numerous conferences and petitions.

By 1915, the political aspirations of the Mahars were also aroused. In their representations before the Southborough Committee in 1918, their leaders demanded that untouchables be represented in legislative bodies in proportion to their numbers. They also asserted that the representatives of the untouchables should themselves be untouchables and be elected by untouchables alone. As a result, in accordance with the provisions of the package of political reforms granted in 1919, a few untouchable representatives were nominated as members of the provincial legislatures. The performance of some of them was truly commendable (Moon 1987: 46-95). For example, Nandgavali made a demand on the floor of the House that representation should be given to untouchables on all statutory bodies and government committees. He urged the government to consider the issues concerning untouchables as civic issues rather than religious ones, and to take the initiative in solving them even against the wishes of caste Hindus.

As stressed above, these early leaders considered British rule a boon, and the British as their real benefactors. They repeatedly stressed their allegiance to them, and eulogized, rather than criticized, them. The Mahar Sabha established by Moon Pande thus earned itself the name of the 'Loyalist Mahar Sabha'. However, this is not to say that the Mahars were not on the side of the nationalists; they merely considered political independence without the emancipation of the untouchables as meaningless.

On the basis of the available evidence one can conclude that the early leaders did not hold religion responsible for their plight. They viewed untouchability as a kind of aberration of which Hinduism must be purged. They certainly thought that it would be possible for untouchables to solve their problems within the framework of Hinduism, a view to which even Ambedkar subscribed in the early stages of his career. Ambedkar, however soon realized the futility of this approach, and began to consider conversion as the only way out, a view which the early Mahar leaders at times had openly opposed.

However, at the same time there is also reason to believe that the early leaders had no faith in the commitment of upper caste reformers to the cause of the untouchables. They preferred to keep at a distance. For example, when V.R. Shinde—a caste Hindu reformer—was invited to represent the case of untouchables to the Southborough Committee, there was a strong protest from the Mahar leaders who insisted that only an untouchable could do so. They also opposed Shinde's recommendations to the Committee regarding the franchise to be given to the untouchables. Phule and Shahu, the latter the ruler of the princely state of Kolhapur, were the only caste Hindu reformers who enjoyed the confidence of Mahar leaders. There was a streak of anti-Brahman feeling in them though it must be stressed that their social reformism was secular in its essence.

The subaltern elites who led the movement undeniably lacked ideological sophistication; yet they were very clear in their minds about their objectives.

Although not highly educated, they were guided by their native wisdom. They certainly understood the competitive and civic nature of the society emerging under British rule, and the means they chose for advancement, such as education, government jobs and internal social reform, were correct. What surprises us is the speed with which they mastered modern techniques of propagation and mobilization. Because of their committed efforts, the untouchable liberation movement in Maharashtra had already achieved a degree of momentum by the time Ambedkar arrived on the scene.

NOTES

1. By making the necessary additions and subtractions in the Census figures of 1901, the number of Mahars in present-day Maharashtra can be estimated at 2.7 million. In some of the districts of the Vidarbha region their population is estimated at 15 per cent of the total.
2. *Vatan* lands were arable plots granted to certain clans of Mahars in each village by the regional rulers for their maintenance, and in return for their administrative services.
3. Weaving was a family occupation by some Mahars in the Vidarbha region long before the opening of textile mills there.
4. The term 'caste Hindu' denotes a member of one of the so-called upper castes.
5. The Southborough Committee was appointed by the British Parliament under the chairmanship of Lord Southborough. The Committee visited India in 1918 to assess the opinions and expectations of different sections of the Indian public regarding political rights and opportunities for political participation to be granted to them.

REFERENCES

Gavali, P.A., 1981, *Peshavekalin gulamgiri va asprushyata*, Kolhapur: Prachar Prakashan.

Gupta, S.K., 1985, *The Scheduled Castes in Modern Indian Politics*, New Delhi: Munshiram Manoharlal.

Khairmode, C.B., 1978, *Dr. Babasaheb Ramji Ambedkar*, vol. 1, Mumbai: Pratap Prakashan.

Kosare, H.L., 1984, *Vidarbhatil dalit chalwalicha itihas*, Nagpur: Dyan Pradip Prakashan.

Moon, V., 1987, *Madhyaprant-Vidarbhatil Dr. Ambedkarpurva dalit chalwal*, Pune: Sugava Prakashan.

Nirmale, H.C., 1987, *Dalitanchi nyatkalike (1908-1950)*, Pune: Sugava Prakashan.

Ramteke, D.L., 1983, *Revival of Buddhism in Modern India*, New Delhi: Deep and Deep Publications.

Zelliot, E., 1970, 'The nineteenth century background of the Mahar and Non-brahmin movements in Maharashtra', *Economic and Social History Review* 7.3.

———, 1973, 'Learning the use of political means: the Mahars in Maharashtra', in *Caste in Indian Politics*, R. Kothari (ed.), Delhi: Orient Longman.

Deshabhakta: The Leaders of the Italian Independence Movement in the Eyes of Marathi Nationalists

E. FASANA

RISORGIMENTO, THE NINETEENTH-CENTURY MOVEMENT FOR THE NATIONAL UNIFICATION OF ITALY

Even as the word *Risorgimento* is never mentioned, the thought and example of the leaders of the Italian nationalist movement made an important impact on the Marathi-speaking intelligentsia from roughly the end of the nineteenth century to the First World War.[1] At that time many Marathi and English publications, including periodicals, dealt with this topic, some of them bearing the brunt of censorship and, occasionally, prosecution. The idea that they could escape this by using foreign examples implied that what was permissible in Britain could have also been permitted in her colonies, but this was not so. The topic was popular for many reasons: many Marathi-speaking intellectuals followed the lead of Bengalis who had known of the lives of Italian leaders for a longer time, having travelled more extensively in Europe. The sympathy towards the *Risorgimento* began among the *bhadralok*[2] and it was moderate in its appeal.

It was Surendranath Banerjea (1848-1925) who fascinated young audiences with his *Lectures* (1876-80) on Mazzini.[3] The message was not for Bengal alone, but for India as a whole. Banerjea came to know Mazzini's work while studying in London for the ICS examinations. From Banerjea the message went to Lala Lajpat Rai,[4] who considered himself one of his disciples, and wrote the first Urdu biographies of Mazzini, Garibaldi and Shivaji (in 1892, 1893 and 1896). The books were also translated into English and other Indian languages.

It is interesting to note in this case, as in many others, that the foreign examples of nationalist heroes came first in time, and were then followed by their Indian counterparts, who at that time were probably considered not national enough. Other Bengalis joined in this hymn of praise and spread the message, for example Romesh Chandra Dutt (1848-1909) who had visited Italy in 1871 and at the end of his career became Revenue Minister of Baroda state (which was ruled by a Maratha, the Gaekwad)[5] and Aurobindo Ghose (1872-1950) who joined him in Baroda as the Principal of the Shri Ganganath Bharatiya Sarva Vidyalaya.[6]

THE SOURCES

Much of the Marathi prose of the period, composed of translations of English works, included biographies of foreign heroes. The impact of this literature (*charitra*) had always been strong in Marathi-speaking areas, but it was mainly hagiographic. Such were the *Bhaktavijaya* or the *Bhaktalilamrita* of the poet-saints of Maharashtra. This literature received a new impetus dwelling on historical heroes of the past, utilizing the old *bakhars* (narratives of famous heroic exploits), letters, *akhbars* and *rojnishis* (diaries); it maintained, on the whole, the poetic flair of the Bhakti hymns and stories, of the heroic ballads (*povadas*) and of the love poems (*lavni*).

During the course of the nineteenth century this material was first translated into standard Marathi and then adapted to a form closer to spoken Marathi, the *nagari* script replacing the *modi* script. Certain forms of traditional literature received the same modifications, for example with the passage from chronicles to historical essays, from the wondrous biographies of saints to those of a Western stamp. They were still called *atmacharitra* (vicissitudes of the soul), but the term no longer carried its original meaning; it was not a question of personal liberation but, on the contrary, of the glorification of even mundane successes.[7] The process, of course, was slow and complex.

THE APPEAL TO THE NATION BY 'MODERATES' AND 'EXTREMISTS'

Two streams of thought were mingled from the start: some underlined the ethical sense of duty of Mazzini, Garibaldi and other Italian leaders towards their country on a highly personal basis, the others stressed Mazzini's concept of the nation. In the first instance the examples could be adopted without engendering a chain of political consequences, while in the second, the stress would have been ideological. There were differences about the concept of the Nation, and thus about the order to be given to a future India. Leaving aside the peculiarities of Gandhian thought, the so-called moderates aimed at a *Nation in the Making*, reflected in the title of Banerjea's famous autobiography.[8] They emphasized the institutional and administrative aspects, favouring the rights of individuals over those of the state. The 'extremists' spoke of the nation as a given historical, social, political and religious fact since time immemorial, and emphasized the duties of individuals towards the community, decrying the presence of foreigners as an obstacle to national unity.

The more the political means were constitutional and representative, the more necessary social reform seemed for the formation of the nation. Unity and independence would follow, with the British model, including its educational institutions, being the favoured one. By contrast, the more the existence of Indian national unity was stressed, the more the British presence was resented. Models of personal and national behaviour were then sought elsewhere, both within India and without.[9] Likewise, interpretations of *mantras* adopted as national slogans, such as *swaraj* and *swatantra*, varied considerably, even though these positions formed not a contrast but a continuum. The concept *in making* already implied a project of a social reality, and social and educational associations helped make one aware of such a reality. Nor was it necessarily true that the so-called extremists were social conservatives; they simply did not want changes to be instituted by a foreign ruling power, a feeling also true of Gandhi.

THE SITUATION IN BOMBAY PROVINCE

The time dedicated to the ideas and examples of European nationalism is limited to a period of fifteen years, up to the outbreak of World War I, which also spans the clashes of the Moderates and Extremists in Bombay Province.[10]

It is important to stress that, in Maharashtra, the social reformers seemed to neglect the Italian Independence Movement in their speeches and in the papers controlled by them. The example of S. Banerjea taught them a lesson, however; after the first emotional reaction he could not accept the revolutionary and violent approach of Mazzini's thought and action.

In Mumbai, where the Utilitarian approach was stronger than in Bengal, and magnified as the symbol of everything new, the intelligentsia stood by the Indian National Congress as an association willing to work inside the political and administrative framework provided by British rule. The so-called moderates were extremely diversified in Mumbai because, on the one hand, the reformist ideas had a relevance within individual communities (chiefly among the Parsis) and, on the other, particular interests were aroused by disparate alliances. The leadership was united by a common Western education, which aimed to reform society and create a political class destined to replace the British in power.

Among the social reformers, interest in the past was severely limited; they did not talk about independence and did not need the examples of other countries apart from England, whose constitutional development remained their main point of reference. However, among the social reformers of Pune, there were contrasts in the management of the education societies in the curricula of the Fergusson and Deccan Colleges, in the opening of the printing presses, in the publication and circulation of books and periodicals. The political, social and cultural atmospheres of these two cities were, in fact, strongly contrasting; Mumbai had an economic *raison d'être* and British inspiration while Pune remained aware of its *Peshwai* historical tradition, its leaders, particularly Bal Gangadhar Tilak (1856-1920),[11] feeling that they could better guide the nationalist movement given their close ties with local society and tradition.[12]

We know that it is difficult to have a clear-cut identification of nationalist leaders, because different streaks overlap in areas, groups and even persons. Furthermore, while the Pune leadership consisted mainly of Chitpavan Brahmans, we cannot be certain that nationalists dominated among them.[13] Chitpavans dominated many political and social movements,[14] but rather as individuals than as an organized group. In fact, individualism among Brahmans has been more evident than among other communities.[15]

One should differentiate between the sociological and ideological aspects of the problem. Sociologically, there is a tendency among Brahmans to accept certain ideas, but this does not mean that there is a definite 'plot'. Certainly, Brahmans on the whole seem to have been more concerned with the *ancien régime*, especially in the Pune area. The images and examples of the past were still vivid in local minds, and probably represented a more clear-cut 'Hindu' way of thought.

Meanwhile, the strong connection, without actual identification, between religion and politics in this area gave the chance of a religious-political recruitment. At the end of nineteenth century Tilak recruited the cult of Ganapati and also revived Shivaji's example.[16] There were also political assassinations by the Chaphekar brothers. The partition of Bengal, the threat of communal divisions, the foundation of the Muslim League, the defeat of Russia by Japan in the same year[17] and the Morley-Minto reforms of political representation all furthered the desire for a local response which had not as yet an ideological frame.

THE ITALIAN EXAMPLES

It is impressive to see how people from a distant country like Italy were adopted as representatives of local grievances and as examples of a sense of duty. Notwithstanding the modernizing factor of these movements, examples from abroad only occurred to some nationalists at a later stage. The title given to foreign nationalists was sometimes *vibhuti* (somebody endowed with creative powers, of divine origin). No wonder that Mazzini could be born again in India as the notion of reincarnation (*avatara*) had always been a factor of local integrations.[18] He was, indeed, a *kavi*, a national bard, just as many Indian nationalists considered themselves to be *kaviraj*, the bards of the nascent nation-state. The *kavya* were contrasted with the ritualists, the Brahmans or *dharmalok*. No longer the legitimizers of royal power, the new *gurus* took into their hands their own destiny.

But why Italy? Evidently there were numerous things in common[19] such as the presence of religion, regional diversity yet with an overriding sense of cultural unity among states (*sansthan* in the Maratha tradition), and the ability to read Italian authors in translation. This last, of course, again shows the percolation of influence through a British filter present in educated Indians. Mazzini spent a large part of his life in London, and Garibaldi had received a royal welcome there. England had helped the expeditions against the Bourbons of Naples and, furthermore, all the *Risorgimento* leaders were staunchly anti-clerical and liberal without being revolutionary.

THE CENTENARIES AND THEIR VARYING IMPACT

The centenaries of the heroes of the *Risorgimento*, Mazzini (1905), Garibaldi (1907) and Cavour (1910), gave the Marathi press the opportunity to cite them as examples that Indians could also follow. The lead came from the weeklies,

Kesari (The Lion) and *The Mahratta*, published in Marathi and English, and edited by Tilak and his lieutenant N.C. Kelkar (1872-1947), respectively. Both weeklies were founded by the Deccan Education Society in 1881, itself founded by Tilak and G.G. Agarkar, the social reformer who left it in 1887 to start his own periodical, *Sudharak* (The Reformer). The *Kesari* was the largest of all weeklies in Maharashtra (at 20,000), *The Mahratta* having a much smaller circulation (1,000).

Kelkar was the first to write a biography of Garibaldi, and it had five editions by 1944, became a standard text for High School examinations, and was the most widespread text on the *Risorgimento* to be allowed by the censors.[20] It was a vast and meticulous list of dates, though it ignores the earlier biography of Lala Lajpat Rai, and is neither very personal, nor attempts any comparisons with India with the exception of the Appendix, since the oath (*shapath*) of the members of Young Italy (*Tarun Italy*) is an evident reference to the possible tasks of Indian nationalists. It also quotes the controversy between the three major leaders, in which Cavour emerges with the most credit, being called *mutsaddi* (statesman) by the author. All in all, the book reflects the Tilakist trend of favouring practical results over abstract ideas.

TILAK'S EDITORIALS AND TRIALS

Tilak's editorials on Garibaldi and Mazzini[21] were translated—among other publications—into English as part of the legal proceedings he instituted against Sir Valentine Chirol. A chapter of the latter's *The Indian Unrest,* published while Tilak was in Mandalay Jail,[22] had portrayed him as one who wished to restore 'the Brahmin dominion', as a 'fanatic racialist' and a major source of inspiration for terrorism.[23] It is interesting to analyse the titles of these articles—Tilak styles Garibaldi *vibhuti*, the same term that he used for Shivaji and which also appears in the *Gita* for 'somebody endowed with creative powers'.[24] The same can be said for *deshabhakta*, used for Mazzini, which is a modernization of *devabhakta* (devoted to God), signalling the transfer of allegiance from God to country.

In the first editorial, Tilak compares the centenary festivities (*utsav*) of Garibaldi and Shivaji. The former was attended by the king of Italy, Victor Emmanuel, and his subjects (*praja*), in spite of Garibaldi's death sentence for high treason (*rajadroh*), while the latter were ignored by the British authorities (*angrezi adhikari*) even though Shivaji had been their friend. Parallels are drawn between Italy and India, geographically and climatically. Italians—like Indians—are by nature affectionate (*premal*), lovers of pleasure (*hausi*), happy (*ulhasi*); the greatness of Rome is compared to that of Ujjain and Delhi; England herself was under Roman dominion, while in later times a divided Italy was subject to the Austrian Empire. These references were not purely casual, but were suggested by Kelkar, since Tilak otherwise had little interest in Italy.

Tilak also dedicated a series of editorials and comments to the Irish Question and the activities of Sinn Fein, the party of armed rebellion. Indeed, he took the idea of *swaraj* from them. This entailed both a boycott of British products and the more positive concept of *swadeshi*, the defence and patronage of locally manufactured goods. Tilak was more interested in *swaraj* than in *swatantra* (independence), a constructive programme as opposed to the negative concept of the Bengali *bhadralok* and the Panjabi Arya Samaj.

Finally, Tilak tried to turn Shivaji—founder of the Maratha *swaraj*—into a pan-Indian hero, in cooperation with Lala Lajpat Rai, who had written a biography of him in 1897. He was successful at least in Bengal, thanks to the ideal alliance between Bhavani and Shivaji. Bhavani was the family deity of Shivaji's clan, the Bhonsle, and at the same time, it is another name for Kali, the most revered goddess of Bengal.

TILAK: GARIBALDI AND MAZZINI AS PARALLELS TO SHIVAJI AND RAMDAS

Tilak cannot separate the personality of Garibaldi from that of his *guru* Mazzini; the *guru*-disciple relationship is indeed characteristic of India, and Shivaji and Ramdas may be offered as a parallel to the Italian case. Mazzini acts against the institutions and the favourable situation of the time, something which Ramdas failed to do. His republican ideas (*prajashakti rajya*), however, are an obstacle for India: in Italy, Piedmont is like a Native State, *sansthan*; the economic support that Tilak received from the native states is well known. On the one hand, a new Chatrapati (king of the *dharma*) may appear, but, on the other, the Maratha nobility may hinder Brahman-non-Brahman unity, as was the case with the Maharaja of Kolhapur.[25]

Tilak also includes in his pantheon of heroes Cavour and Victor Emmanuel, whose practical spirit he appreciates. The king and Garibaldi are portrayed as brothers, while the clash between the latter and Cavour is seen as exclusively motivated by the transfer of Nice (Garibaldi's native land) to Austria (*sic*!). Both Mazzini and Garibaldi are appreciated for their principled behaviour and sense of sacrifice; for example, Mazzini remained a bachelor and made a vow of chastity (*brahmachari*) for the good of his country. While Mazzini was seen as a poet (*kavi*) with the power of vision, Cavour was the *mutsaddi* (diplomat).

Garibaldi as a soldier and farmer was not interested in the material aspects of life; he is *rashtrabhakta vira* (national hero) who prepares his followers for the sacrifice in the *homakunda*. Victor Emmanuel is *rashtrabhakta sansthanik* (the national ruler) who prepares himself for the initiation (*diksha*) of war to the benefit of his country, and behaves in general like Yuddhisthira, the personification of Duty in the *Mahabharata*. Indeed, the whole Italian experience is assimilated to Vedic sacrifice and the holy war described in the epic. The anti-clerical aspect of Garibaldi is almost ignored: Hindu institutions are different and the only negative hint is addressed to the Pope whose authority is likened to that of the four Shankaracharyas, the representatives of Brahmanical orthodoxy.

As we can see from these examples, the protagonists of the *Risorgimento* were successfully adopted to meet Indian requirements; yet Tilak's interpretation greatly differs from Gandhi's, expressed in *Hind Swaraj* in 1909. The latter felt that no attempt was made to change Italians either before or after Independence, and that Mazzini's ideals were sacrificed to political results.[26] But what mattered most to Tilak was the recovery of the Indian tradition. The six years spent in Mandalay Prison (1908-14) enabled him to complete those researches which he started with *The Orion: Researches into the Antiquities of the Vedas* (1893) and *The Arctic Home of the Aryans* (1903). From the Vedas he moved on to Bhakti, from the scripts of revelation to those of tradition, with his articulated interpretation of the *Bhagavad Gita*.[27]

N.C. KELKAR'S EDITORIALS ON ITALY AND HIS POLITICAL PRAXIS

Kelkar too wrote on the occasion of the centenaries of Garibaldi and Cavour,[28] besides his interest in Ireland.[29] He was known as *sahitya samrat* (emperor of literature) and was a Chitpavan like Tilak who moved from the *sansthan* of Miraj to Pune. As chief editor of *The Mahratta* from the outset, he twice submitted his resignation due to disagreements with Tilak (1897 and 1907), but withdrew it on both occasions. He frequently acted as bridge between the Moderates and the Extremists, and was even accused by some of the latter (e.g. S. M. Paranjpe) of being a Moderate himself. He certainly preferred to work through established channels like the press, the associations of caste and interests, and the Indian National Congress. As he preferred to harmonize the various strains of nationalism, his approach was much more flexible than Tilak's, though he followed in his footsteps during the final stages of the Lokamanya's life (Cashman 1975: 191), and succeeded him as leader of the Swarajist Party in 1924, supporting electoral participation in the local assemblies. Opposition to the non-cooperation movement later led him to join the Hindu Mahasabha.

The contradictions between Garibaldi and Mazzini are not highlighted in Kelkar's works, nor are there many references to the Indian scene. It is the Italian celebrations that make good news and Kelkar is a good journalist. Both heroes feel the charm of Rome,[30] Mazzini sees it as the capital of the world, Garibaldi in the Italian context. They go back to the ancient past of their country to find their identity, a clear allusion to Indian trends. Cavour is the politician and statesman, the brain behind Italian unity and the one who succeeds in blending the heterogeneous, discordant elements of Italian patriotism. Kelkar likens him to Bismarck, though he prefers Cavour for his maintenance of constitutional liberties ('Italy was created with liberty, Germany with authority'). Prussia is likened to the Piedmont, with the hint that Maharashtra could play a similar role in India.

Kelkar was not specifically interested in Mazzini, though he wrote an introduction to one of his Marathi biographies.[31] The same biography refers to English sources on the *Risorgimento*: Trevelyan for Garibaldi, W.R. Thayer for Cavour, Bolton King's *Life of Mazzini*, Marriott's *The Makers of Modern Italy*; all standard works and full of praise for the movement. Kelkar's Introduction clearly sets Mazzini against Cavour, the man of practice (*pratyaksha*) against the man of *kalpana* (imagination, fantasy) and the statesman (a term he also used for Garibaldi) against the saint. The reference to Gandhiji in 1923 was not purely casual. The desire for political results, be it independence or self-government, led many of Tilak's followers to join the 'Hindu Revolutionaries'.

KRANTIKARI, THE REVOLUTIONARIES

It is significant that on the basis of Mazzini's thinking it was the revolutionary idea that became the most popular in Maharashtra, especially in Pune. Neither *jahal* nor *nemast* (moderate or extremist) but *krantikari* (revolutionary) was the favoured term describing the Italian nationalists.[32] For those who wanted to reject the British example from the beginning, the Italian Nationalist Movement was the most closely akin to the feelings of Bhakti and Sakti (inner and vital force), though more in personal behaviour than in belonging to any established social or religious organization. Mazzini's best assets were his sense of duty, that he was a *deshabhakta*, an organizer of *ganimi yuddha* (guerilla bands) and of *gupta mandalis* (secret associations like Young Italy). In an environment like India, where there is no established church but where spirituality as a way of liberation had a particularly personal character, Mazzini became the standard bearer of all 'religious' nationalisms, which were not religious in any identifiable way but possessed a very general spiritual feeling.

THE SAVARKAR BROTHERS

Among the Revolutionaries, the one who spread the name and example of Mazzini most was Vinayak Damodar Savarkar (1883-1966)[33] along with his brothers Ganesa Damodar (1879-1945) and Narayan Damodar (1886-1949). They were Chitpavans from Bhagur, not far from Nasik, and were initially spurred by the killing of Dr Rand, an ICS officer-in-charge of anti-plague measures in Pune, by the Chaphekar brothers,[34] who were hanged for their crime. British reprisals and the counterreprisals against police informers were among the dramatic consequences of this case, and various secret societies were formed on the Carbonari model by the Savarkars and their friends, first the Rashtra Bhakta Samutha (the body of devotees of the nation, 1899), then the Mitra Mela (the gathering of friends, 1900). Vinayak was a student at that time in Fergusson College, where, in 1902, he made speeches on the revolutions of Holland, Italy and America, and held a seminar on the history of Italy. In 1905, he founded Abhinav Bharat (modern India) with his friends, probably inspired by Mazzini's Young Italy. In 1906, on Tilak's recommendation, he went to London with a scholarship from Shyamji Krishnavarma, who had founded the India House, a hostel for Indian students.[35]

SAVARKAR'S BIOGRAPHY OF MAZZINI

Asaf Ali (1888–1953), a Muslim nationalist, student at Lincoln's Inn writes:

> Savarkar's mind was totally saturated with Mazzini's teachings. Well before he proceeded to England and the free atmosphere of the British Isles, his Sunday speeches served to nourish and ripen the lessons which he had imbibed. . . . The meetings were liberally leavened with the revolutionary ethic of the Indian patriot.[36]

Savarkar himself writes in *Shatruchya Shibirat* (in the country of the enemy)[37] that as soon as he arrived in London he had the unexpected fortune of finding an entire set of Mazzini's works[38] in the library of India House. He goes on: 'I am convinced that the history of the Italian revolution will be able to guide the Indian revolution in many ways.' In a few months, Savarkar translated the passages interesting to him, particularly the autobiographical ones, and sent a selection to his brother Baburao (Ganesh Damodar) who published them in Nasik in 1907 in the name of Vinayak.[39]

The text appeared in 2,000 copies which were sold out in two months, before the book was banned. From the letter of a prisoner, Patankar, which was shown as evidence in the subsequent trial of Savarkar, dated 30 December 1908, and addressed to Ganesh (Baburao), it seems that the latter planned a new edition of 3,000 copies (Srivastava 1983: 272–3)—which did not materialize until 1946 in Pune, a third edition appearing in Mumbai only in 1979.[40] In places like Nasik and Pune, the book was wrapped in silk, placed in a palanquin and taken in procession to show its importance and to spread its message, thus treated almost like a deity in a *ratha yatra*. Its contents, moreover, were learnt by heart by members of Abhinav Bharat. The actual spread of the printed word and its impact has to be evaluated with local conditions in mind: a person who reads it often becomes the spokesman for a much larger group, and single copies may be reproduced by many newspapers. The prestige of an informer can further enhance the circulation of any news.

Savarkar's book was dedicated to Tilak, who had advised against its publication,[41] and to Shivram Mahadev Paranjpe (1864–1927), editor of *Kal*, the most influential weekly after *Kesari*, considered to be much more extremist than the latter, for which Savarkar was the London correspondent.[42] Disowned by Tilak during the Chirol trial, the second edition was dedicated to 'The revolutionaries of the entire India in 1857–1946'. Most of the nationalist papers published reviews of the book.

In the Introduction Savarkar underlines the parallels between Mazzini and Ramdas, the bard of national and political unity of *deshabhumi*, and the close connection expressed by Mazzini between religion and politics (*dharma* and *rajkaran*). The concept of duty of Mazzini is emphasized and compared to the rights inculcated by the French Revolution.[43] Duties unite while rights are individual and competitive. There is a great difference as regards the ideas previously formulated by the nationalist milieu, and the *duties of man* are seen as more adaptable to Indian tradition than the *rights of man and of the citizen*. Life is not a pleasure but a duty (*kartavya*); the idea of sacrifice prevails just as in Tilak's case. *Kartavya* is no longer the religion of birth or *dharma*; the action must be done by man; destiny is in his hands.

The first duty of man is to fight for a *swatantra rashtra*; the form of future government is postponed until this goal is attained, as suggested by Aurobindo and Lajpat Rai, though not by the latest writings of Tilak. Savarkar agrees with Mazzini on the republican ideal, and opposes monarchy to democracy, *rajasatta* to *loksatta*, something which Tilak was careful to set aside. He also insists on the concept of nation (*rashtra*); nations do not die, and liberation must not stop within one country, but carried on until all slaves are liberated. Furthermore, liberty cannot be obtained through charity as a result of begging, a stance which Moderates and Extremists were both felt to have taken.

THE CHOICE OF MAZZINI'S WRITINGS: AN INTERPRETATION

In order to gain national freedom, the formation of secret societies was needed. Mazzini had founded Young Italy (*Tarun Italy*).[44] Through these, it is necessary to penetrate the army and for war bands to attack the enemy. The writings on the 'war of the bands' and on the insurrectional attempt by the Bandiera brothers are the most emphasized parts of Mazzini's work apart from the autobiographical notes. One should note that these were precisely the aspects of Mazzini's legacy that both Moderates and Hindu Revivalists of the Arya Samaj, not to mention Gandhi, rejected.[45] Savarkar called Mazzini *bhagwan*, *mahatma*, one who behaves like a far-sighted eagle. By contrast, Savarkar says little about the 'valiant soldier' Garibaldi, and ignores Cavour and Victor Emmanuel altogether. Everything is centred on Mazzini, although reinterpreted to suit India.

The selection of other texts is also consistent with the editor's comments. The appeal to the religious, *dharmalok*, *dharmaguru*, with the consequent attack on the established church,[46] the appeal to poets and men of letters, pleased Savarkar, whose national ideal is really a subterfuge for the religious ideal. Even if the use of symbols remains Sanskritic, the religious aspect of the past falls within a monistic and philosophical interpretation, which, too, is reduced to politics. This equation of religion and politics is, indeed, without known parallel in India. M.R. Lederle (1976: 287) calls Savarkar 'agnostic' for his *mantra* of God and people. It is difficult to say how much of the equation was to do with God and how much with people: the Indian immanentism played its part here.

THE BANNING OF THE BOOK

For sometime, the police had been keeping an eye on Savarkar. A summary of the Introduction was translated into English and handed to the Judicial Department by the Political Department for an opinion from the Advocate General. The latter, E.B. Raikes, wrote on 19 July 1907:

> On the summary before me I have no doubt that the Preface was written with a directly seditious intention and that almost every native of this country who reads it will know

this, but at the same time it is very difficult to point to a single line of it which can be said to be directed against the British Government. . . . A regular attempt is being made to preach sedition under the guise of teaching historical lessons in this and many other articles. . . . I cannot, however, advise that such a prosecution is certain of success. . . . I incline to think that if the accused person were skillfully defended, he would have a good chance of getting off.[47]

Raikes concluded that any prosecution would have to be instituted in Mumbai, rather than in London.

Despite such caution, the book was banned, due perhaps to the specific choice of Mazzini's writings, such the 'war of the bands' and the insurrection of the Bandiera brothers, which marked a definite affinity between the Indian and Italian situations. It is the sole volume of Mazzini ever to be banned in India,[48] although quotations on the *Risorgimento* were often taken as proof of sedition. An excerpt from Savarkar's *Atmavritta* (autobiography)[49] served as part of the Introduction of the 1979 edition (pp. 18-23). It ends with a poem by Meredith on Italy:

Italia to vindicate thy name—Mazzini, Cavour, Garibaldi three—Thy soul, thy brain, thy sword—They set me free—from ruinous discord with one lustrous aim—May he bless thee and them.

1857

In 1907, on the fiftieth anniversary of the so-called Mutiny of 1857-8, Savarkar was invited to hold some lectures in India House. Comparisons with Italy remained popular and the lectures were warmly received by Indian students.[50] After revising his speech Savarkar then published the text after about a year. The Marathi manuscript having been purloined by police informers, the book was immediately proscribed on its appearance in English in 1909.[51]

In the book, Savarkar again quotes Mazzini on page 3: 'every revolution must have a fundamental principle' and again on page 9: 'if we forget this . . . we cannot appreciate the vast difference between the empire-building wars of Alexander the Great and Italy's fight for liberty under Garibaldi'. It was the first book to deal with the Mutiny as a war of national liberation, and all subsequent nationalist accounts of it followed in Savarkar's footsteps.[52] Thus the popular reverence now accorded to the martyrs of the Mutiny have much to do with Savarkar's work. In the previously mentioned *Shatruchya Shibirat* Savarkar even asserts that Garibaldi himself volunteered to fight for Tatya Tope, the Maratha general, but had to give up his resolve due to the worsening situation in Italy.

THE CONVICTION OF THE SAVARKAR BROTHERS AND INTERNATIONAL INTEREST

G.D. Savarkar was arrested in 1909 for seditious libel and remained in jail until 1921.[53] Madanlal Dhingra, of the India House Group, shot dead Sir Curzon Wyllie, political aide-de-camp to Morley, Secretary of State for India.[54] In 1910,

A. Kanhere, a Chitpavan like the Chapekar brothers, shot the District Magistrate of Nasik, Jackson. The Intelligence Department proved the connection between the London group and the terrorists in Nasik; explosives and manuals for their preparation were found in India House.[55] Savarkar was extradited to India for trial, and although he managed to escape from the boat in Marseilles he was caught again at the sea-front. This episode in Marseilles seemed once again to unify him and Mazzini.[56]

The Indian nationalist group, which had taken asylum in Paris and included Shyamji Krishnavarma, S.S. Rana and Madame Cama, tried in vain to find an echo in French public opinion and at the International Tribunal in The Hague. But the escape to Marseilles and the interest of the Indian refugees in Paris led to the involvement of Assoziano Mazziniana Italiana, in the person of Maria Zandrino, professor of French in Genoa, and correspondent of numerous French and Italian newspapers.[57] In 1912, Zandrino wrote a letter to Pierre Khorat, a socialist who had written a biography of Savarkar in French, asking for information on the possibility of his release.[58] Nevertheless, Savarkar was given a life sentence and transported to Port Blair in the Andamans. After remaining there for eleven years, he was returned to the mainland in 1921 for a further three years in Yeravada Prison in Pune, and subsequently for a period of forced residence at Ratnagiri (until 1937).

HINDUTVA, HINDUPADPADSHAHI

In 1921, while in prison, Savarkar in a poem *Maranonmukha Sanyevara* (on the death bed) once more identified Mazzini with Ramdas.[59] The morally good nations are those which have solidarity (*lokasangraha*) and spiritual welfare (*atmahita*). In his view, the present self, 'I', is not permanent. It will disappear in the absolute self (Lederle 1976: 288). Then, under the pseudonym of 'a Maratha' Savarkar had *Hindutva* published in Nagpur in 1923, with the intention of it becoming his national ideological project. In it he states that the Hindus are a Nation held together by a common culture, history and religion: 'A Hindu is one who looks upon the land that extends from the Indus to the Sea (from *Sindhu* to *Sindhu*) as the land of his forefathers (*pitrbhu*) . . . and who addresses this land as his *punyabhu* (Holy Land).' The three main factors of unity are territorial ties (*rashtra*), blood ties (*jati*) and cultural ties (*samskrti*). The concept of a nation of equals departs from the idea of *dharma* and its practical counterpart, the integration of different groups with their own characteristics and functions.[60] The maximum concession to the caste system is its interpretation as a functional, egalitarian way of life, part of national *samskrti*. The autonomy of *dharma* and *artha* has no place here; the role of the political leader is absolute and replaces that of the *guru*. *Ram-rajya* is much more the kingdom of a king called Rama than of the god of *bhakti*. *Hindutva* becomes politics (*rajkaran*) and, as in Mazzini, politics mingles with ethics and religion is seen as a factor in citizenship of the country.

In 1925, Savarkar wrote *Hindupadpadshahi: a Review of the Hindu Empire in*

Maharashtra, published in Nagpur.[61] The example of the Marathas as 'restorers' of national independence is underlined. In his historical introduction before the events which led to this 're-awakening', Vedic Hinduism is glorified to the detriment of Buddhism and Jainism, which are considered too pacific.[62] The Maratha-Mughal antagonism is highlighted and Shivaji is presented as the ideal Hindu sovereign. Though the stand resembles Tilak's, the Lokamanya was, in fact, more ready to compromise, as shown by the Lucknow Pact of 1916 with the Muslim League leaders. While Tilak and Kelkar had preferred Garibaldi and Cavour as their spokesmen, Savarkar opted for Mazzini and his idealism.

NARAYAN DAMODAR SAVARKAR AND S. A. JOGLEKAR: *THE DUTIES OF MAN*

Narayan, the younger brother of Vinayak and Ganesa, who was still at large, pleaded the cause of his brother even with Gandhi.[63] The latter took up the case of the Savarkar brothers in the pages of *Young India*.[64] Meanwhile, Narayan wrote on Mazzini's birthday, on 22 June, the Preface (*prayojan kathanak*) to Joglekar's Marathi translation of the *Duties of Man* (Joglekar 1921). This preface is very cautious: Narayan wonders if he should write it. In a crescendo he remembers the *Duties of Man*: 'The country as a God, God at the summit, a nation of equals at the base.' He opposes *rajasatta* to *loksahi*, monarchy to the power of the people, but appears more interested in Maharashtra than in the idealized Indian nation (*bharatvarsha*). He underlines the intellectual and spiritual aspects of Mazzini, the great seer, his activism, the universal brotherhood and liberty as a gift of God. Mazzini's combination of religion and politics is here brought closer to the Gandhian stance. Narayan also published a book on Tatya Tope, one of the leaders of the Mutiny, and, like his brother, gave his interpretation of the Mutiny as the First War of Independence, though without suggesting Garibaldi's involvement.

Joglekar belonged to the Tilak school and his attitudes are closer to Kelkar's. His translation enjoyed a second edition in 1924. The stanzas inserted as a preface to the individual chapters are taken from the *Gita*, Eknath's poems, Ramdas' *Dasabodh*, Tukaram's *Abhangas*, and the *Kathopanishad*. Joglekar's notes on the texts support the opposition between Rights and Duties, and how the Rights asserted by the French Revolution could not be exercised without sufficient preparation (Joglekar 1921: 19ff.). The translation employs terms of the Hindu tradition: *har har mahadev* (a warlike invocation to Shiva) becomes the hymn of the crusaders (ibid.: 42), Dante's title is *mahakavi* (ibid.: 96) or an inspired poet like Vyasa.

THE PERIODICAL PRESS

There was an emphasis on the *Risorgimento* in periodicals other than *Kesari*. During British rule, reports on 'native press' were regularly compiled stating the name and caste of the author and the title, contents and circulation of the work. From 1900 onward, the *Bombay Native Newspapers Report* became a part of this.[65] The figures of circulation vary from year to year. The most controversial among those responsible for such periodicals was Shivram Mahadev Paranjpe, the editor of the weekly *Kal* with a circulation of 7,000 between 1898 and 1910. Paranjpe, a Chitpavan from Mahad, followed in Tilak's footsteps but was more inclined to extremism, with a particular interest in Irish nationalism and Russian anarchists.[66] He wrote a preface to N.S. Phadke's *Terence McSweeney* (Pune, 1923),[67] took an active part in *Abhinav Bharat*, wrote a review of *Mazini Atmacharitra va Rajkaran*[68] and defended Savarkar from accusations while the latter acted as his London correspondent. In 1908 he too was sentenced to eight months in prison. Even his successor, Purshottam Bapuji Khare, was arrested and convicted[69] and the newspaper was forced to close after the Press Act of 1910.

On 13 April 1908, Ramchandra Narayan Mandlik (1881-1958), editor of the *Vihari* (Rambler), a Marathi weekly of Mumbai with a circulation of 1,000, was likewise sentenced to two years of rigorous imprisonment and a fine of 1,000 rupees, for publishing a poem by Mazzini entitled *Awakening*.[70]

Awake o fools! Why are you sleeping? Open your eyes for a moment and see who sits on your chests. Your motherland who gives you nourishment has fainted. . . . A cruel ruler is governing you; why do you submit to his authority? Why did you lose your independence?. . . . When God created the universe, he created all persons free. . . . When freedom, which is man's birthright, is lost how can you remain quiet? You should die on the battlefield for the sake of Independence!

Ramachandra Mandlik[71] had also written a review of Savarkar's book on Mazzini in *Vihari* (17 July 1907). Savarkar, incidentally, had been sub-editor of the paper, along with Balkrishna Narayan Phatak,[72] before leaving for London.

On 1 June 1909, Bhaskar Balwant Bhopatkar, a Karhade Brahman from Thane, close to Tilak's position, brother of the more famous Laksman (1880-1960), leader of the Hindu Mahasabha and editor of the weekly *Bhala* (Spear) with a circulation of 2,300-6,000, was convicted to six months' imprisonment, for an article on Ramdas.[73] He also wrote a long article on *The Emancipation of Italy: the Preliminaries of the Great Rise*, with an invocation to Italy by the poet Swinbourne.[74] It is a detailed history of the Neapolitan Carbonari in 1820. The reference to India was clear to British censors and they asked for the opinions of T.J. Strangman, Advocate-General and L.C. Crump, Remembrancer of Legal Affairs.[75] Strangman's reply was, 'There is no doubt in my mind that the writer's intention was to contrast the conditions of Italy under the Austrians with that of India under the English and to extol a resort to secret societies and rebellion with a view to obtain Independence in India.' Crump wrote:

On the whole, viewed as an historical sketch, it cannot be said that the article is seriously inaccurate, the passage in praise of independence is germane to the matter; more particularly so as it is based on the doctrines expounded by Mazzini. . . . There is not a word that can be hasted upon as pointing in any way to the existing state of affairs in India. The truth or falsity of an historical sketch is clearly relevant as bearing on the intention of the writer. It is for this reason that I have discussed the accuracy of the article.

Neither of them recommended prosecution and advised the authorities to 'wait and see'.

A Marathi weekly of Satara, *Pratod* (The Whip), with a circulation of 300-400 copies, followed in *Kesari*'s footsteps and regularly published articles and excerpts for local readers. It was shut down in 1892 and again in 1897 for sedition, and its owner and editor were fined. The paper was again banned in 1907 and in 1908; its editors were Karhade Brahmans: Ganesh Ramchandra Kusalkar and Vasudev Damodar Mundale (1880-1947). The latter is the Marathi biographer of Cavour.[76] The publisher, J.N. Oak, proposed the Italian example following Italy's entry into World War I; a country which fought for its independence, then became powerful. Mundale's work became part of a series of schoolbooks, among which he also produced Bismarck's biography.[77]

In the Introduction to Cavour's biography, the historian V.K. Rajvade (1863-1926)[78] invites readers to understand the history and geography of different countries; government by experts is preferable to monarchy, or *pratinidhisatta* (representative) or *mahajansatta* (commercial) government. In the footsteps of Rajvade, Mundale also stresses how history is *magistra vitae*: history is only *uttam*, the best means, of inculcating *rastriya guna* (national qualities). It is interesting to note how in Mundale's book the Ramdas-Mazzini pair is replaced by Ramdas-Cavour. In Tilak's realistic hypothesis, which Mundale follows, Mazzini remains a Utopian, whilst Ramdas is the embodiment of a kind of realpolitik, even if with a superior aim.[79] Cavour the statesman has the best gifts for that: *swarthayoga* (personal sacrifice) and *swadesha priti* (love of one's country). The fact that Cavour is not married is a demonstration of his attachment to the fatherland.[80] The term used for Mazzini was *brahmachari* (a chaste, religious man).

GIOBERTI AND CAVOUR: FEDERALISTS AND UNITARIANS

The opposition between Moderates and Extremists in Italy, according to Mundale, is not between Cavour and Mazzini, but rather between Federalists and Unitarians. Gioberti and his followers are *nemast*, moderates, while Cavour and his cohorts are *jahal* or extremists. The ideas of Goberti (*sic*) are described in detail and his federal hypothesis amply appreciated. The term used for the Sardinian-Piedmontese kingdom is *sansthan*, already applied to Princely States in Maharashtra; one cannot forget that until the 1930s all nationalists tried to attract the Princes to their cause. Only the policy of the new Congress leadership, in particular Nehru, led to the establishment of Congress units in the Princely States. Mundale, like Kusalkar and Bhopatkar, was a Karhade Brahman, the smallest of the Maharashtrian Brahman groups, which may explain his eclectic ideology and sympathy for the federalist hypothesis, *sansthancha sangh* (union of states).[81] Cavour is also a journalist like Mundale and several Indian nationalist leaders, and his struggle against religious institutions (*dharmopadeshak*) and the ecclesiastical world in general (*padri mandal*)[82] was shared by Moderates and

Extremists alike, who wished to reform traditional Hindu society. The support given to Cavour by England invited reflection. If England supported Italian independence, it might do the same for India. Garibaldi and Cavour are therefore not opposed but complementary; the former has *mutsaddegiri* (the art of diplomacy), the latter *shaurya* (heroism).

VARIATION AND DECLINE OF THE IMPACT

In Maharashtra Cavour too had his say. In fact, someone even likened Sayajirao Gaekwad of Baroda to Victor Emmanuel.[83] Nepal, also, could have been the Piedmont of the subcontinent, a representative of whose ruling family met Savarkar during his exile in Ratnagiri. However, the interest in Italy declined as local substitutes were found: Ramdas for Mazzini and Cavour and Shivaji for Garibaldi and Victor Emmanuel. Also, Italy entered the war with the Ottoman Empire, and since nationalist papers such as the *Kesari* and *The Mahratta* wished to preserve Hindu-Muslim unity, they had to stop referring to Italy. Instead, *Hindutva* and *Hindupadpadshahi* concepts won over the revolutionary circles, and the history of Maharashtra became tantamount to the history of India. The *Maharashtra Dharma* of Ramdas changed into *Hindupadpadshahi* of Savarkar. The specifically royal functions of *kshatriyadharma* and *rajadharma* became the duty of every Hindu, who now had to militarize. On the other side, Gandhiji took over with his message of *satyagraha* and *ahimsa*. However, his influence in Maharashtra remained weak. From the pages of *Hind Swaraj* (1908) Gandhi had written with sympathy for Mazzini but at the same time had declared the example of Italian unity a failure. *Swaraj* took the lead over *swatantrata*, the positive answer with a new structural reform-plan for society, over the merely political aim. Gandhiji's self-rule and self-respect were considered primary to Independence.

A SHORT ANALYSIS OF THE TERMS OF REFERENCE

Let us consider the four main leaders of the *Risorgimento* who were the primary targets of nationalist writers. From the terms of reference and their designations, the differences between Italy and India in interpreting their role become evident. Mazzini was throughout named *deshabhakta* (Ghanekar, Tilak and Ketkar[84]); *bhakti* was such a part of the Marathi tradition, though *deva* was, of course, outweighed by *desa*. V.D. Savarkar called Mazzini *bhagwan* and *mahatma*, his brother Narayana called him *maharishi*, which implied his sense of suffering (and final liberation) for a cause. Kelkar also stressed the word *mahatma*, but considered Mazzini as a man of *kalpana* (imagination) compared with the *pratyaksha* (practical mind) of the *mutsaddi*, Cavour. Both Tilak and Savarkar further compared Mazzini with Ramdas, stressing the latter's ideology more than his activism, the man behind Shivaji, the *swaraj*-maker.

Garibaldi was *vibhuti* and *rashtrabhakta vira*, the hero-incarnate. Tilak extolled his heroism as high as that of Shivaji. Savarkar tried to etablish Garibaldi's connections with Tatya Tope in 1857. Kelkar and Tilak contrasted Cavour, the *mutsaddi* (the practical statesman), with Mazzini the idealist. Mundale compared Cavour to Ramdas, depicting him as a man of action. Finally, Victor Emmanuel was, for Tilak, the *rashtrabhakta sansthanik* (kingly patriot), who was held as an example to Indian princes, *sansthan* being the Marathi term for princely administration.

THE IMPACT

If we have to measure the impact of the Italian nationalist movement on the Indian, the British certainly thought much of it, judging by the ban on works dealing with Mazzini and the heavy sentences imposed on those who printed, edited and published them. They were equally harsh on those who wrote on Garibaldi and other Italian leaders. The Savarkar brothers certainly felt the impact, Vinayak and Ganesh having been sentenced to hard labour in the Andamans, and Vinayak being further detained on the mainland.

Biographies of the leaders of the *Risorgimento* circulated in the so-called National Schools as part of the curriculum; Aurobindo Ghose was responsible for one such school in Baroda until its closure. But while many of these schools were closed, the impact on Hindu nationalism was profound: attacks against the official power and traditional religion now went hand in hand, and religious symbols became part of a new national ideology. Thus Italian nationalism was probably the outstanding European source of legitimation; more so in Maharashtra than in the rest of India, as here interest seemed wider and included all relevant characters of the *Risorgimento*. The Indian (Maharashtrian) nationalists embraced the *Risorgimento* as a shining example for their own struggles. Mazzini, Garibaldi and Cavour became the *karma yogi* (men selfless in action). This is in tune with the general Hindu outlook of setting examples in life, structural as well as saintly, though the 'Hindu' nationalist goal was rather one of exclusion than one of integration.

NOTES

1. For the research work I am indebted to V.S. Anand, V.S. Godbole, V.G. Kale and M. Sonpatki.
2. J.H. Broomfield, 1968, *Elite Conflicts in a Plural Society; Twentieth Century Bengal*, Berkeley: California University Press.
3. The first being the Uttarpara Hitakari Sabha of 2/4/1876, reproduced in *Speeches and Writings of the Hon. S. Banerjea, Selected by Himself*, Chennai, 1918: 391-416.
4. Lala Lajpat Rai (1865-1928), a Panjabi *vakil*, was a principal Indian nationalist and an influential member of the Congress and a great supporter of the Arya Samaj.
5. Dutt's *Baroda Administration Report of 1902-3 and 1903-4* (Mumbai, 1905) remains a classic example of an economic-adminstrative analysis of an Indian state.
6. Founded by Aurobindo, Kesavrao Deshpande and others near Baroda, its name was taken from a temple on the banks of the Narmada. The British Resident intervened,

however, and both the school and the association promoting the school (*Bhav mandir*) were forced to close down.

7. G.D. Sontheimer, 'Biography and autobiography in Marathi literature: an introduction', 54-7; S.G. Tulpule, 'Spiritual autobiography in Marathi: a tradition lost and renewed', 57-68, I. Rothermund, 'Biographical writings in Marathi', 69-80—all in *Biography and Autobiography in Modern South Asian Literatures*, vol. 5 (1976) of South Asian Digest of Regional Writing, Heidelberg, 1979.
8. *A Nation in the Making, Being the Reminiscences of Fifty Years of Public Life*, Mumbai, 1925.
9. The spectrum ranges from the Carbonari of Italy to the Prussia of Bismarck, from the Piedmont of Cavour to Mazzini's bands, from Sinn Fein to the Russian nihilists. Interest focussed on people, however, as *exempla vitae*, on their personal life and sense of duty rather than their political activities or writings. Often vision (*darshan*), even without the articulation of thinking, was sufficient.
10. For the history of Marathi literature then see Deshpande, 1954; as well as G.C. Bhate, 1939. *History of Modern Marathi Literature, 1800-1938*, M.V. Rajadyaksa, 'Marathi literature from 1800 to 1920' and T.V. Parvate, 'Marathi literature during 1920-1970' in 'Language and Literature' sections of the *Maharashtra State Gazetteers*, Mumbai, 1971.
11. For biographies, refer to Cashman, 1975; see also D. Keer, 1959. *Lokamanya Tilak, Father of the Indian freedom struggle*, Mumbai; S.L. Karandikar, 1957, *Bal Gangadhar Tilak, the Hercules and Prometheus of Modern India*, Pune; T.L. Shay, 1956, *The Legacy of the Lokamanya; the Political Philosophy of Bal Gangadhar Tilak*, London.
12. 'Pune is rich in its political tradition.... Bombay, we speak of native Bombay, is richer than Pune but the attention as well as the time of our Bombay commercial men is entirely taken by their pursuits, and in consequence, the work of formulating a scheme of commercial revival must be done by other hands', Tilak in *The Mahratta*, 6 September 1891 and 22 September 1895, quoted in Cashman, 1975: 169.
13. For analysing the success of many Chitpavans, their family histories (*kula vrttanta*) must be consulted. See M. Patterson, 1968, 'Chitpavan Brahman family-histories: sources for the study of social structure and social change in Maharashtra', in *Structure and Change in Indian Society*, M. Singer and B. Cohn (eds.), Chicago.
14. It was thanks to Chitpavans migrating to the Peshwa court in the eighteenth century that the memory and often the nostalgia of the time of Maratha independence, which was destroyed by the British in 1818, remained alive. See G. Johnson, 1970, 'Chitpavan Brahmans and politics in Western India in the late Nineteenth and early Twentieth centuries', in *Elites in South Asia*. E.R. Leach and S.N. Mukherjee (eds.), Cambridge: Cambridge University Press, 95-118; also R. Tucker, 1970, 'From Dharmashastra to politics: aspects of social authority in nineteenth century Maharashtra', *Indian Economic and Social History Review*, VII.3, 325-46.
15. See V.D. Divekar, 1981, *Survey of Material in Marathi on the Economic and Social History of India*, Pune, Bharatiya Itihas Samshodhan Mandal, esp. 26-30 and 54-76. There was no Chitpavan caste journal until 1940.
16. R. Cashman, 1970, 'The political recruitment of God Ganapati', *Indian Economic and Social History Review*. VII.3, 347-73. The Ganesa *utsav* remains even today the most impressive mass manifestation of religious feelings in Maharashtra.
17. No European state, however, supported Russia, which was considered an Oriental state by many. The Pan-Asian feelings are effectively described by B.K. Sarkar, 1922, *The Futurism of Young Asia and other Essays in the Relations Between East and West*, Berlin.
18. It may be mentioned that Muslims, unlike Hindus, found it difficult to seek inspiration outside their culture.

19. See, for example, Anand, 1969 and Srivastava, 1982. With the aid of the Greater London Council, Anand helped to preserve the house in which Mazzini lived in London, as well as install a commemorative plaque. Srivastava was a student of Emilia Morelli, Professor of History of the *Risorgimento* in Rome.
20. N.C. Kelkar, 1902, *Ghiaribaldi*, Pune.
21. *Eka vibhutichi satsanvatsarik jayanti* (Centenary of the birth of a hero), *Kesari* 9/7/1907, and *Italian desabhakta Mazini* (The Italian patriot), ibid., 23/7/1907.
22. Valentine Chirol, 1910, *The Indian Unrest*, London: Macmillan & Co.
23. *In the High Court of Justice: Tilak Plaintiff, Chirol and McMillan & Co. defendant*, 2 vols., Mumbai, 1917. The articles on Garibaldi and Mazzini are found on 911-17 and 926-30 of vol. 2. It doesn't seem that the translation of B.R. Kudalkar, Chief Translator for H.M. High Court of Bombay, emphasizes Tilak's anti-British sentiments any more than necessary.
24. Again, in 1927, V.B. Kale calls Mazzini *vibhuti*, along with eleven other Indian and European heroes, in his book, *Bara vibhuti*, published in Aundh *samsthan*. The rendering of *vibhuti* in this paper follows Varma (1980: 227).
25. J.F.S. Coupland, 1973, 'The Maharaja of Kolhapur and the non-Brahman movement', *Modern Asian Studies*, VII.2, 209-25; G. Omvedt, 1976, *Cultural Revolt in a Colonial Society: the Non-Brahman Movement in Western India 1873 to 1930*, Pune.
26. *Hind Swaraj*, Chapter XV; *Italy and India* (Ahmedabad, 1938), 97-102.
27. In *Srimad Bhagavadgita rahasya* (The secret of the Gita), Pune, 1915. For an interpretation of Tilak's works, see Varma, 1980: 261-81. For a comparison of Gandhi and Tilak on the same topic see E. Fasana, 1988, *Gandhi, Mahatma e Uomo Politico*, Trieste, 58-62, and D.K. Gosavi, 1983, *Tilak, Gandhi and Gita*, Mumbai.
28. In *The Mahratta*, 7 July 1907 and 9 February 1910. Reproduced in his *Pleasures and Privileges of the Pen*, Pune, 1929 (vol. 1, 28-45), along with other editorials on Tolstoy, Ramdas, Spencer, Max Müller and Mark Twain.
29. See his *History of Ireland*, Pune 1910.
30. Kelkar himself was a lover of Dante and of the Italian artistic heritage in general.
31. S.A. Joglekar, 1923, *Joseph Mazzini, italicha janak* (progenitor), Pune, 1923. Joglekar (1879-1963) was a close associate of Tilak and translated Mazzini's *The Duties of Man* into Marathi.
32. For much of the so-called seditious activities and banned literature I have relied on *Sources for a History of the Freedom Movement in India*, vol. 2: 1885-1925 (Mumbai, 1958), henceforth called *Source Material*.
33. His first English biographer was Chitra Gupta (*Life of Barrister Savarkar*, Chennai, 1926), who was in fact C. Rajagopalachari, the first Indian Governor-General. See also D. Keer, 1950, *Savarkar and his Times*, Mumbai; V.S. Anand, 1967, *Savarkar, a Study in the Evolution of Indian Nationalism*, London.
34. For the Chapekhars see *Source Material*, 955-1015 for D.H. Chapekar's autobiography, as well as E. Kedourie, 1970, *Nationalism in India and Africa*, for their impact on future nationalist movements.
35. M. Sonpatki, 1980, *Daryapar* (On the sea), Pune; Srivastava, 1983.
36. S.L. Karandikar, 1947, *Savarkar charitra*, Pune.
37. His autobiographical writings started at that time, and he mentions his knowledge of Mazzini from the writings of Banerjea and Lala Lajpat Rai, and from the first Marathi biography by L.G. Ghanekar, Collector of Baroda State [*Prasiddh italian desabhakta Mazini yanche charitra* (The famous Italian devoted to the country, and his life), Vadodara, 1899].
38. *Life and Writings of Joseph Mazzini*, London: Smith, Elder & Co., 1864-70, rpt. 1890-1. The text of *The Duties of Man*, is found in vol. 4, 209-378. He never hints at any other source in English, except Trevelyan.

39. *Joseph Mazini yanche atmacharitra va rajkaran* (Autobiography and politics of Joseph Mazzini), with an Introduction of 26 pages by Savarkar himself.
40. Savarkar states in his Introduction to this work that it was written in a series called 'Laghu Abhinav Bharat Mala', in which he had already published two *povadas* on Maratha heroes.
41. During his legal proceedings against Chirol, Tilak denied recommending Savarkar to his friends in London, but accepted that he had probably countersigned the latter's request for a scholarship, which was already endorsed by the Principal of Fergusson College, of which Savarkar had been a good student. See Srivastava, 1983: 9.
42. Apart from writing articles for the *Gaelic American* of New York on the Irish Question.
43. Mazzini had, in fact, expressed reservations on the French Revolution, even if he considered it an indispensable step towards progress. In the Indian context one mustn't foget the impact of Burke's *Reflections*, and the favouring of continuity and reform rather than fracture and revolution.
44. Savarkar differentiates here between 'young' and 'modern'.
45. G. Srivastava, 1982, 'Mazzini and Gandhi', *Gandhi Marg*, March 1982: 734-41.
46. On this he is close to Lajpat Rai and at variance with the much subtler and more complex stand of Tilak *vis-a-vis* orthodox Brahmans.
47. *Opinion of the Honourable the Advocate General in Regard to the Preface to a Translation of Joseph Mazzini's Autobiography*, in *Judicial Department (Confidential) Proceedings*, October 1907, Mumbai, 31-4.
48. None of Lajpat Rai's writings were proscribed. See G. Barrier, 1976, *Banned: Controversial Literature and Political Control in British India 1907-1947*, New Delhi.
49. From *Savarkar sahitya navnit*, op. cit., 276-83.
50. Not, however, by Gandhi, who simply called a speech of Savarkar's, given on 24 September 1909 'spirited' (Gandhi, 1963: IX: 499). See Srivastava (1983: 25-8) about the Gandhi-Savarkar relationship.
51. V. Savarkar, 1909, *The Indian War of Independence, 1857*, Mumbai. The second edition had to wait until 1947, while a German translation appeared in Berlin in 1940 as *Indien im Aufruhr* (The Indian War of Independence by an Indian nationalist).
52. With some exceptions such as R.C. Majumdar's 'The Mutiny and the revolt of 1857-58', in *The History and Culture of the Indian People. Vol. XII: British Paramountcy and Indian Resistance*, 467-650, Mumbai, 1963. For an analysis of this theme see also G. Borsa, 1977, *La Nascita del Mondo Moderno in Asia Orientale*, Milano, 170-5.
53. Prosecution of G.D. Savarkar of Nasik for the publication of certain poems and verses, in *Judicial Department (Confidential) Proceedings*, March 1909, Mumbai, 91-8.
54. He was later executed. See V.N. Datta, 1978, *Madan Lal Dhingra and the Revolutionary Movement*. New Delhi.
55. *Source Material*, op. cit., 359-437; B.C. Kunte, 1974, *Nasik District Gazetteer*, Mumbai, 152-201.
56. See *Source Material*, op. cit., 437-81.
57. For example, La Sera, Scaena Illustrata, Le Soleil du Midi, Le Petit Niçois. I have been unable, so far, to find a French biography of Savarkar, the notes here having been provided by Adelina Negri in Genova on 3 June 1983.
58. See I. Yajnik, 1950, *Syamji Krishnavarma: Life and Times of an Indian Revolutionary*, Mumbai, 304-5.
59. V.C. Maydev (ed.), 1943, *Savarkaranchi kavita*, Mumbai.
60. L. Dumont, 1964, 'Nationalism and communalism', in *Contributions to Indian Sociology* VII, 30-70 and in *Homo Hierarchicus*, Paris, Appendix D, 376-95.
61. Later reissued as *Story of the Maratha Struggle to Re-establish Sovereign Hindu Power*, Mumbai, 1974.

62. Just as Gandhian *ahimsa* is considered 'unalloyed nonsense'. See A.S. Bhide, 1941, *Veer Savarkar, Whirlwind Propaganda*, Mumbai, 432. Also see V.P. Varma, op. cit., 386-91.
63. Letter to Gandhi, 18 January 1920. Gandhi 1963: XIX: 507.
64. 26 May 1920; 18 May, 26 June, 28 July 1921; and 1 September 1924—in Gandhi 1963: XIX: 460-3; 1963: XX: 104, 284-5 and 431-2 and 1963: XXV: 118.
65. Both of them are excellent complements to Bhate's *History of Marathi Literature* (op. cit.) and to S.G. Date, 1961, *Marathi niyatkalikanchi suchi 1800-1950* (General Index of Marathi Periodicals 1800-1950), Mumbai. Nearly a quarter of all periodicals were edited by Chitpavans between 1901 and 1921, showing their intellectual predominance.
66. By contrast the supporters of non-violence preferred Tolstoy and the Russian 'religious pilgrims'.
67. Mayor of Cork who died in a hunger strike in Brixton Jail in 1920.
68. *Kal*, 12 July 1907.
69. Prosecution of P.B. Khare, editor of the *Kal* newspaper, in *Judicial Department (Confidential) Proceedings*, February 1909, Mumbai, 57-63.
70. Ker 1917: 102 and *Source Material* (op. cit.), 659-60.
71. M.B. Sahasrabuddhe, 1959, *Desabhakta Rambhau Mandlik yanche jivan charitra* (Life and works of the patriot Rambhau Mandlik), Pune.
72. He, too, as editor, along with his successor Bhaskar Vishnu Phadke, both Chitpavans, was convicted and fined. See Comments on the sentence passed on the editor of *Vihari*, *Report of Native Papers for week ending 4th July 1908*, 34-5.
73. *A Darbar in Hell*. The word *darbar* evidently referred to the British Raj.
74. It was also inscribed in the Preface to Kelkar's *Ghyaribaldi*.
75. Opinion of the Law Office on an article in the *Bhala* newspaper of 1 June 1909. *Judicial Department (Confidential) Proceedings*, July 1909: 343-7.
76. *Kavhur urf italicha Ramdas*, Pune, 1915.
77. *German rashtrapurus prins Bismarck: charitra va rajkaran*, Pune, 1917.
78. A Chitpavan of Pune and a founder of Bharat Itihas Samsodhak Mandal, V. K. Rajvade dedicated much of his time to the role of Ramdas in the history of Maharashtra. He eventually settled in a *math* (monastery) of *Ramdasi* (disciples of Ramdas' teachings) in Dhule. See E. Fasana, 1987, 'Samarth Ramdas e il Dharma: un santo indiano nella vita, nella storia e nell', immagine', *La Realizzazione Spirituale Dell 'Uomo*, Milano, 75-122.
79. A.N. Deshpande (1954: II: 424) who is little inclined towards foreign examples, considers Mundale's work mediocre, and he pairing of Cavour and Ramdas as irrelevant to India.
80. Mundale evidently follows the biographies of Cavour by W.R. Thayer, and Pietro Orsi, the latter having evidently been translated into English.
81. It is interesting to note that Mundale also wrote *Karl Marx va tyachen karya* (Marx's life and works, Kolhapur, 1945) along with biographies of Thomas Paine (1924) and William of Orange 1925).
82. The term *padri* was adopted from the Portuguese.
83. See *Source Material*, op. cit., 555-601 for the period of 'sedition' in Vadodara, as well as D. Hardiman, 1978, 'Baroda, the structure of a progressive state', in *People, Princes and Paramount Power; Society and Politics in the Indian Princely States*, R. Jeffrey (ed.), Delhi, 107-35.
84. S.V. Ketkar (1884-1937), another Chitpavan, founder and editor of the *Maharashtra Jnanakosa*, the Encyclopaedia of Marathi knowledge, published in Pune in 23 vols. between 1920-7. *Kavhur*, 'The Italian *mutsaddi*' is found in vol. 14 (1924): 447-9, *Garibaldi, Ghiuseppe* [*sic*], 'the Italian *desabhakta*' in vol. 12 (1925): 40-2, and *Mazini*, also *Desabhakta* in vol. 18 (1926): 95-6.

REFERENCES

(NB: Only works that are repeatedly cited appear in this list; the rest of the references are quoted in full in the notes.)

Anand, V.S., 1969, 'L'Italia di Mazzini nel Risorgimiento Indiano', in *Il Pensiero Mazziniano*, XXIV.6.

Cashman, R.J., 1975, *The Myth of the Lokamanya: Tilak and Mass Politics in Maharashtra*, Berkeley.

Deshpande, A.N., 1954, *Adhunika Marathi vangmayacha itihasa* (2 vols.), Pune.

Gandhi, M.K., 1963, *Collected Works of Mahatma Gandhi*, New Delhi.

Ker, J.C., 1917, *Political Trouble in India 1907-1917*, Shimla.

Lederle, M., 1976, *Philosophical Trends in Maharashtra*, Mumbai.

Srivastava, G., 1982, *Mazzini and His Impact on the Indian National Movement*, Allahabad.

Srivastava, H., 1983, *Five Stormy Years, Savarkar in London*, New Delhi.

Varma, V.P., 1980, *Modern Indian Political Thought*, Agra.

Bhau Mahajan and his *Prabhakar*, *Dhumketu* and *Dnyan Darshan*: A Study in Maharashtrian Response to British Rule

J. V. NAIK

How did the nineteenth-century Maharashtrian intellectuals perceive the social, political and economic realities of their time? How did they respond to British rule and the new challenges that came in its wake? On these and other related questions contemporary newspapers and journals, especially vernacular journals owned and edited by those who were actually involved in the reform movement, form a major source of information.

This paper studies three such periodicals—*Prabhakar, Dhumketu*, and *Dnyan Darshan*—founded and edited by one of the pioneers of Marathi journalism and reform in Maharashtra, Govind Vitthal Kunte, *alias* Bhau Mahajan. An early product of the Elphinstone Institution, Bhau Mahajan was the first Maharashtrian intellectual to start an exclusively Marathi newspaper, *Prabhakar*, in 1841, and make journalism his full-time occupation. With a pragmatic mind he diligently sought out the causes of injustice—political, economic, and social—and made the vernacular press a force to reckon with in Maharashtra long before the young lions of *Kesari*.[1] He showed a keener perception of the seamy side of British rule than most of his contemporaries and severely criticized it. With equal vigour he exposed the social evils that beset contemporary society. However, he never allowed himself to drift with the tide, and his criticism was never one-sided. Another striking feature of his journalism were the serious attempts he made to arouse interest in science, disseminate scientific knowledge and promote scientific studies. A liberal spirit and the extraordinary courage and steadfastness with which he conducted his journals make him one of the outstanding editors of his time.

His journalistic career lasted a little over two decades (1841-62), during which period Bhau Mahajan's writings, urging this or that cause, form one of the most critical descriptions of Maharashtrian response to new challenges. In 1862 he decided to wind up his business in Mumbai and, for some unknown reason, retired to his son's home at Nagpur, where he was to die on 4 January 1890.[2]

Strangely, for a man of his achievement, biographical information about Bhau Mahajan is scanty.[3] He was born at Pen in Raigad District, in a well-to-do Brahman family of Kuntes or Bhau Mahajans (also known as Havaldars as they were the supervisors of salt-pans in Konkan during the Peshwas' rule). When

Bhau Mahajan was about eight, his brother-in-law, Sadashiv Kashinath *alias* Bhau Chhatre, the Native Secretary of the newly-established Bombay Native Education Society,[4] brought him over to Mumbai for his education. Bal Shastri Jambhekar (1812-46), the noted scholar and social reformer, was also then living with the Chhatres for his education. Bhau Mahajan found in Jambhekar a gifted teacher and guide. He also benefitted from the private tutors employed by Bhau Chhatre to educate his own son, Vireshwar, in various subjects, including music. His interest in science and scientific knowledge may have been first aroused by his close companionship with Bhau Chhatre's two cousins, Vishnu Sunder and Ramkrishna Wyjeenath (also spelt Wiswanath), who had the distinction of being the very first students of the newly established Engineer Institution (1823) under the headship of Captain G.R. Jervis.[5] This institution moved in 1830 from Mumbai to Pune, and was closed in 1832. However, the institution marked the beginnings of science education in western India.[6]

Such were the formative influences on Bhau Mahajan. In 1827, he completed his primary education at the Bombay Native School Book and School Society, where among his classmates were the two Tarkhadkar brothers: Dadoba, the Marathi grammarian and founder of the Paramahansa Sabha; and Bhaskar, the severe critic of British colonial rule. Later, as the editor of *Prabhakar*, Bhau Mahajan fully identified with their socio-political cause.

There is no record of his activities over the next ten years. The death of his guardian, Bhau Chhatre, perhaps interrupted his education. In 1837, Bhau Mahajan joined the Elphinstone Institution and in the following year the Elphinstone College Council 'elected' him and two other students, Wamanrao Trimbak and Sakharam Balkrishna, to a scholarship of 20 rupees. In January 1839, the three of them were brought before the Scholarship Examination Committee headed by A.B. Orlebar, Professor of Mathematics and Natural Philosophy. The Committee did not form a favourable opinion of Bhau Mahajan's progress, Professor Orlebar remarking that 'Bhao Wittul had made a study of history as an excuse for the little attention he paid on his classes.' He was thus not given a raise on his scholarship, while the others were promoted to scholarships of 40 and 30 rupees, respectively.[7] That he showed little interest in his classroom studies is indicated in Orlebar's report dated 21 January 1839 to the Elphinstone College Council:[8]

> With regard to Bhao Wittul I cannot persuade him either to write down what I notice in the class, or to answer any questions; and although he sits and listens I am unable to say what he does or what he does not know. Although I have reason to hope that he is making some progress.

Obviously, Bhau Mahajan had other ideas. The deplorable state of his poverty-stricken, enslaved country was agitating his resilient mind. He knew that the claims of government service were not for him. He was well read and acquired a good command over both Sanskrit and English; proud of his mother-tongue, he wanted Marathi rather than English to be the language of the new intelligentsia.[9] He left the Elphinstone Institution in 1841,[10] and, significantly, on *Vijaya Dashmi* day (24 October) of the same year, launched his Marathi weekly *Prabhakar*.

To appreciate his journalism, which was at its best when inveighing against injustice, it is important to know the conditions in the region. The British takeover from the effete Peshwa Bajirav II was relatively smooth, but the old elite could never fully reconcile to the loss of power in 1818. During the nine years of his benevolent reign Mountstuart Elphinstone introduced some studied measures, which to a large extent helped to conciliate the old ruling classes as well as the general populace. His aim was not to destroy, but to transform the old traditions. But the colonial state had its own logic and followed its own course. Elphinstone's successors, however hard they tried, could not live up to his ideals. John Malcolm, who followed him, permitted missionaries to open their centres in the Presidency. Though the government formally adhered to the policy of religious neutrality, some high officials like James Farish, the acting Governor of Bombay in 1839, were openly guilty of abetting conversions.[11] The full impact of colonial economic policies came gradually to be felt. Old occupations were lost and new opportunities were slow in coming.

Economic distress, the threat of Christianity, the imposition of British law and administration, and a limited exposure to Western ideas of rationalism and humanism through English education all combined to produce a new social and political awareness among a small educated elite. Their response to British rule was a mixed one. They admired and despised the English: admired them for their military strength and administrative acumen, and for the secular-scientific world-view they represented; hated them for being usurpers and aloof overlords who pursued policies in the interest of their mother-country, depriving Indians of their just dues. Bhau Mahajan was one of the earliest Indian journalists to come to grips with this new situation. Englishmen in India, in his words, behaved like 'freemasons'.[12] Nevertheless, much had to be learnt from them, the old institutions needed to be reaccessed before the tables could be turned, and the lost grounds recovered.[13]

A new consciousness found expression in the newly founded Mumbai press. The *Bombay Samachar*, a Gujarati weekly, started in 1822, made a modest beginning. Since then, the newspaper became an important vehicle for the dissemination of knowledge and social criticism in western India. Bhau Mahajan's mentor, Bal Shastri Jambhekar, established the first Anglo-Marathi newspaper, the *Bombay Durpun*, in 1832. In its first issue, on 6 January 1832, the *Durpun* stated its objectives 'to open a field for free and public discussion on points connected with the prosperity of the country, and happiness of its inhabitants'.[14] The *Durpun*, which catered to both English and Marathi speakers, was well-received by the educated and the government. Governor Clarke said: 'The *Durpun* is, I think, a very interesting publication and I shall be glad to give it every reasonable help.'[15] The government's patronage, however, did not extend beyond subscribing to the paper.[16] The *Durpun* did not last more than eight years. In its last issue published on 20 June 1840, the editor said the main aim of the paper had been 'to spread liberal sentiments in matters of religion and politics that might promote the improvement of our countrymen'. Though the paper did not give any reason for its sudden closure, there is some evidence to suggest that its editor, Balshastri Jambhekar, had to face a libel case which possibly threatened his position in the government educational service.[17]

The void created by the demise of the *Durpun* was soon filled by the *Prabhakar*. Possessing an independent bent of mind, Bhau Mahajan was in a better position to make use of the freedom of the press granted by Charles Metcalfe in 1835. In his running of the *Prabhakar*, Bhau Mahajan seems to have been particularly influenced by the short-lived pro-Indian editor of the *Bombay Gazette*, to whom he often made laudable references. The editor of the *Gazette*, on 1 July 1841, had pronounced that his paper

> would unremittingly advocate those measures which appeared likely to benefit the Indian people, regardless of the source whence they emanate. . . . 'Measures, not Men' will be the motive by which we will be actuated and fair and impartial will be the principles we will unflinchingly advocate: while everything which may be inimical or injurious to the happiness, liberty and prosperity of India will be fearlessly censured.[18]

The Anglo-Indian community was up in arms against the *Gazette*, forcing its pro-Indian editor to resign. The news was reported in the *Prabhakar* with the greatest regret.[19] The tradition of fearless journalism initiated by the *Bombay Gazette* was, however, continued by Bhau Mahajan through his Marathi periodicals. The *Prabhakar*, while stating that it was not the organ of any community or vested interest save *vox populi*,[20] invited its readers to voice their grievances against British rule. It was in response to this invitation that Bhaskar Tarkhadkar, wrote his 'eloquent epistles' under the pen-name 'A Hindoo', in which he criticized almost every aspect of British colonial rule, thereby earning for himself the sobriquet of 'A Second Junius'.[21]

PRABHAKAR

The first issue of Bhau Mahajan's *Prabhakar* appeared on 24 October 1841, and then on every Sunday. Until 17 July 1842, when Bhau Mahajan established his own Prabhakar Press, it was published at the Ganapat Krishanji Press. The weekly, 11" x 9" in size, contained eight pages of two columns each. Its monthly subscription was one rupee.

All important local events were written about with incisive editorial comments. It announced important official appointments in the Bombay Presidency; also included were the news of the arrival and departure of steamers at Mumbai port. From 11 September 1842 onward, at the suggestion of a reader, it started giving Mumbai market news, thus making itself useful to the business community.[22] The paper wrote on matters concerning education, and occasionally published book-reviews. The weekly covered important national and international events, mostly culled from prominent Indian and foreign papers of the time.[23] More important, the weekly discussed the political, economic and social maladies of India, and introduced subjects concerning the fundamental problems of eking out a living. Its blistering criticism of political and social wrongs, written in epigrammatic Marathi style, became popular all over Maharashtra; the paper was hailed by its readers as a major source of informed opinion.[24]

The distinctive feature of the paper was that it provided a forum for all segments of Maharashtrian society, including Christian converts, to express their views freely and frankly. In fact, letters from readers on various subjects, some of which Bhau Mahajan answered in editorials, became a routine part of the paper. However, the published letters were carefully selected to produce the desired effect on readers, and to generate a dialogue between the writers of the coloums and their readers.

Deshkalyan, or 'welfare of the country' was evidently the central theme of Bhau Mahajan's journalism.[25] Contemporary political issues which he took up for discussion show him as an uncompromising critic of British imperialism. The *Prabhakar* covered, in great detail, the sordid episode of the deposition of Raja Pratap Singh of Satara. According to the *Prabhakar*, because Pratap Singh was a competent ruler, much loved by his subjects, the British found him intolerable in their game of power politics. Therefore, they fraudulently invoked Article 5 of the Satara Treaty of 1819 to depose him, and put the 'weak and imbecilic' Appasaheb, his brother, and their protege, on the Satara throne. The long legal battle that ensued brought no justice to Pratap Singh. The *Prabhakar* exposed what it considered an act of British political chicanery and hypocrisy, though not in as strong a language as did Bhaskar Tarkhadkar in the *Bombay Gazette*.[26] The *Prabhkar* published a number of letters describing the low character of Appasaheb, and the deplorable condition of Satara under his misrule. The letter of the *spashtavyakta* (candid speaker) regarding the influence of a 'vicious prostitute' named Saraswati on Appasaheb was particularly revealing. 'She is not Saraswati (goddess of learning), but *avadasa* (vixen)', lamented the letter-writer, and predicted, 'as Sagunabai earlier ruined Bajirao II and the Maratha kingdom, so will this Saraswati ruin Appasaheb and the kingdom of Satara'.[27]

When Pratap Singh died in exile in 1847, the *Prabhakar* carried a touching obituary in which the British claims of fair play and justice were severely criticized: 'To hell with your justice. It is better to go without justice, rather than having your kind of justice. . . . Even the Muslim rulers of India were better dispensers of Justice.' The obituary significantly concluded with the following apocryphal anecdote:

> In the court of an English official in the Ratnagiri Taluka, immediately after the overthrow of Peshwa rule, portraits of two men were prominently displayed, the one stark-naked, the other in a loin-cloth. When asked to explain the significance of the portraits, the official replied that they were symbolic of the would-be fate of those who come to 'our courts' for justice. While the loser is stripped of everything, even the winner is left only with the loin-cloth.[28]

The *Prabhakar* joined the chorus of criticism of the First Afghan War with the British, but with a difference. Unlike most Anglo-Indian and all English papers, it presented the Indian point of view of Auckland's 'totally unjust and unprincipled' Afghan policy.[29] Bhau Mahajan stated that apart from being unethical, this disastrous war was draining India of its wealth. Bhau Mahajan endorsed the letter of *ek swadesh abhimani* (a patriot) which gave the motive behind the war: secure as they were on three sides of India on account of their control of the seas, the British wanted to establish their firm sway over the North-West Frontier so that they could loot India at will without any threat of outside interference.[30] The *Prabhakar* reported that the war, by the middle of 1842, had already cost the Indian treasury 17 crore rupees.[31] The final cost of the war in terms of men and money was estimated at '20,000 lives and fifteen millions sterlings'. Such a huge sum of Indian money Bhau Mahajan complained, could well have been used to improve the lot of the impoverished Indian people. The ill-effects of British imperialist policies on the India economy also came in for severe criticism. The *Prabhakar* wrote:

> Having emptied the Indian treasury on ill-conceived wars, the Government has issued bonds worth more than 75 crore rupees at 5% interest. Even big businessmen cannot afford to pay 5% interest. They will, therefore, be naturally tempted to invest their money in bonds, instead of lending it to private enterprise at a lower rate, which would eventually ruin business and spell doom to *ryots*. And if, in 1852, the Crown takes over the Government of India, it will be obliged to pay the Company's debts. The Queen's Government will ultimately recover that debt from the people of India. If such a thing happens, then the people of India will recollect Aesop's fable, 'The Fox and the Porcupine'.

Bhau Mahajan exhorted people to stop moaning over their fate and start doing things which would lead to the progress of their own country.[32]

Long before Dadabhai Naorojee had begun his comprehensive survey of the *Poverty of India*, Bhau Mahajan made 'drain' the dominant theme of his economic analyses in *Prabhakar*. He lost no opportunity to show how England was prospering at the cost of India. He reported the christening of Queen Victoria's son in March 1842, and gave a vivid account of the wealth displayed and the huge expenditure incurred. This, he bitterly complained, was possible because of the regular drain of India's wealth in various forms to England.[33] He published a number of letters on the subject and praised 'A Hindoo' for his brilliant letters to the *Bombay Gazette* of 1841, which were written primarily 'to show how rigorous the present policy of the British has been in operation in regard to draining India of its wealth and reducing it to poverty'.[34] He also published, in 1843, Ramkrishna Wiswanath's book, *Hindusthananchi prachin va sampratachi shiti va pudhen kaya tyacha parinam honar hyavishayin vichar*, the first work in Marathi on political economy, which contained a severe indictment of the economic ruin of India that Great Britain wrought.[35]

These writings were the forerunners of Naorojee's drain theory, and he acknowledged this fact in his opening lecture on the theme, entitled 'England's Duties to India', delivered before the East India Association, London, on 2 May 1867.[36]

> More than twenty years ago, to my knowledge a small band of Hindu students and thoughtful gentlemen used to meet secretly to discuss the effects of British rule upon

India. The home charges, and the transfer of capital from India to England in various shapes, and the exclusion of children of the country from any share or voice in the administration of their own country, formed the chief burden of complaint.

In one of his editorials, entitled 'Freemasons', Bhau Mahajan wrote:

The Englishmen of India, the missionaries, the military men, the civil servants, the naval officers, and. also the businessmen, all unite and act in unison. Whatever they write about this country is readily believed in England, and accordingly Indian administration is conducted. This has led to the ruination of the land. . . . The Natives do not show any enterprise, and do nothing for the progress of their country. The Englishmen take advantage of this, and openly say that there are no wise and learned men among us. Our people ought to feel ashamed of this.[37]

To substantiate the charges of 'freemasonry' he cited three examples. First, he said that all Englishmen in Mumbai united to persecute Sir Edward West, the Chief Justice of the Supreme Court of Bombay, for his taking up cudgels on behalf of natives who were 'treated as nothing' by his countrymen. 'It was rumoured that Sir Edward was poisoned to death and Englishmen continued to speak ill of that noble man even after his death.' Second, Englishmen stopped buying the *Bombay Gazette* for it published the letters of 'A Hindoo', severe in criticizing them and their rule in India, as a result of which that paper went into liquidation and its editor, himself deep into troubles, had to leave Mumbai. Third, the Rev. Wilson, in order to please the rulers, 'published utter lies' describing Appasaheb, the reigning king of Satara, as a good man and an able administrator, and the deposed king, Pratap Singh, as an evil man, when everybody knew that the facts spoke to the contrary. Bhau Mahajan concluded that 'Englishmen, after coming to India, form themselves into *chandalchowkadi* (a pack of wild rascals). The honest among them are afraid to speak the truth and thus incur the displeasure of their countrymen, lest they meet the fate of Sir Edward West.'[38]

It is not merely the oppressive Colonial rule that came in for bitter attack. He was equally unsparing in his criticism of the rotting political and social system of India, which had made British conquest possible. He published a number of letters delineating the causes of British success[39] and was ready to acknowledge the positive aspects of British rule. He lavished praise on those British officials who in their individual capacity did some good work for the welfare of the Indian people. Thus, he offered a eulogistic obituary for Major Lancelot Wilkinson, Political Agent at Sihor, who died on 15 November 1841:

This generous man took great pains to spread education among the people of Sihor. Though he was not rich, he spent a lot from his own pocket in running a school at Sihor. In that school he maintained a teacher well-versed in Astrology, Geography, etc. He himself taught a number of students. He published a book on geography and was planning to translate the Sanskrit work of Bhaskaracharya into English. While serving in Malwa, he exhorted the Rajputs there to give up their cruel customs. To have such a man, among the selfish English, is truly a great wonder![40]

It is foolish, said Bhau Mahajan, simply to fume and fuss over British rule.

He urged the people to put their own house in order first and then resist injustices. In his writings he never delved deep into the question of religion or took up abstract philosophical issues for discussion. His aim was to make practical suggestions which would lead to the progress of the country and help people live a healthier life. He made his paper a conduit of genuine public grievances. He appreciated *eka navo surati* (a newcomer from Surat) and *dakshina pranthasta* (the man from the South) for their letters criticizing the wasteful expenditures on *sankranti, Ganesh utsav* and other festivals. The same money, he pleaded, could be better utilized on education and medical care of the poor and needy.[41] For the same reason he deprecated raising of memorials to important men in the form of expensive statues and busts. He reported that a *babu* in Calcutta spent thirteen lakhs on the *sraddha* of his mother. 'How much better it would have been', he wrote, 'if the Babu were to put that money in some bank in the name of his mother and utilise the interest on that amount to establish an educational institution or a house for the rehabilitation of the physically handicapped or a hospital or some useful industry.' He asked people to change their concept of charity and said that 'English charities do not cater to the lazy and idle people as Indian charities do.'[42]

The *Prabhakar* attacked social obscurantism and the evil customs practised in the name of religion. It was in order for people, Bhau Mahajan wrote, to celebrate religious festivals like *shimga* and *holi*, according to the Shastras, in their own homes. But if they caused a public nuisance, as they invariably did, the government must step in to ban the evil customs.[43] He praised Bhau Daji for his prize-winning work on the inhuman custom of female infanticide in Malwa.[44] He questioned the concept of *Kaliyuga* and laughed at the unscientific predictions of the so-called *jyotisha shastra* of ignorant pundits on rainfall, *sukal, dushkal* and such other things.[45] In this context he published a letter of 'A Hindoo' who doubted the historicity and hence questioned the propriety of Krishnashastri Sathe's *kirtan* on the subject of *kaliyuga*.[46] He appealed to the people to develop a rational and a scientific outlook on life.

The letters of 'Satkale' and 'Eka loka hittechhu' which the *Prabhakar* published raised, perhaps for the first time, a public protest against the Hindu social ban on sea-travel, and also against the compulsion to follow none but one's hereditary profession. 'Whether these restrictions', the letter-writers protested, 'are according to our Shastras or custom we cannot say, though we feel that they are mostly due to custom'. For achieving social progress, they pleaded, Hindus must give up such pernicious customs. For the good of self and society, every individual irrespective of caste or creed, should be free to travel wherever he liked and to choose any trade or profession that suited his talent best.[47]

On 16 May 1847, the *Prabhakar* published a letter of *hinduchen kalyan icchinara* who pleaded that for the good of Hindu society, the marriageable age for girls and boys be fixed at 16 and 21, respectively. This was long before Behramji Malbari began his campaign for raising 'The Age of Consent'. Contrary to the general belief that Bhau Mahajan was not in favour of widow remarriage,[48] there is evidence to show that he was a strong supporter of widow remarriage.

As early as 1845, in an editorial note, *vidhavancha punarvivaha,* he gave the gist of a paper prepared by the pundits for the Bengal East India Association on the question of widow-remarriage:

With extensive quotes from many Hindu Shastras, the paper established that the Shastras permit widow-remarriage in all castes. The pundits, however, are of the opinion that there is greater merit in committing *sati* or in abstaining from remarriage after the death of the husband. But the Shastras themselves do not prohibit widow-remarriage; on the contrary, they prescribe rules for performing it in the proper manner. We hope that the Brahmins will now accept the Shastric view, and perform marriages of their widowed daughters with suitable bridegrooms, and let them live with dignity. Even many Brahmins would agree that the introduction of the custom of widow-remarriage in this country will put an end to numerous evil deeds and sins. In an earlier issue of our paper, we had reported the marriage of a widow from a Kulin Brahman of Calcutta. It is our earnest wish that many more such marriages take place.[49]

Bhau Mahajan often wrote in defence of Hinduism, especially against missionary attacks; but he was not a religious fanatic. He appreciated the magazine *Upadesha Chandrika* started by Moreshwar Dandekar to counter missionary propaganda, and praised it for its rebuttal of Reverend Nesbit's interpretation of the *Geeta*. He however told the *Chandrika* that it is not enough merely to counter missionary arguments; the magazine should also educate Hindus in their own religion.[50] In his review of Gangadhar Shastri Phadke's book, *Sanskrit bodha vachan*, he complimented the author for making a case for Sanskrit learning, as against merely concentrating on English, for a proper understanding of Indian tradition, and also for a good summary of Vedic ideals. However, he also said that the author should not have gone to the extent of asserting that 'Hindu religion is superior to all religions.' Such statements, he said, 'damage the objectivity and credibility of the book'. 'The author at the most could have said "This is my opinion". Just because other religions do not have books like the Vedas, *Jnaneswari, Amritanubhav*, and their books are not in Sanskrit, it is not scientific to say that they are inferior to Hindu Dharma.'[51]

Though critical of the evangelistic activities of the Christian Missionaries, Bhau Mahajan showed no bitterness against those who embraced Christianity of their own volition. He published in his *Dhumketu* Baba Padmanji's account, 'Why I became a Christian.' But he did not approve of the law giving right of inheritance to the converts. He debated this issue with *Dnyanodaya*, the Christian missionary paper. The latter argued that 'if a person converts himself to faith which he thinks to be the true religion, why should he be deprived of his right to inheritance?' Bhau Mahajan's counter-argument, by the same logic, was: 'If the eldest son of the King of England were to become a Catholic, will he be allowed to inherit the throne? As the established law of England denies that right to the Prince, so does ancient Indian custom denies it to converts.' 'Long-established custom,' Bhau Mahajan told *Dnyanodaya*, 'has a greater force than Law.'[52]

The missionary contribution in the field of education, especially female education, was duly acknowledged by *Prabhakar*. However, Bhau Mahajan was against educational institutions being turned into centres of Christian religious propaganda. When *Jam-e-Jamshed* reported that a professor in the Native Education Institution was suspected of giving religious instruction to pupils, with a view to converting them to Christianity, the *Prabhakar* asked the Director of Public Instruction to initiate the necessary inquiry into the matter.[53] In his review of Laxman Ganpat's book, *Hindusthananche lokancha prapanchika sudharana*, which was essentially a missionary production sponsored by the *Oriental Christian Spectator*, Bhau Mahajan complimented the author for making female education the central theme of his work. But at the same he chided Laxman Ganpat for falling bait to his 'Christian gurus', and for indulging in such wild generalizations as 'There is no mutual love among the Hindus; Hindu parents do not teach morals to their children.' Bhau Mahajan concluded his review on a significant note: 'There are many defects in Hindus, and they should be removed. This, however, does not mean that everything about Hindus is bad.'[54]

Bhau Mahajan's appreciation of the Manav Dharma Sabha of Surat (1844), and his close association with the Paramahansa Sabha of Bombay (1849), both of which had rejected not only idol-worship but also the infallibility of the scriptures, suggest that he had much in common with the deistic rationalism of Durgaram Mancharam and Dadoba Pandurang.[55] In this he seems to have made a departure from the Bal Shastri School of Reform, which wanted reform to grow from within, on evolutionary lines, conforming as far as possible to the Shastras and Hindu tradition. The *Prabhakar* was the only contemporary newspaper to give a fairly detailed account of the objects and activities of the Manav Dharma Sabha,[56] and to defend the Paramahansa Sabha against the scurrilous attacks of its orthodox opponents.[57] The *Prabhakar* zealously espoused the cause of modern education. Bhau Mahajan was one of the earliest Maharashtrian advocates of female education and also technical and industrial training. Commenting on the 1843 Report of the Board of Education, he said:

> To this date, the Government has not started any school for girls. This must be done without delay, for so long as our women remain in ignorance, there is no hope for the progress of this country. How can ignorant mothers educate their children?. . . It is difficult to estimate how much this country has suffered due to the ignorance of women.[58]

He also stressed the importance of science education for the progress of the country and the welfare of its people. He was, however, unequivocal in his assertion that Indian languages, not English, should be the media of instruction.[59] He deprecated the tendency in government schools to focus on English to the neglect of regional languages. He suggested to the Board of Education of the Bombay Presidency that it should provide special incentives for competent teachers like Durgaram Mancharam, who conducted local schools with great success.[60] He wanted Indians to get positions in government service commensurate with their learning and talent and, therefore, hailed the appointment of Bal Shastri Jambhekar as Professor of Mathematics in the absence on leave of Professor Orlebar in 1842.[61]

Any move to start professional courses was reported in the *Prabhakar* with great enthusiasm. The paper gave wide publicity to the Civil Engineering class started in Elphinstone College in 1842, as well as to the Grant Medical College established in 1845.[62] In one of his editorials, Bhau Mahajan gave the etymology of the Greek word *polytechnic* and expressed satisfaction over the formation of a Native Association with the object of starting a polytechnic to train students in the useful arts.[63] He published a letter from 'A Hindoo', who said that Hindus would not be able to derive benefits from such institutions unless they give up their stupid notion of the division of labour, the basis of the pernicious caste system, and take up a trade or profession involving hard labour.[64] In fact, no educational development in western India went unnoticed in the columns of the *Prabhakar*. It regularly published the reports of the Board of Education, reviewed the history of Poona Sanskrit College through diverse phases of its development,[65] announced the formation of new associations like the Literary and Scientific Society, and constantly urged the government and the people to promote the cause of education.

It is not merely the problems of new elites and of a small, urban middle class that caught the attention of the *Prabhakar*. It also showed genuine concern for the impoverished rural economy, and the endless suffering of peasants and landless labourers. The harassment of poor peasants by revenue collectors, especially by such native officials as the *mamlatdars* who wanted to prove their loyalty to their foreign masters, came in for sharp criticism. The *Prabhakar* in 1847 published a 'heart-rending' eyewitness account, of the sufferings of tenants under the *khoti-zamindars*, and said that this 'true account' should receive the immediate attention of people in authority.[66]

Earlier, the *Prabhakar* had also published, in the form of readers' letters, a fairly detailed account of how the British mode of revenue collection placed the poor peasants totally at the mercy of rapacious Marwaris. By way of a partial solution, it was suggested that the government should have a scheme for the procurement of food-grains. The scheme, which was modern in its conception, would have required the government to purchase at the time of the harvest, which was also the time of revenue-collection, the surplus from the peasants at a reasonable price, and in time of scarcity it should sell its stored surplus to the peasants at an equally reasonable rate, thus neutralizing the exorbitant price-hikes which the Marwaris effected during such times. There began a fairly lively debate on the merits and demerits of the scheme.[67]

Between 1848 and 1850, the *Prabhakar* published Lokahitvadi Gopal Hari Deshmukh's celebrated *Shatpatre*, a critique of contemporary Hindu society. Bhau Mahajan welcomed it. However, Lokahitvadi almost unreservedly hailed British rule as 'divine dispensation'. It would have been interesting to know how Bhau Mahajan, a severe critic of British colonial rule, reacted to this aspect of Lokahitvadi's writings, and also to know the general reaction of readers, who normally expressed their views on all important matters published in the *Prabhakar*. Unfortunately, the relevant files of the *Prabhakar* dealing with this area are irretrievably lost.

Those of Bhau Mahajan's writings examined here belong to the pre-1850 period. They show that he foreshadowed almost all movements—political, social, economic—that characterized the subsequent history of Maharashtra. Bhau Mahajan also introduced some subjects of wider historical interest. He was the first, for example, to introduce the French Revolution to the Marathi-speaking public. In giving a serialized account of it in over twenty-five instalments,[68] he perhaps wanted to drive home the lesson that 'too much oppression breeds revolution'. When *Dnyan Sindhu*, a contemporary of the *Prabhakar*, questioned the utility of such an account, a reader of the *Prabhakar* gave a fitting reply: '*Dnyan Sindhu* perhaps equates the French Revolution with Umaji Ramoshi's revolt. What great changes that Revolution brought in all walks of life, and what profound lessons we should learn from that mighty upheaval, are beyond the comprehension of the *Dnyan Sindhu*.'[69] In yet another series of articles entitled 'Administration of Great Britain', Bhau Mahajan traced the development of democracy in England.[70] He also gave a brief account of the history of America.[71]

DHUMKETU

On 6 May 1853 Bhau Mahajan started another newspaper, *Dhumketu*, which was a low-priced weekly of four pages. Charaterized by the same liberal spirit as that of the *Prabhakar*, this new weekly, it appears was started basically to counteract *Vartaman Deepika*, patronized by the disciples of Vishnubawa Brahmachari. The extant issues of *Dhumketu*,[72] which lasted until 1862, throw some light on how Bhau Mahajan reacted to Vishnubawa's *magnum opus*, the *Vedokta Dharmaprakash*, which 'set a pattern for later Hindu revivalist movements'. The *Dhumketu* also gave some interesting information on the revolt of 1857 and its aftermath.

Vishnu Bhikaji Gokhale, *alias* Vishnubawa Brahmachari (1825-71), who has been described as 'the first great revivalist'[73] and a 'Utopian Socialist',[74] was an ardent champion of 'Vedic religion'. He wanted to propagate Vedic *dharma* and fight Christian ideas and secular Western ideology. To this end he wrote his famous work in 1859, which became the subject of a lively controversy, showing how people reacted to his interpretation of Vedic *dharma*.

Vishnubawa, for all his eccentricities, was an earnest and practical man. In a signed advertisement in *Vartaman Deepika*, he explains the purpose of his *Vedokta Dharmaprakash* with the acumen of an astute salesman:

> This is to inform all the people of Bombay that I have written a new book with a view to imparting knowledge of, and clear doubts about, Vedokta Dharma, what people now call Hindu Dharma, to all; to fight atheism is yet another aim of the book. Read the whole book and feel free to ask me for any clarification. I shall immediately give a satisfactory explanation. This is my request to all. BRAHMACHARIBAWA

The advertisement carried full details about the book, its printing, size, language, form, price and the places where it was on sale.[75]

The *Vedokta Dharmaprakash* is divided into twenty-four chapters dealing with various religious and metaphysical issues. Its main argument is that Vedic religion is superior to all other religions, and the only road to salvation.

Vishnubawa did not confine the term 'Vedic' to the four Vedas, but extended it to include later religious literature, including the Puranas. Accordingly, the *Vedokta Dharmaprakash* sought to explain 'the meaning of traditional religion, its thought, its moral code and its rituals'. Vishnubawa asserted that the Vedic *dharma* is the store of all knowledge, and Hindus need not look anywhere else for enlightenment. He said that people in Vedic times were rich in spiritual insights and also in scientific achievement. In this respect, Vishnubawa marked the beginning of revivalism in Maharashtra, which was basically a reaction to Western influence coming in the wake of British rule.

The book had a mixed reception. In a number of articles the *Dhumketu* exposed its fallacies and contradictions. The main criticism against Vishnubawa was that he had neither read the Vedas, nor understood them. The whole book, the critics complained, was a jumble of confused ideas. 'If Vishnubawa had given a correct picture of Vedic religion, the people would have understood that the difference between Vedic *dharma* and current Hinduism is as great as that between a cow and a donkey.' The critics further argued that people did not even know the names of Vedic deities such as Indra, Agni, Brhaspati, Vayu and the Maruts; they challenged Vishnubawa to show that the gods he adored and worshipped—Dattatraya, Jagadamba, Shankar, Parvati, Vitobha—ever existed in Vedic times. If the people want to follow Vedic *dharma*, the critics asserted, the existing temples should be demolished and idolatry extirpated. Contemporary Hinduism, they told Vishnubawa, was a conglomeration of diverse views which had left the Hindus in a state of utter confusion.[76]

The *Dhumketu* gave equal opportunity to Vishnubawa and his followers to defend themselves. His anti-intellectualism notwithstanding, Vishnubawa showed a remarkably open mind with regard to the problems of social reform. He was ahead of the reformers so far as the emancipation of women was concerned. And, his assertion that it was qualities, rather than birth, that should determine caste, supported the stand of the Paramahansa Sabha with which Bhau Mahajan was closely associated. Interestingly, after reading *Vedokta Dharmaprakash* many people of lower castes applied to Vishnubawa, expressing their desire to become Brahmans. One Pandurang Kashinath Shimpi wrote that he was strictly following the norms of personal behaviour as laid down in Chapters 18 and 19 of the *Vedokta Dharmaprakash*, and, therefore, should be raised to the status of a Brahman;[77] his example was followed by others.[78]

Bhau Mahajan conducted his journals in a spirit of objectivity; 'measures not men' was the principle he scrupulously followed. In his biographical sketch of Raja Rammohun Roy, he wondered how the Raja amassed his vast fortune, but said that there was absolutely no reason to believe that he had done by unfair means.[79] Bhau Mahajan, though a friend of Baba Padmaji, published letters which were very critical of the latter's novel, *Yamuna Paryatan*.[80]

A nationalist, and a severe critic of colonial rule, Bhau Mahajan guardedly presented what may be called the Indian view of the happenings of 1857. The *Dhumketu* reported, without comment (for obvious reasons), Lord Canning's speech in the Imperial Legislative Council on 3 June 1857, recommending that the freedom of the press be further curbed to meet the new situation.[81] It regularly followed the course of the rebellion and gave accounts of the battles between English forces and the rebels. As regards the role of Sikhs, *Dhumketu* on 27 August 1857, observed that

> thus far the English were confident of the loyalty of the Sikhs and did not anticipate trouble in the Punjab. But that confidence is now shaken, for the Sikhs, who hitherto stood by the British, are now showing signs of rebellion. . . . On investigation, it was found that some 130 'Malwai Sikhs' were instigating their comrades in the regiment at Dera Ismail Khan, to rise in revolt against the English. Though the plot was nipped in the bud, the English have now lost their confidence in the Sikhs, and have strengthened their forces in Lahore Fort by posting an additional company (it must be of European soldiers) there.[82]

Bhau Mahajan published in the *Dhumketu* the Proclamation of the Begum of Oudh, which was a rejoinder to the Queen's Proclamation. The Begum analysed the latter clause by clause, and told the people not to be misled by it. 'Though the Company's Government is formally taken over by the Crown,' the Begum warned, 'the conduct of actual administration, its laws, judicial, and personnel have remained the same. Therefore, the people should not trust the English.'[83]

DNYAN DARSHAN

A striking feature of Bhau Mahajan's journalism was the interest that it sought to awaken in scientific knowledge. He owned and edited, for a while, the first Marathi monthly magazine, *Dig-Darshan*, started by Raghoba Janardhan, very probably under the influence of Bal Shastri Jambhekar, in 1840.[84] This magazine, mostly devoted to the discussion of scientific subjects,[85] received the token patronage of the government.[86] Nevertheless, for want of adequate public support it was forced to close sometime after 1843.

Bhau Mahajan started a quarterly of 100 demi-size pages, the *Dnyan Darshan*, in July 1854. Its declared objectives were to acquaint the Marathi knowing public with new ideas and discoveries in the social and physical sciences.[87] The magazine lasted three years and folded in April 1856.[88] It published writings on jurisprudence, ethics, psychology, chemistry, geology, political economy, history and geography. These writings, as stated in the Director of Public Instruction's Report for 1854-56, were mostly 'able translations and accommodations of standard English works'. The magazine serialized the 'History of Modern Europe' and 'The Story of Napoleon Bonaparte'. It carried a piece on the 'Great Men Theory' to which Bhau Mahajan did not appear to subscribe. The magazine also carried some science jokes, like 'how the cat was used as a clock in China', which were both amusing and instructive.

Interestingly, the *Dnyan Darshan* serialized *Paraganda jahalelya gruhastachi kanya* (Daughter of an Errant Householder), which seems to be the first social novel attempted in Marathi. This novel, although heavily rhetorical and moralistic in tone, vaguely portrays the transition from the old feudal ideas to a new way of life, and speaks of the Panjab as a land of opportunities.

Bhau Mahajan was one of the ablest editors of his time and created a high standard of Marathi editorial writing. He showed a rational outlook and fought social obscurantism. He raised his voice against every form of injustice. He welcomed the growth of modern science and pleaded for the industrialization of the country. It is not, however, easy to assess the precise effects of his writings on Maharashtrian society. Strangely, the *Nibandhamala* does not make any mention of him, nor does the *Kesari* or the *Sudharak* in their hey-day. Only recently attempts have been made to do justice to this pioneer of Marathi journalism on the basis of a careful and dispassionate study of his writings.

NOTES

1. Vishnushatri Chiplunkar, G.G. Agarkar and B.G. Tilak.
2. Curiously, the press hardly took any notice of the death of this pioneer journalist. It may perhaps be due to the long gap of twenty-eight years between his retirement and death. The only noteworthy obituary of him appeared in *Vividha Dnyan Vistar*, 22.1-2 (January 1890): 24a-b.
3. The only contemporary sketch is by K.S. Bhavalkar, which is both incomplete and desultory. It is given in the Appendix to B.S. Pandit (ed.), *Raosaheb Keshav Shivram Bhavalkar Yanche Atmavritta*, Nagpur: Vidharba Samshodhan Mandal, 1961: 110-17. The same, with critical notes, is given in *Memoirs and Writings of Acharya Bal Gangadhar Shatri Jambhekar* (henceforth Jambhekar) ed. by G.G. Jambhekar, vol. 3: Appendix. Jambhekar, n.d.: III: Appendix 3. For a modern estimate see G.B. Sardar, 'Bhau Mahajan', *Maharashtra Sahitya Parishad*, 13. 4 (October 1940): 195-310. Also, G.D. Khanolkar, 'Nispruha Vruttiche un Pattiche Patrakar', *Maharashtra Times, Sunday Supplement*, 13 March 1988: 8. For the family history of the Kunte-Mahajan see *Kunte Kula Vrittanta*, ed. by G.V. Vartak, Mumbai, 1981.
4. For a contemporary estimate of Bapu Chhatre see A.K. Priyolkar, 1947, *R.B. Dadoba Pandurang: Atmacharitra va Charitra*, Keshav Bhikaji Dhavale, Mumbai, 60-2. See also M.K. Chhatre, *Chhatre Kula Vrittant*, enlarged and reprinted by R.K. Chhatre, Pune, 1984, 63. G.G. Karve, 1957, Sadashiv Kashinath Urfa Bapu Chhatre, *Marathi Sahityantil Upekshit Mankari*, Venus Prakashan, Mumbai, 1-6.
5. Their names in the official records appear as Visnoo Soonder Bhut (Chhatre) and Ramcrutsna Wyjeenath (also spelt Ramkrishna Wiswanath Bhut Chhatre). They qualified themselves as 'Surveyor and Builder' on 1 May 1826 and on the same day they were absorbed in Government service. Visnoo Sunder was appointed as Tutor in the Engineer Institution, and Ramakrishna Wiswanath was posted in the Executive Engineer's office, Khandesh. See *Maharashtra State Archives* (henceforth *MSA*) *General Department* (henceforth *GD*), vol. 24.394 (1837): 45, 294. In another paper I have advanced the hypothesis that it was Ramakrishna Wiswanath who had to face strange vicissitudes in Government service wrote the book *Hindusthanachi Prachin Va Sampratachi Sthiti Va Pudhen Kaya Tyacha Parinam Honar Yavishayin Vichar*, which was published in Bhau Mahajan's Printing Press in 1843.
6. Under the orders of Sir John Malcolm, Governor of Mumbai, 'The Engineer Institution' was shifted to Pune in 1830 and renamed 'The Government Engineer Institution'. It was closed down in 1832.

7. The Committee consisted of Orlebar, the Reverend Dr Stevenson, Eisdale and Brennan. *MSA GD*, 16.485 (1839): 13-15.
8. Ibid., 16-17.
9. Baba Padmanji, 1968, *Arunodaya*, Mumbai: Bombay Book Tract and Book Society. 3rd edn., p. 8; Bhavalkar, op. cit., 114.
10. *MSA GD*, 24A.749 A (1843): 189.
11. See Letter of 'A Third Hindoo', *Bombay Gazette*, 20 October 1841 (vol. 53: 432).
12. *Prabhakar* (henceforth *PR*), 4 January 1846, vol. 5, 11: 1750-5.
13. For a perceptive analysis of Maharashtrian response to British rule, see K. Mukerji, 1962, 'Renaissance in Bengali and Maharashtrian Thought from 1850 to 1920', *Artha Vijnana*, 4.4: 331-41.
14. The *Durpun* was a forthnightly until 27 April 1832, becoming a weekly from 4 May. Its prospectus was issued on 12 November 1831. Jambhekar, n.d., 2: 1-2.
15. *MSA GD*, 14.259 (1832): 95.
16. *MSA GD*, 21.538 (1840).
17. Ibid., 3: Appendix 3: 17, 37-8.
18. *Bombay Gazette*, 1 July 1841 (vol. 53: 3).
19. *PR*, 12 October 1841 (1: 60-1).
20. Ibid., 30 August 1841 (vol. 53: 203).
21. For a detailed analysis of the letters of 'A Hindoo', which appeared in the *Bombay Gazette* between 30 July and 27 October 1841, see J.V. Naik, 1975-6, 'An Early Appraisal of the British Colonial Policy', *Journal of the University of Bombay*, Arts Numbers. 44-5, 81-2: 241-70.
22. Ibid., 4 September 1842 (1.46: 361).
23. Extracts and news were often given from the following: The *Bombay Times*, the *Bombay Gazette, United Service Gazette* of Bombay, *Christian Advocate, Harkaru, United Service Gazette* of Madras, *Government Gazette, Calcutta Courier, Delhi Gazette, Agra Akhbar, Bengal Herald, Spectator, Dnyanodaya, Englishman, Canton Press, Canton Register* and some newspapers from Great Britain.
24. 'Eka Swadeshbhimani', *PR*, 21 November 1842 (1: 36-7).
25. See *Deshkalyan*, *PR*, 4 January 1846 (5: 1748-9).
26. *BG*, 20 September 1841 (53: 275).
27. *PR*, 27 March 1842 (2: 188-90).
28. Ibid., 31 October 1847 (6: 2502-3).
29. Ibid., 23 October 1842 (2: 419-20).
30. Ibid., November 21, 1842 (1: 36-7).
31. Ibid., 21 July 1842 (2: 317-18).
32. Ibid., 8 May 1842 (2: 230-1).
33. Ibid., 20 March 1842 (2: 174-5).
34. *BG*, 30 July 1841 (53: 103).
35. This book is republished in D.K. Bedekar (ed.), 1969, *Char June Arthasastriya Grantha*, Pune: Arthasastra Samstha. Ramakrishna Wiswanath was the first Maharashtrian to attempt an analysis of Hindu society from an economic point of view.
36. *Essays, Speeches and Writings of D. Naoroji*, ed. by C.L. Parekh, 1887, Mumbai, 32-3.
37. *PR*, 4 January 1845 (5: 1750-1).
38. Ibid. The *Memoirs of Edward West* (ed. by F. Dawtrey Drewitt) do not mention any rumours regarding the poisoning of Sir Edward, but show how he was persecuted by Englishmen in Mumbai. See *Bombay in the Days of King George IV*, London: Longman Green, 1907.
39. See, for example, the letter of 'Eka Hindu', in *PR*, 12 January 1845 (4:1337-8); of 'Vidyabhivruddhicchu', in *PR*, 2 February 1845 (4: 1362); of 'Eka Nyayadarshi', in

PR, 29 March 1846 (5: 1841-2); of 'Vat Saru Hindu', in *PR*, 23 August 1846 (5: 2011-12).

40. *PR*, 28 November 1841 (1: 44-5).
41. Ibid., 30 January 1842 (2:118-20); 22 September 1844 (4: 1213).
42. Ibid.
43. Ibid., 7 March 1847 (6: 2233-5).
44. Ibid., 1 December 1844 (4: 1291).
45. Ibid., 9 October 1842 (1: 406).
46. Ibid., 10 November 1844 (4: 1265).
47. Ibid., 25 September 1842 (1: 387); 9 October 1842 (1: 402-3).
48. G.B. Sardar, Bhau Mahajan, *Maharashtra Sahitya Patrika*; op. cit., p. 307; R.K. Lele, 1984, *Marathi Vrittapatrancha Itihas*, Pune: Continental Prakashan, p. 80. This may be because of his remark made in the heat of debate with *Dnyan Sindhu*: 'I am not concerned with the matter whether widow-marriage should be allowed or not. Nor do I necessarily hold the view in favour of widow-marriage. While presenting the views of both the sides on this issue, I refrain from expressing my opinion but leave the matter for the consideration of our readers.' *PR*, 13 March 1842 (2: 168).
49. *PR*, 11 May 1845 (4: 1478-9).
50. Ibid., 14 December 1845 (5: 1717).
51. Ibid., 8 May 1842 (2: 228).
52. Ibid., 22 June 1845 (4: 1523).
53. Ibid., 29 June 1845 (4: 1532).
54. Ibid., 11 and 15 September, and 2 October 1842 (1: 376, 388-9, 396-7).
55. For a detailed account of the Manav Dharma Sabha and the Paramahansa Sabha, see J.V. Naik, 1974-6, 'Early anti-caste movement in western India: the Paramahansa Sabha', *Journal of the Asiatic Society of Bombay*, 19-51: 136-61.
56. Ibid., 145.
57. Ibid., 156-7.
58. *PR*, 4 May 1845 (4: 1467).
59. Ibid., 3 November 1844 (4: 1262).
60. Ibid., 27 March 1842 (1: 183-4).
61. Ibid., 15 May 1842 (1: 239).
62. Ibid., 26 January 1845 (4: 1357-9).
63. Ibid., 2 May 1847 (5: 2297-8).
64. Ibid., 7 February 1847 (6: 2201-2).
65. Ibid., 6 December 1846 (6: 2129-33).
66. Ibid., 4 July 1847 (6: 2365-7).
67. Ibid., 23 March, 27 April, and 25 May 1845 (4: 1417-18, 1493).
68. Beginning with the issue of 10 April 1842, the account of the French Revolution is serialized in the subsequent 22 issues.
69. *PR*, 14 August 1842 (2: 338-9).
70. Ibid., 27 March-24 April 1842 (2: 177-80, 185, 193, 201 and 209).
71. Ibid., 28 February 1847 (6: 2230).
72. The following issues of *Dhumketu* (henceforth *DK*) are available in the *Bharat Itihas Samshodhan Mandal*, Pune, 12 June 1857; 17 August, 27 September, and 26 November 1858; 25 February, 22 April, 3 June, 22 and 29 July, 23 and 30 September, 28 October, 4 November, and 11 and 16 December 1859.
73. Matthew Lederle, 1976, *Philosophical Trends in Maharashtra*, Mumbai: Popular Prakashan.
74. S.V. Puntambekar, 1945, 'Vishnu Bawa Brahmachari (1825-71)—Utopian Socialists', *Indian Journal of Political Science*, 6.3: 154-66.
75. *Vartaman Deepika* (henceforth *VD*), 25 June 1859 (7: 109).

76. *DK*, 22 July 1859 (7: 116).
77. *VD*, 9 July 1858.
78. *VD*, 2 July 1858 (7: 108).
79. *DK*, 3 June 1859 (7: 88).
80. *DK*, 12 June 1857 (5: 93).
81. *DK*, 3 July 1857 (5: 107).
82. *DK*, 27 August 1858 (6: 139).
83. *DK*, 25 February 1859 (7: 31-2).
84. In official records the name of Raghoba Janardhan is given as the editor of *Dig-Darshan*; see *MSA GD*, 23.54 (1843): 129, 424. The ownership of the paper was trasnferred to Bhau Mahajan in 1843; see *GD*, 41.766 (1843): 111.
85. For scientific articles in the *Dig-Darshan* (henceforth *DD*) see Jambhekar, n.d., II: 189-238.
86. The Government subscribed to 20 copies of the magazine. *MSA GD*, 540 (1840): 135.
87. See Preface in *DD*, 1.1 (July 1854): 1.
88. All issues of *DD* are in the Mandlik Collection of the Fergusson College Library, Pune; some are also found in the Mumbai Marathi Grantha Sangrahalaya, Mumbai.

REFERENCES

Bedekar, D.K. (ed.), 1969, *Char June arthasastriya grantha*, Pune: Arthasastra Samstha.

Chhatre, M.K., 1984, *Chhatre kul vrittant*, Pune.

Jambhekar, B.S., 1950, *Memoirs and Writings of Acharya Bal Gangadhar Shastri Jambhekar*, ed. by G.G. Jambhekar, Pune.

Karve, G.G., 1957, 'Sadashiv Kashinath Urfa Bapu Chhatre', *Marathi Sahityantil Upekshit Manakari*, Mumbai: Venus Prakashan.

Khanolkar, G.D., 1988, 'Nishpruha vruttiche un patiche patrakar', *Maharashtra Times, Sunday Supplement*, 13 March 1988.

Lederle, M., 1976, *Philosophical Trends in Maharashtra*, Mumbai: Popular Prakashan.

Lele, R.K., 1984, *Marathi vrittapatrancha itihas*, Pune: Continental Prakashan.

Mukerji, K., 1962, 'Renaissance in Bengali and Maharashtrian thought from 1850 to 1920', *Artha Vijnana*, 4.4: 331-41.

Naik, J.V., 1974-6, 'Early anti-caste movement in western India: the Paramahansa Sabha', *Journal of the Asiatic Society of Bombay*, 19-51: 136-61.

———, 1975-6, 'An Early Appraisal of the British Colonial Policy', *Journal of the University of Bombay*, Arts Numbers 44-5, 81-2, 241-70.

Padmanji, B., 1968, *Arunodaya*, Mumbai: Bombay Book Tract and Book Society (3rd edn.).

Pandit, B.S. (ed.), 1961, *Raosaheb Keshav Shivram Bhavalkar yanche atmavritta*, Nagpur: Samshodhan Mahal.

Parekh, C.L. (ed.) 1887, *Essays, Speeches and Writings of D. Naoroji*, Mumbai.

Priyolkar, A.K., 1947, *R.B. Dadoba Pandurang: atmacharitra va charitra*, Mumbai: Keshav Bhikaji Dhavle.

Puntambekar, S.V., 1945, 'Vishnu Bawa Brahmachari (1825-1871)—an Utopian Socialist', *Indian Journal of Political Science* 6.3: 154-66.

Sardar, G.B., 1940, 'Bhau Mahajan', *Maharashtra Sahitya Parishad*, 13.4: 295-310.

Vartak, G.V. (ed.), 1981, *Kunte kula vrittanta*, Mumbai.

The *Bombay Chronicle*: Competing Images of Division and Unity in the Indian Nationalist Movement, 1920-30

MILTON ISRAEL

The 1920s were a time of experimentation when national leaders and local politicians competed for control of the freedom struggle. This was not a new situation, but the struggle became more critical with the arrival of M.K. Gandhi at the centre and the establishment of an all-India base that appeared to have a life of its own. The newly-enlivened Congress was required to mobilize support in old and new areas of activity while carrying on its confrontation with the British state. By the end of the nineteenth century, colonial rule had come to be a system which attracted cooperation and participation without the continuing use and threat of force, and provided as well the primary stimulus for the nationalist movement which sought its overthrow. At the focal point of this complex set of competitive forces, the press played an essential role facilitating communication between those who determined the strategies of confrontation and mobilization—both official and nationalist—and their target constituencies.

This paper concerns one newspaper, the *Bombay Chronicle*, and one locus of competitive action and response, what is now Maharashtra. It will consider the *Chronicle's* presentation of the struggle and the goal in the 1920s, as reflected in responses to such major issues as working the Reforms, Non-Cooperation and Gandhian leadership, and competing conceptions of national unity. As was the case in every region and locality in the subcontinent, there was a particular Mumbai debate and perspective, the product of the concentration of industrial and commercial interests, local communal issues, and the perceived tradition of a Maharashtrian response to challenge, tested by the British since 1818, and more recently by the nationalist movement itself. There were approximately 250 papers published in the Bombay Presidency in 1925, and the *Chronicle* was among the eight or ten with a circulation above 10,000. It was read and quoted beyond its metropolitan and provincial borders, and a deliberate participant in the work of nation-building as well as nationalist/Raj confrontation. It was, in this context, an important focus for the exchange of information and viewpoint within the Presidency, and between Mumbai and the rest of India. The *Chronicle*, like the *Tribune, Hindu, Amrita Bazar Patrika* and other papers with a national perspective, attempted to play a mediating role by advocating and describing a coalescence of viewpoint and interest between the all-India and provincial leadership and the constituencies they sought to mobilize.

The *Chronicle's* endeavour through the 1920s to remain loyal to Gandhi and the mainstream Congress programme made it the principal English-language nationalist paper in the Presidency. It also placed it in competition with other local nationalist papers representing conflicting views and constituencies such as the liberal *Indian Daily Mail* and the responsivist *Kesari*. In the context of the changing pattern and content of nationalist action in this period, the *Chronicle's* desire to be a national voice tended to deny it a stable base in Mumbai, with its range of camps opposing the leadership at the centre. This made the paper too a continuing candidate for take-over by various groups and individuals, both within the Congress and outside. The *Chronicle* sought to limit its distance from what was perceived as a Maharashtrian perspective, but its position on the margin of the local/national exchange was a continuing source of instability.

Unlike the *Tribune* of Lahore which had been endowed by a founding Trust, or the *Hindu* and the *Amrita Bazar Patrika* with their Iyengar and Ghosh owner-editors, the *Chronicle* had to be concerned about its financial support, and its editors were employed by a Board conscious of the connection between resources and viewpoint. The result was recurrent crises, usually the reflection of political action at the Congress centre or within the Presidency. Viewpoints in ascendance would be represented by changes in Board membership, and new sources of funding would replace the gifts of disenchanted financiers. Identification with the Congress was no guarantee of security, as the paper was confronted with policy choices which divided Congressmen and ran the risk of of offending some large and influential constituency. The Congress might be able to subsume a vast array of differing viewpoints under its spacious umbrella, but an editorial position, reiterated daily in print, tended to antagonize—especially those who found no home at the centre and sought loyalty from opinion-makers when they were at home.

The *Chronicle* tried to respond to the different viewpoints and, as a result, was continually attacked for its lack of a 'settled policy';[1] for those whose political views were principled convictions wanted loyalty and propaganda. Over time, the *Chronicle* supported the Moderates, the Extremists, Non-Cooperation, Swarajists, No-Changers and Pro-Changers, leaving in its wake anger and disappointment. This was particularly the case in Mumbai which had played such a major role in initiating the all-India movement. Its leaders had carried all-India viewpoints and strategies evolved out of local experience and tradition, and factional struggle at the centre could often trace its lineage to earlier confrontations within the Presidency.[2] In the early 1920s, however, the Maharashtrian content of the national programme and its advocates lost their privileged position, and the *Chronicle's* loyalty to the new leadership antagonized old constituencies which had once considered the paper their own.

Gandhi's apparent appropriation and synthesis of Maharashtra's mixed nationalist legacy (calling Gokhale his political *guru* and adopting confrontational techniques more akin to Tilak's methods), did not attract an easy transfer of loyalty and support. Many of these local heirs of the founders of the Congress—Moderate or Extremist—were now described as 'slackers', plotting to regain control from a new generation, whose lineage and political base were alien and distant. Soon after the adoption of Non-Cooperation, N.C. Kelkar, the editor of the *Mahratta*, had insisted that Maharashtra was not opposed to Gandhi's leadership, and that their differences concerned only details of the programme. Over time, while asserting his loyalty to Congress, he reiterated his concern about the impracticality of viewing Non-Cooperation in terms of principle, rather than as a temporary tactic to achieve a specific, attainable objective, and associated this pragmatic view with a Maharashtrian perspective.[3] In response, the *Chronicle* utilized well-known images of local political identity in order to isolate the opponents of Gandhi's leadership as either collaborationists in the case of Moderates, or disgruntled reactionaries in the case of the leaderless Tilakites.

In a continuing exchange of leader and editorial charges and responses, the *Chronicle*, speaking for the Congress centre, and the *Mahratta*, for the Maharashtra branch, carefully directed their rhetorics at the heart of the opposing programmes. In response to a *Chronicle* suggestion in July 1922 that those who opposed the mainstream Congress view cherished the ambition of reviving Peshwa rule in Pune, Kelkar insisted that he spoke for 'the real mind of the whole of Maharashtra'. Citing the all-India contributions of Ranade, Gokhale and Tilak, he insisted that those who shared his views were the descendants of that tradition of 'true Indian nationalism'. The reference to the Peshwas was interpreted as an attack both on this Maharashtra-based national accomplishment, and on the Pune-based Brahman elite which was its source. Kelkar reminded his readers that the *Chronicle* was no longer the paper founded by Perozeshah Mehta, 'a truly cosmopolitan Parsee', financed by many 'catholic Hindus'. It was, he lamented, now run 'more in the interests of pan-Islamism than the *Mahratta* or the *Kesari*, founded by Brahmins, are in the interests of the Peshwa's rule'.[4] Kelkar's vision of a pragmatic, cosmopolitan and enlightened Hindu Maharashtrian nationalism was often recast in *Chronicle* commentary as unprincipled, parochial, and communalist. For him, and M.R. Jayakar, at whom the Peshwa charge was directed, such views confirmed the *Chronicle* as an enemy of Maharashtra.[5]

The Indian Newspaper Company had been established by Mehta in 1907 to provide a voice for another presumed Maharashtrian perspective: the moderate nationalist politics of the Westernized urban intelligentsia and business establishment. Mehta considered himself the spokesman for a progressive and enlightened viewpoint, threatened by reaction from an aggressive, indigenous revivalism represented by Tilak's *Mahratta* and *Kesari*, and a defensive, alien colonialism supported by the powerful *Times of India*. The *Chronicle*, which first appeared in 1913, was meant to occupy the middle ground. Mumbai was a city founded on accommodation with the lifestyle, values, and norms of its alien governors,[6] and the *Chronicle* was a Mumbai paper—confidently associating with the centres of power, the Government of India and the Indian National Congress, on its own terms.

If Tilak, and subsequently Kelkar, from their base in Pune were not seeking the restoration of the Peshwas, they did seek a place for their heirs, and a stake at the bargaining table where the new Indian nation was being envisioned, and the campaign designed. While Mumbai city had its own distinctive life reflected in its heterodox mix of British businessmen, Parsee industrialists, and Gujarati traders and shroffs, Pune remained dominated by a Brahman elite, the self-professed designers, beneficiaries and representatives of a Maharashtrian viewpoint reflected in the peculiar mix of Kshatriya and *bhakti* traditions, and symbolized in the achievements of Shivaji and Ramdas. Tilak's Ganapati and Shivaji festivals were as much a challenge to Mehta's moderate moderns, who perceived themselves to be the beneficiaries of British rule, as to the British themselves, and he brought his defensive struggle to the heartland of both adversaries—Mumbai.[7]

In the period of its ascendancy in nationalist politics, Mehta's Mumbai tradition and his city newspaper lived on the margins of Pune's Maharashtra. In 1915, however, both Mehta and Gokhale died, and Tilak, after six years in exile, had managed to integrate his confrontationalist style into a constitutional context on the form of the Home Rule League. In response, *Chronicle* policy, now controlled by its editor, B.G. Horniman, moved away from the orthodox liberal creed of its founder to support home rule. It was a relatively small change, merely a 'deviational angle', in the view of its associate editor Pothan Joseph,[8] but it required a choice between the two major factions. In the view of the Tilakites, the paper had finally come home, while Mehta's old colleagues on the Board considered the *Chronicle* lost to their party. There were a sufficient number of resignations and replacements to create a new Board, described by M.R. Jayakar as 'now flooded with Mr Horniman's friends and allies'. Jehangir Petit, one of the founders of the Indian Newspaper Company, resigned, lamenting that the *Chronicle*, after ten years of difficulties and hardships, had been 'handed over to a noisy minority'.[9] This 1917 confrontation and internal reorganization established a pattern for change in the *Chronicle* over the next thirty years, as it continually moved to accommodate the dominant forces within the Congress leadership, with a Maharashtrian base. In 1917, it remained a Maharashtrian choice—Tilak or Gokhale—and only indirectly a choice of national policy as well. Both Maharashtra and the Congress were, however, soon caught up in the transition that would bring Gandhi to power, and with it a reversal of the relationship. Maharashtra, or at least those who believed that they represented its interests and viewpoint, found themselves in the minority, attempting to keep up with and influence a movement that appeared to be going out of control.

B.G. Horniman, the first editor, was brought in from the *Statesman* on the recommendation of Gokhale and S.N. Banerjea, the latter noting that he was 'as good an Indian as myself'.[10] Notwithstanding this spotlessly moderate pedigree, it was Horniman who became associated with the evolving extremism of the Home Rule League, and with the early Satyagraha experiments in Kaira and Ahmedabad. He severed the paper's allegiance to the Moderate formula of the Congress founders, and likewise destroyed the accommodative relationship with the government, which Mehta had considered essential for a powerful and influential organ on the pattern of the *Times of India*. For the next year and a half, officials in Mumbai and Delhi carefully recorded the increasingly antagonistic editorials and political coverage of the *Chronicle*, filing them away for future use. In April 1919, they finally moved to arrest Horniman, who was subsequently deported.

Although Horniman was supposed to be safely back in England, and no longer able to participate in Indian politics, his presence seemed hardly diminished. Over the next seven years he was the editor across the water—filing stories regularly, acting as the London correspondent of the paper, publishing articles in *India*, the journal of the British Committee of the Congress, and in the *Catholic Herald*, for subsequent reprinting in the *Chronicle*. As President of the Indian Press Association in London, his speeches and writings on the repression of press freedom in India attracted large audiences, and he was generally included in any Congress delegation in London. Throughout the last half of 1919, stories about Horniman—his services to India, his arrest, rebuttals concerning the charge which led to his deportation, and descriptions of his London-based activities—appeared regularly. In subsequent years the stories diminished, but no regular reader of the *Chronicle* was allowed to forget that Horniman languished in exile in Britain and wished to return. The campaign was carefully orchestrated from London, and Horniman corresponded with his former colleagues in the *Chronicle* regarding issues that required greater coverage.[11] The paper seemed always willing to give him as much space as necessary. In large type, and often with a portrait of 'the king across the Ḳala Pani',[12] the anniversaries of his deportation were noted with special messages;[13] his inability to obtain a passport was attacked and his return demanded,[14] and his absence was regularly associated with the general denial of fundamental rights in India: in short, Horniman's return was a matter of 'national self-respect'.[15]

While Horniman was carrying on his personal struggle in London, and committing himself as well to Gandhi, Non-Cooperation and the struggle against the Reforms, his old responsibilities were shared briefly by Syed Hussain and S.A. Brelvi. Both recognized that they were only temporarily filling in for their exiled master, and neither had the experience and influence that allowed for strong, independent control of editorial policy. In any case, the paper remained in danger of closure for some time, and the Board was committed to re-establishing a working relationship with the government that would at least allow for uncensored publication. Both M.A. Jinnah and M.R. Jayakar, who alternated in the chairmanship in 1919-21, were critics of Non-Cooperation and it appeared that the paper might return at least in the direction of the Moderate camp, from which Horniman had carried it away in 1917. As was often the case, however, it remained difficult to assign the *Chronicle* to a specific camp, since its messages were always mixed. The continuing flow of Horniman's colourful prose shared space with Brelvi's more measured political comment, and neither reflected the conservative priorities of the Board.

In 1920, however, any confusion regarding the policy of the *Chronicle* was resolved with the appointment of Marmaduke Pickthall as Editor. Pickthall was a novelist and religious writer, particularly well-known for his interest in the Middle East, his conversion to Islam, and his pro-Turk position on the post-war treaty concerning the remnants of the Ottoman Empire. He took the job because he needed the money, and because his political views denied him the opportunity of using his expertise in London.[16] In Mumbai, he was quickly recognized as a Khilafatist leader, and, in that context, a staunch non-cooperator as well.

The *Chronicle* had taken a strong pro-Turk position under Horniman, who insisted that the question could only be regarded from a Muslim point of view, and that it was 'absurd and perverse' for non-Muslims to quarrel with Muslim views. The history of the conflict was rehearsed in a flow of editorials associating the issue with the Muslims of Mumbai, and all India.[17] Pickthall now carried on the campaign with the fervour of a true believer. Although initially reluctant to accept the appointment, he discovered an ideal opportunity for using his writing talents in support of his religious and political convictions. During the first year of his appointment, however, Pickthall's acclaim in the Khilafat Committee was not reflected in the *Chronicle's* Board, where concern with the paper's unrestrained support for the whole of Gandhi's programme led to resignations and reorganization. Jinnah resigned in April 1921 and Jayakar, who seemed to enter and withdraw at regular intervals, resigned again from the chairmanship and the Board at the end of the year. On this occasion, he was angered by Pickthall's appointment as Chief Leader Writer in addition to his Editorship without consultation with the Board. He considered his position to be 'very anomalous if not humiliating' and decided not to continue as a 'rubber stamp' for actions and views he could not support.[18]

The changes in the Board were greeted enthusiastically by Pickthall, who felt that he had been forced to be guarded in his views. He now looked forward to 'boldly uttering the Gandhian sentiments and views, *insh'allah*'.[19] Any constraint had been more evident to Pickthall than to his critics, who had already concluded that the *Chronicle* had been lost again. The hoped-for rapprochement with the government was stillborn. At his first interview with Sir George Lloyd, the Governor rejected a constructive relationship with a 'vile rag' and the Pickthalls experienced an almost total European social boycott.[20] Within the Board, Jamnadas Dwarkadas, a Gujarati dye-importer, Home Ruler and, by 1921, anti-Gandhian, spoke for the loyal opposition. He dissociated from the editorial policy of the *Chronicle*, noting that it was in conflict with the agreed policy of the directors. The paper was not meant to be an active protagonist of Non-Cooperation and Dwarkadas was particularly angered by implied attacks on his patriotism for retaining his membership in the Legislative Council. He further lamented that Pickthall had 'allowed his pro-Muslim leanings to convert the paper into practically an Islamic organ'.[21]

Gandhi, Non-Cooperation and Khilafat arrived in Maharashtra as a single package, concentrating a range of concerns and grievances, defined as Maharashtra's response;[22] and the *Chronicle*, the declared voice of the Congress in the Presidency, helped to entrench the communal focus of the new politics. The inordinate emphasis on Khilafat was particularly offensive in Pune, where

Tilak's heirs perceived a combined attack on their cultural heritage. Among the major national newspapers published by Indians, the *Chronicle* was virtually alone in its uncompromising stand on the Turkish Question. Britain's policy was variously described as 'mad and idiotic',[23] 'a crusade against Islam',[24] and an 'insult to the Muslims of India and to the Indian people'.[25] The Khilafat and Punjab wrongs were twinned as inseparable grievances which had to be jointly redressed.[26] While the campaign continued throughout the early 1920s in the *Chronicle*, others attempted to put the issue into perspective and distance it from the mainstream of Indian nationalism. By the spring of 1920, the *Hindu* asked 'What can Musalmans of India do?' and suggested that Montague and Chelmsford had sincerely tried to help, while Gandhi's use of Non-Cooperation on their behalf would lead to bloodshed and rioting and 'innocent people, who have nothing to do with the Treaty, would be the only sufferers'.[27] The *Leader* agreed. While recognizing the pain caused to Mohammedans in India and throughout the Islamic world, there seemed no alternative but 'swallow the hard pill'.[28] The *Bengalee* suggested 'philosophic patience and calmness' to its Muslim readers,[29] and even the loyal *Independent*, while supporting the Khilafat cause, noted ominously that it was not possible to 'control the forces created by this movement by any sudden change of its temper or ideals'.[30]

Criticism of its apparent Muslim bias poured into the *Chronicle's* office and much of it was published. Pickthall met his opponents directly in a December 1922 editorial noting concerns about his emphasis on the Turkish Question. In response to the argument that the *Chronicle* ought to be a national organ and not concern itself with such issues, Pickthall insisted that what was being asked for was a 'provincial organ concerned with the opinions of Mr This and Mr That of local fame, rather than with those of India in relationship to the world at large'.[31] There was no lack of support. At a Khilafat Conference in the following week, the delegates noted their appreciation of the work of Pickthall, and the *Chronicle* appealed to all Muslims to help the paper. A Mumbai participant, Seth Khatri, noted that the *Chronicle* had brought a 'message of hope' and 'sustained the faith of Muslim India'. It was, he insisted, the duty of all Muslims to 'stand by the *Chronicle* under all circumstances'.[32] As in the case of his critics, Pickthall shared such applause with his readers.

Pickthall's enthusiasm for Gandhi's leadership and programme was no less fervent than his commitment to righting the Khilafat Wrong, and he surely tested his command of laudatory adjectives to describe him. In a 1922 editorial Gandhi was styled 'the greatest leader in the East', 'the national leader', the 'strategic chief', 'the leader', the 'absent general', 'Mahatma', 'the great commander', and 'Mahatmaji'.[33] He delighted in the opportunity to share a platform with Gandhi, always dressed on such occasions in *khaddar* and Gandhi cap. To his correspondents in England he described Gandhi as a saint and his movement as a form of 'self-purification',[34] and the religious nature of his enthusiasm was always evident in his *Chronicle* stories. 'Our weapon, thank God, is a clean one', he noted in applauding the Bardoli decision in 1922.[35]

It was in this context that Kelkar had rebutted the charge that Gandhi's opponents in Maharashtra were reactionary dreamers, seeking to retain power, symbolized in the restoration of Peshwa rule. In retrospect, Jayakar described in his autobiography the viewpoint of the defenders of Maharashtra who had experienced injustice in this period, a situation which in his view had continued throughout the balance of the nationalist period.[36] The fault, Jayakar lamented, was largely their own because Pune had not openly attacked Gandhi but settled instead for 'halting and disingenuous conversion'.[37] Jayakar had noted in 1922 the 'marked dislike of Maharashtra and its politics' evinced by the editor of the *Chronicle*,[38] and he continued throughout his life to reiterate the same defensive theme: 'the non-receptivity of the Maratha mind to Gandhian fancy and asceticism', 'the essential incompatibility between the Maratha mind as moulded by Tilak's doctrines and Gandhi's teachings', 'the practical Maratha genius'.[39]

In 1924, a series of legal disputes and substantial financial losses led to a takeover of the *Chronicle* by a group considered to be more sympathetic to Maharashtra. As had been the case after the 1917 Horniman coup, and again in 1921 when additional Gandhian supporters removed any constraint on the *Chronicle's* advocacy of Non-Cooperation and the Khilafat Movement, Pickthall resigned along with three other Gandhi loyalists on the Board: L.R. Tairsee,[40] Shankerlal Banker,[41] and N.H. Belgaumwalla.[42] In their place Jayakar returned again with Swarajist Party leader Motilal Nehru, and V.D Govindji.[43] It appeared that the Swarajists were about to gain control of a Mumbai paper that would support and advocate their views.

It was a slow transition. In January 1922, commenting on the desire of Motilal Nehru and C.R. Das to enter the Councils for the purpose of obstruction, the *Chronicle* called on 'our friends of Maharashtra' to explain their position. Did those who advocated Responsive Cooperation accept this goal, or were they likely to cooperate with the bureaucracy when a 'beneficial measure is brought forward'.[44] Throughout the year the *Chronicle* attacked Council Entry in general, and the Maharashtra PCC in particular, for apparently more traitorous plans. In response, Kelkar challenged the *Chronicle* for attempting to make him and the Maharashtra party the 'scapegoat for NCO fire eaters', noting that he reserved the right to be a critical Congressman under the orthodox Non-Cooperators, just as he had been at one time under the orthodox moderates. In contrast to the *Chronicle's* uncompromising attack, he noted the 'mild and genial fire of *Young India*' that had been directed against the Maharashtra Party in the last two years.[45]

In January 1923, the *Chronicle* began a slow migration by noting that the new party was at least within the Congress,[46] but the Maharashtra participants remained less trustworthy. They were again pressed to formally and publicly state their allegiance to, or deviation from, Das' obstructionist priority. Kelkar responded by noting his rejection of both 'the blind chelas of the Mahatma' and the 'selfish group of moderate politicians'.[47] Throughout the year the growing accommodation within the Congress of the reality of Swarajist Party success was reflected in reticent enthusiasm in the *Chronicle*: 'At least Swarajists have gotten rid of the moderates.'[48] By January 1924, in a lead editorial entitled

'Forward to Work', the *Chronicle* formally withdrew from the battle, adopting along with the Congress a policy of benevolent neutrality.[49] The desire of the Swarajists for advocacy awaited the takeover in July.

The new Board met on 30 July, under the chairmanship of Motilal Nehru. He recognized that the Swarajists still lacked a loyal majority and, therefore, declined the permanent chairmanship. He also warned his Mumbai Swarajist colleagues that there would be no party money for the *Chronicle* until their control was solid. With regard to the Editorship, there was still a preference for Horniman if he were allowed back into the country. It was agreed, however, that his editorial skill would have to be complemented by a commitment to the Swarajists after Nehru reminded them that Horniman's contributions had been 'in support of the orthodox Gandhian doctrines'. K.M. Panikkar was proposed but he refused to keep the seat warm for Horniman. The Board finally agreed to turn to S.A. Brelvi.[50] He had been introduced to Perozeshah Mehta by Lallubhai Samaldas and appointed Assistant Editor in 1915. Throughout all the subsequent crises and changes Brelvi was available to fill in: Acting Editor after Horniman's deportation, Joint Editor under Pickthall, Acting Editor again after Pickthall's resignation, and, finally, Editor, but only until 'the King across the Kala Pani' returned.

While the struggle for secure funding and party loyalty continued within the Board and in the offices of selected Mumbai moguls, Brelvi eased the paper back from the confrontational style of his predecessor. He shared, however, Pickthall's loyalty to Gandhi as well as his concern for Muslim issues, and his *Chronicle* never satisfied those in the Swaraj Party who wanted their own paper like Das' *Forward*. Brelvi's solution to the problem of competition and conflict within the Congress was to provide a forum for all positions.

In January 1925, the partial support the Swarajists had been receiving from the *Chronicle* was threatened by its continuing insolvency and another takeover bid. Nehru and Jayakar attempted to rally support from F.E. Dinshah, Lalji Naranji, Purshottamdas Thakurdas and other members of the Mumbai business establishment, to prevent the paper from 'being acquired by people who will not run it on independent, progressive, nationalistic lines'.[51] Discussions were held in R.D. Tata's home and a financing package to allow for a competitive bid was tentatively arranged.[52] The anticipated support did not materialize, however, and N.H. Belgaumwalla, with the support of a group of investors that included Lalji Naranji, took control. Belgaumwalla had been a director with Pickthall, and had left the Board with him. Jayakar was convinced that the Swarajists and Maharashtra had lost again, and the *Chronicle* would become 'the organ of Mr Gandhi's devoted followers'.[53]

Once again the loss was not complete. Belgaumwalla offered Jayakar a directorship and some control over the paper's editorial policy. The *Chronicle* would not be a Swarajist paper as proposed in the losing takeover bid of Jayakar's group,[54] but it would not be orthodox Gandhian either. Formal terms of agreement were prepared by Jayakar, providing for support of Swarajist Council activities, without precluding other forms of political agitation. It was also noted that should Swarajists decide to accept office in the unreformed government, the *Chronicle* was at liberty to be critical, provided that its criticism was 'dignified and decorous' and did not 'ascribe motives to persons or indulge in any unbecoming abuse of individuals'. Belgaumwalla and Jayakar also agreed to meet regularly and Jayakar was given the right of approval of any future directors.[55]

These measures for the interests of the party should have been adequate, but the resulting performance of the paper clearly did not measure up to Jayakar's expectations. There was too much of Gandhi, too many Muslim stories, too much evenhandedness and too little loyalty to the Swaraj Party. By March, Jayakar returned to his old theme of the need for a party paper in Mumbai.[56] The need was becoming ever more compelling, as Jayakar's wing slowly moved towards full responsive cooperation and office, likely bringing renewed isolation for Maharashtra.[57] Relations with Belgaumwalla soured, and it seemed that the paper would finally make its return to the orthodox Gandhian camp.[58]

In January 1926, however, the *Chronicle* supported the new Responsivist Party. Gandhi's willingness to accommodate deviationist views had reduced the ranks of the orthodox, and the mixed signals emanating from the centre made it easier to remain pure, while experimenting at the same time. Belgaumwalla, who returned to control the paper in 1925 after his resignation in the previous year with the rout of the Gandhians, had become more flexible. He also could not antagonize potential backers. And Brelvi's view of Congress loyalty had already demonstrated a measure of tolerance for a range of tactics and viewpoints.

In January 1926, B.G. Horniman returned to India and to the editorship of the *Bombay Chronicle*. 'I am not changed. I am not aged', he declared to the large crowd that welcomed him home, and he prepared to carry the *Chronicle* back to Gandhian orthodoxy.[59] The Board, however, though willing to use Horniman's editorial talents and nationalist prestige, refused to admit him into its ranks as that would have made a repetition of the 1917 coup possible. On 2 March Horniman resigned from the editorship in a flurry of charges and counter-charges, proclaimed in public meetings and published in the press.[60] He founded and edited the *Indian National Herald*, from which he continued his attack on NCO heretics including Gandhi himself, and after losing control of that paper in another celebrated contest, ended his career with the *Bombay Sentinel*. The commitment to support the Responsivists, given by Belgaumwalla in January, was restored, and Responsivist Party workers continued their efforts to collect funds for the *Chronicle's* support.[61] In April, the paper's precarious financing required another reorganization and another flurry of correspondence and meetings to gather support for its current policy.[62] In October, the paper was sold, again to Belgaumwalla who was now associated with a group of investors including L.R. Tairsee who had sat on Pickthall's Board and had been moving away from confrontational politics.[63] Jayakar was able to assure Pandit Malaviya that the *Chronicle* promised to be 'the bulwark of the old world nationalism as we understand it',[64] and received a pledge of support to stabilize its finances in the face of the threat from Horniman's *Indian National Herald*.

Brelvi used the announcement of the sale of the *Chronicle* as an opportunity to reiterate the paper's commitment to the national cause and to the Congress. After thirteen years of advocating a particular viewpoint—Moderate and anti-Extremist, Extremist and anti-Moderate, Orthodox Gandhian, marginal Swarajist and so on—the *Chronicle* declared a unilateral peace. Brelvi noted his commitment to 'the old, undiluted, creed of Mahatma Gandhi' and his aversion to Councils and Office, 'those playthings of designing bureaucracy'. But he recognized that the growth of national consciousness had produced 'a richness and variety of views regarding new ways and means'. In this context, he argued, the Congress ought to be sufficiently broadly based 'to welcome and absorb every shade of nationalist opinion'. There was room enough for all mainstream views, Brelvi suggested, and the *Chronicle* would find room to deal with them fairly and critically.[65]

By the end of the year, the *Chronicle* was urging Swarajists to modify their policies on the Government of India Act rather than moving in a disorganized way—and through the backdoor—towards cooperation. It suggested that 'the shrewd Swarajists may be well advised to request the Gauhati Congress (meeting at the end of the month) to frame a practical programme of such coordinated action as may enable them to cooperate with all independent parties for the good of the people'.[66] As if to certify the rapprochement between Mumbai and Pune, Jayakar spoke to Kelkar about the paper's continuing financial problems, and it was agreed that the *Kesari* would recommend the *Chronicle* to its readers.[67]

The dominant theme of Brelvi's editorship, was the dominant theme of the decade, a search for unity, its achievement and loss, its friends and enemies. As he settled back into the Editor's chair, which would never be denied him again until his death in 1949, he lamented the lost opportunities and the obvious difficulties ahead:

> If a modern Diogenes were to hunt out for Indians with his lantern in these days, he would be sure to come across fervid Hindus, bigotted Muslims and fanatical souls deeply engrossed with the problem of tirelessly finding out how unjustly their own particular community was being treated, and he would have to ask in sorrow: 'Where are the Indians!'[68]

As the only Muslim editor of a major national English-language paper, Brelvi was especially sensitive to the communalist context of the political debate. He tried to keep the paper's comments on the high ground, but unlike Chintamani, Iyengar and Kalinath Roy, he did not have absolute control of his paper. Deeply felt divisions, violent confrontation and emotional reaction surrounded him in his office, and were evident in the pages of the paper. Often Brelvi's impatient and defensive idealism on the editorial page debated with an article in the same issue.

Hindu-Muslim amity and socialism were the two essential elements in Brelvi's unity mandate. But however idealistic his personal commitment, in the editorials of an influential newspaper they invariably attracted and helped to entrench divisiveness. His designation of Muslim participation and agreement as essential for any significant political progress or change of strategy tended to overshadow his commitment to political tolerance in the minds of defensive Maharashtrian leaders. Brelvi assured readers that Shivaji had no quarrel with Muslim rule in the north, but was solely—and justifiably—concerned with incursions into Maharashtra. He pressed his Hindu readers to reject the communalization of their history, and that of all of India, whose heroes were Ashoka, Akbar, and Shivaji.[69] Brelvi attempted to redirect the debate among Indians to confrontation with the British—'they will try to divide us in regard to the Simon Commission';[70] the bureaucracy would be the greatest loser if separate electorates were abolished[71]—but there was clearly no united front to carry on the fight. He was particularly derisive about the apparent fanaticism of some No-Changers, who pressed for a return to Non-Cooperation but ignored its essential component, 'complete cooperation between Hindus and Muslims'. Without it, without the cooperation of peasants and workers, the Congress would remain, he lamented, 'a paper organization'. In a conclusion that might have been written by Kelkar eight years before, Brelvi insisted that Congress desired 'no more spectacular fireworks which end in smoke'.[72]

Brelvi was particularly concerned that Jawaharlal Nehru gave too little attention to the communal question as a fundamental constraint on further progress.[73] Nehru agreed; in the political lull of 1933, following two years of active confrontation, he admitted that the diversion of public attention to the positive economic and political side of the struggle had not made any impact on the problem. He was now ready to speak out forcefully and noted that he was accused of using unnecessarily strong language. 'I think the right line to take', he suggested, 'is that communalism is merely a cover for political reaction.'[74] Brelvi was pleased that Nehru had become an activist, but believed that his diagnosis was far too simplistic. Throughout the late 1920s, Brelvi had attempted to deal with communal identity on its own terms, understandable if not laudable. During the extended negotiations concerning separate electorates and the Nehru Report, he agreed that there was disagreement among Muslims and that Hindus were reticent about making a deal. But, he insisted, there was no possibility of making any progress unless the risk that the Muslims had taken was matched by the Hindus. 'Complete unity and trust do not exist', he declared; and India had to accept this reality.[75] Even so, however much he tried to be balanced in his arguments on this issue, the *Chronicle* remained for many a Muslim paper, and a permanent candidate for takeover. In February 1930, Jayakar heard a rumour, which turned out to be incorrect, that the *Chronicle* was to be auctioned off at a reasonable price. He immediately contacted a potential buyer in Mumbai, who might be interested in 'acquiring the paper for the Hindu Cause'.[76]

In 1935 Jayakar, Tej Bahadur Sapru, and representatives of some Princely States established a syndicate with the help of the manager of the *Times of India* to start a new paper for propaganda in favour of working the new constitution. In Brelvi's view the scheme was designed to kill two birds with one stone: suppressing the *Chronicle* and starting their own paper. Jayakar had first attempted to buy the *Chronicle* but the price was too high. Now the paper was on the market, and since the Congress could not afford to buy it, Brelvi considered the possibility of starting another. But he needed the support of Vallabhbhai Patel and Bhulabhai Desai, the conservative Mumbai Congress leaders, who had been critical of the *Chronicle's* 'socialist' bias for quite sometime.[77]

Brelvi contacted Gandhi, and asked him to intercede with Patel and Desai, and Gandhi duly urged them to support the establishment of a Congress paper in Mumbai, which should, if possible, be 'ready on the very day the *Chronicle* changes hands'. Gandhi advised Brelvi that if he were otherwise eligible, his 'socialistic inclinations ought not to be regarded as a bar' to his selection as Editor.[78] This was not the unreserved support Brelvi had sought and anticipated, but he was doubtless used to his idealism being categorized as someone else's enemy. In a subsequent conversation with Patel and Desai, they agreed that a Congress paper should be started, but they denounced the *Chronicle's* support for the socialist programme. They insisted that their paper would be a party paper, 'giving publicity and support only to the majority view of the Congress and suppressing the minority view altogether'.[79]

Brelvi had argued with Patel and Desai that the function of a newspaper was to publish all views in its news columns while reserving the editorial for its dominant policy. But in response to his query whether they would allow him even to report a Congress-Socialist meeting, they said no. He was astounded by their narrow-minded and reactionary views about the function of a newspaper, 'and did not think it would be possible to work under their control'. Happily, the sale of the *Chronicle* fell through and Brelvi was able to finish his life and career in its Editor's chair. But the interview was 'an eye-opener' for him, demonstrating yet again the particular difficulties for a Congress newspaperman.[80]

There was a complex mix of assumed and envisaged unity subsumed in the words 'Indian Nationalist Movement'. In this context, nationalism for many was part of the problem as well as the solution. In the case of Maharashtra, the *Bombay Chronicle* was one locus of the internal struggle for control of means and ends—an expropriated voice of one party or another fending off opposition, or a professional institution attempting to assert a margin of independence. At exchange points like the *Chronicle*, choices had to be made to represent 'Pune' or 'Mumbai' or 'Delhi', using these three terms as paradigms for three distinctive viewpoints. Although the overlap was, in fact, substantial, a mix of fear, defensiveness and intolerance produced demands for loyalty, and concern for any accommodation.

While Horniman and Pickthall were willing representatives of Gandhian orthodoxy, as reflected in the Khilafat Movement and Non-Cooperation, Brelvi's idealism and Muslim identity moved him and his paper to seek an accommodation of viewpoint with the reality and presumed legitimacy of division. This was not, however, reflected in support for a Maharashtrian reluctance to become a fragment of an aggressively asserted all-India entity. Brelvi's concerns concentrated on nationwide categories: Muslims and the poor. As a result, he antagonized those who chose to speak for Maharashtra, and denied the *Chronicle* an easy relationship with all the orthodoxies: Gandhian, socialist, capitalist, communalist. His paper was categorized as 'socialist' by the Congress right, 'Islamic' by defensive Hindus and anti-Communalist, and 'undependable' by all who measured loyalty in terms of absolute acceptance of their position. By the early 1930s, the *Chronicle* had become more like the *Tribune* and the *Hindu*, a Congress supporter with a mind and life of its own—a good representative of the mix of pragmatism and passion of heterodox Mumbai.

NOTES

1. Vaikunth Mehta to S.A. Brelvi, 21 January 1931, *Brelvi Papers.* See also *Annual Report on Indian and Anglo-Vernacular Newspapers Published in the Bombay Presidency for 1925*, Home-Poll, No. F 261/1926.
2. G. Johnson, *Provincial Politics and Indian Nationalism: Bombay and the Indian National Congress, 1880 to 1915*, Cambridge: Cambridge University Press.
3. N.C. Kelkar, 1918. What is passive resistance? *Sarvajanik Sabha Quarterly Journal.* Reproduced in Kelkar, 1925: 6. He continually returned to this theme and opposition to the *Chronicle*, insisting that Non-Cooperation was a political movement and it was necessary not to overdo the spiritual side. See *Mahratta*, 3 December 1923 (Kelkar 1925: 178).
4. N.C. Kelkar, 1922, 'The Chronicle and Maharashtra', in Kelkar, 1925: 86-90.
5. M.R. Jayakar, to S.A. Brelvi, 19 July 1922, *Brelvi Papers.*
6. *Capital*, 4 January 1919. Quoted in Gordon, 1978: 60.
7. See Cashman, 1975, for an extended discussion of the Mumbai-Pune dichotomy. Gordon Johnson (1973: 116-17) has also noted that Gokhale's Moderate career was dependent upon an alliance with Mumbai's politicians. His political base was the Bombay Presidency Association, which provided the money and influence to launch his all-India career.
8. P. Joseph, 1959, *Glimpses of Yesterday*, Chennai: The Madras Premier Co., 33.
9. Home-Poll, 47, 1918. See also M. Israel 1980. 'M.R. Jaykar and the Bombay Nationalist Movement', in *Images of Maharashtra*, N.K. Wagle (ed.), London: Curzon Press, 13.
10. S.N. Banerjea to P.S. Mehta, quoted in *Dictionary of National Biography*, S.P. Sen (ed.), 1973, Calcutta, 170.
11. *Bombay Chronicle*, 13 March 1920. (Horniman wrote to the *Chronicle's* manager, Umar Sobhani, regarding his passport difficulties.)
12. Ibid., 26 April 1920.
13. Ibid., 28 April 1921.
14. Ibid., 6 March 1920.
15. Ibid., 17 March 1924.
16. A. Fremantle, 1938, *Loyal Enemy*, London: Hutchinson and Co., 322.
17. The Moslem Demand. *Bombay Chronicle*, 21 March 1919. Horniman was committed to pan-Islamic nationalism. In 1917, in response to a request from Jinnah to prepare remarks for the Raja of Mahmudabad's speech as the presiding officer of the Muslim League meeting of December 1917 in Calcutta, he 'drafted a speech, instilled with the spirit of Islam, which contained references to the Khilafat in terms very objectionable to the Government'. The Raja of Mahmudabad refused to read that speech. See Bamford 1974.
18. Jayakar to the Hon. Secretary, Board of Directors, Indian Newspaper Company, 19 December 1921, *Jayakar Papers*, 364.
19. Fremantle, *Loyal Enemy*, 339.
20. Ibid., 322, 331.

21. Mr Jamnadas' Grievance, *Bombay Chronicle*, 18 April 1921.
22. Richard Gordon (1975: 162) has noted that Mumbai was the treasury of the Khilafat Movement, but the Maharashtra was never reconciled to Gandhi.
23. Bombay Chronicle, 9 October 1922.
24. Ibid., 10 October 1922.
25. Ibid., 18 March 1922.
26. Ibid., 3 October 1921.
27. *Hindu*, quoted in the *Bombay Chronicle*, 22 May 1920.
28. *Leader*, quoted in the *Bombay Chronicle*, 22 May 1920.
29. *Bengalee*, quoted in the *Bombay Chronicle*, 22 May 1920.
30. *Independent*, quoted in the *Bombay Chronicle*, 22 May 1920.
31. The *Chronicle* and some critics. *Bombay Chronicle*, 21 December 1922.
32. *Bombay Chronicle*, 1 January 1923. Pickthall wrote to a friend about his attendance at the Nagpur Congress as the guest of the Central Khilafat Committee. 'We travelled up in the Khilafat Special Train, bedecked with Muslim flags, and full of what the ordinary onlooking Englishman would doubtless have mistaken for a crowd of wild fanatics.' Fremantle 1938: 332.
33. *Bombay Chronicle*, 31 March 1922.
34. Fremantle, *Loyal Enemy*, 339.
35. *Bombay Chronicle*, 14 February 1922.
36. M.R. Jayakar, *The Story of My Life*, vol. I: X.
37. Ibid., 377.
38. Ibid., vol. II: 16.
39. Ibid., vol. I: 378-9.
40. Laxmidas R. Tairsee: social worker, landlord, shroff and merchant. He was an active Home Ruler and a radical member of the Indian Merchant's Chamber.
41. Shankerlal Banker: Home Ruler and active Congress politician throughout the 1920s.
42. N.H. Belgaumwalla: Parsee businessman and speculator. During most of the decade he was either a director or the owner of the *Chronicle*. He sold it to the Cama family at the end of the decade.
43. Director's Report; the Indian Newspapers Co., 28 November 1922, *Jayakar Papers* 365.
44. A Pune explanation. *Bombay Chronicle*, 11 January 1922.
45. A statement of personal explanation. *Mahratta*, 3 February 1923.
46. *Bombay Chronicle*, 26 November 1923.
47. 'Walk into my parlour, eh?' *Mahratta*, 4 February 1923.
48. *Bombay Chronicle*, 26 November 1923.
49. Ibid., 2 January 1924.
50. Motilal Nehru to M.R. Jayakar, 30 July 1924. *Jayakar Papers* 365.
51. M.R. Jayakar to F.E. Dinshaw, 14 January 1925. Ibid. 404, Pt.1.
52. Jayakar to Umar Sobhani, 16 January 1925. Ibid. 365.
53. Jayakar to G.S. Raghavan, *Hindustan Times*, 16 January 1925. Ibid., 404, Pt. 2.
54. Memo of January 1925. Ibid. 365.
55. Jayakar memorandum. Ibid.
56. Jayakar to J.K. Mehta (Secretary, Indian Merchants' Chamber), 9 March 1925. Ibid., 404. Pt. 2. Also, Jayakar to Jairamdas Doulatram (editor, *Hindustan Times*), 30 August 1925. Ibid. 405.
57. Jayakar to Motilal Nehru, 10 March 1925 and 16 March 1925. Ibid., 404. Pt. I.
58. Jayakar, op. cit., vol. II: 595-6.
59. *Bombay Chronicle*, 12 January 1926.
60. *Bombay Chronicle*, 3 and 4 March 1926.

61. Jayakar's general letter to Kelkar (Pune), Dr B.S. Moonje (Nagpur), M.S. Aney (Yeotmal), R.C. Pradhan (Nasik), Mr. Ketkar (Nasik) and N.B. Patankar (Nasik) on 5 January 1926. *Jayakar Papers* 365.
62. Belgaumwalla to Jayakar, 12 April 1926; Jayakar to Lalji Naranji, 29 September 1926. Ibid.
63. Auction of the *Bombay Chronicle*, 1 October 1926. Ibid.
64. Jayakar to Malaviya, 5 October 1926. Ibid.
65. *Bombay Chronicle*, 12 October 1926.
66. Ibid.
67. Jayakar to D.V. Gokhale (editor, *Mahratta*), 9 December 1926. *Jayakar Papers*.
68. *Bombay Chronicle*, 20 May 1926. Belgaumwalla did offer Jayakar the editorship in December 1926, but he refused.
69. Ibid., 3 May 1927.
70. Ibid., 27 April 1927.
71. Ibid., 16 May 1927.
72. Ibid., 25 April 1927.
73. Brelvi to J. Nehru, 29 November 1933. *Jawaharlal Nehru Papers*, vol. X.
74. Nehru to Brelvi, 3 December 1933. Ibid.
75. *Bombay Chronicle*, 14 April 1927.
76. Jayakar to Raja Narain Lal Bansi Lal, 26 February 1930. *Jayakar Papers* 365.
77. Brelvi to Nehru, 14 November 1935. *Jawaharlal Nehru Papers*, vol. X.
78. Mahadev Desai to Brelvi, 26 October 1935. *Brelvi Papers*.
79. Brelvi to Nehru, 14 November 1935. *Jawaharlal Nehru Papers*, vol. X.
80. Ibid.

REFERENCES

Bamford, P.C., 1974, *Histories of the Non-Cooperation and Khilafat Movements*, Delhi: Deep Publications.

Cashman, R., 1975, *The Myth of the Lokamanya*, Berkeley: University of California Press.

Fremantle, A., 1938, *Loyal Enemy*, London: Hutchinson and Co.

Gordon, A.D., 1978, *Businessmen and Politics, Rising Nationalism and a Modernising Economy in Bombay 1918-1933*, Columbia: South Asia Books.

Gordon, R., 1975, 'The Hindu Mahasabha and the Indian National Congress', *Modern Asian Studies*, 9.2.

Israel, M., 1980, 'M.R. Jayakar and the Bombay Nationalist Movement', in *Images of Maharashtra*, N.K. Wagle (ed.), London: Curzon Press.

Johnson, G., 1973, *Provincial Politics and Indian Nationalism: Bombay and the Indian National Congress 1880 to 1915*, Cambridge: Cambridge University Press.

Joseph, P., 1959, *Glimpses of Yesterday*, Chennai: The Madras Premier Co.

Kelkar, N.C., 1925, *A Passing Phase of Politics*, Pune: A.W. Awati.

Dr George Buist of the *Bombay Times*: A Study of the Self-Proclaimed Messianism of an Anglo-Indian Editor, 1840–57

AROON TIKEKAR

Among the Anglo-Indian[1] editors of western India, George Buist (22 August 1805–1 October 1860)[2] of the *Bombay Times* (precursor of the *Times of India*), merits the attention of historians on account of his significant contributions to Indian journalism in its infancy,[3] his contributions to the civic life of Mumbai in the first half of the nineteenth century,[4] and the unexpected circumstances which led to his ignominious exit.[5]

Buist's career in Mumbai between 1840 and 1857 provides excellent material for the study of the failure of self-proclaimed Messianism.[6] This paper attempts to describe his journalistic achievements and bring out his zeal and pioneering contribution to 'every enterprise for educating the people, ameliorating their condition and rescuing the guilty from persistence in crime'.[7] It also analyses the causes of the undoing of his great work of nearly two decades. It is one of the ironies of the history of Mumbai that a man of such rare natural abilities, who might have achieved so much and retired from India with glory and popular respect for sowing the seeds of public development, accomplished in reality so little that it is now difficult even to conjure his memory. It is a matter of surprise to many researchers of nineteenth-century western India that something should have come between the testimonial due to him and its actual bestowal. This paper suggests that 'that something' was the disappointment of a self-appointed messiah, who lost his bearing and his emotional balance upon the rebellion of a people for whose welfare he had toiled for two decades. His was the case of a renowned journalist who, unlike his later counterparts, mingled journalism with self-imposed responsibility for the socio-cultural transformation of a defeated nation and thus confused the role of catalyst with that of Messiah. By thus overstepping the bounds of journalism he precipitated the catastrophe of his dismissal from the editorial chair he held for eighteen long years. The main theme of this paper, therefore, is an examination of how Buist's judgement was swayed by waves of emotionalism and prejudices.

Son of the Reverend J. Buist, George was educated at St. Andrew's Seminary and at Edinburgh and, in July 1826, he was licensed by the Presbytery of Forfar, of which his father had been a lifelong member. He would, no doubt, have become a priest had he not opted for journalism; he preferred to remain a licentiate in the clergy and continued to officiate in the pulpit until 1836.

However, as soon as the duties of preacher and editor became incompatible, at a period of great political excitement, he restricted his career to journalism (Buist 1857: 17). He was not a 'Reverend', as the *Gentleman's Gazette*, a contemporary of the *Bombay Times,* designated him on his arrival in India. Nor was he a physician, as stated by one of his adversaries, but a Doctor of Laws. Before he was 'selected from the midst of many applicants to take charge of the *Bombay Times*' (ibid.: 5) in 1840, he had been the young and promising editor of provincial newspapers in Fifeshire and Perth in Scotland. At the *Bombay Times*, in addition to an allowance of 150 Pounds for his (overland) travel expenses to India he was to receive 600 Pounds, together with a sixth of the profits. This engagement was to last for five years (Buist 1846: xi).

Buist reached Mumbai on 6 May 1840. He was not the first editor of the *Bombay Times*, the paper having been founded in 1838, inspired by the newly obtained freedom of the press, and initially edited by J.E. Brenan, whose contributions to contemporary medical and scientific journals in England had been greatly appreciated. The *Bombay Times*, in a sense, was a product of its day. Gone were the days of rigorous censorship under the Marquis of Wellesley (1798 to 1805), administered in Mumbai by Lord Clare. Then a government secretary read all the proofs before they went to press; editors were subjected to strict adherence to the laws of censorship and to penalties if they did not comply. In 1811, for example, the Editor of the *Bombay Gazette* was asked to apologise for having reprinted an English newspaper article about the Duke of York. In 1824 C.J. Fair, Editor of the same paper was deported for a misreport. His successor, Francis Borden was threatened with the same action for publishing a letter complaining about the rates of exchange allowed to soldiers (Jejeebhoy 1932: 285). James Silk Buckingham (1786 to 1855) was also deported in 1826, for having censured the appointment of a stationary agent (Buist 1857: 27). The press in India was finally emancipated by Governor-General Charles Metcalfe, in 1835, though only over the strong objections of Lord Clare.

The year 1835 proved to be a landmark in the history of Indian journalism. Along with two papers already in existence, *The Bombay Courier* and the *Bombay Gazette*, which made the most of their freedom, a third appeared, stimulated by the desire of the merchant class. As the *Times of India* reported,

> The city was full of energy. The founding of the Chamber of Commerce in 1836 was the main, and most successful, outlet of that energy. The Company's Charter had been abolished [i.e. renewed] in 1834, and trade had been thrown open to private enterprise. The Bank of Bombay was being projected. The establishment of a steamship service and of the Overland Route to Europe were the subject of daily discussion and heated argument. Never was there a better time for a newspaper venture in Bombay, and the men who seized the opportunity were for the most part connected with the merchant houses which had come to Bombay to share the profits of trade and banking previously monopolised by three old East India firms.[8]

Brenan, who was to be both editor of the *Bombay Times* and Secretary to the Chamber of Commerce, had stated in the very first issue of the paper (3 November 1838) the objectives before him. Deploring the fact that England gave little attention to India, he pointed out that few Englishmen thought of visiting this country, yet India in any aspect presented a wide field not only for philosophical investigation but also for practical excursion. 'Arrangements', said an advertisement of the *Bombay Times*, setting forth the objectives before the new paper,

> have been already made for securing the earliest possible intelligence upon all subjects of politics, science and literature. All changes and promotions in the Civil, Military and Naval services, and everything of interest connected with these, will be regularly and correctly recorded, and a portion of its columns will be set apart for giving to the mercantile community, both here and in England, the fullest and most authentic commercial intelligence. Complaints relative to public or individual grievance will meet with all due notice and enquiry and be discussed in a free and independent spirit, and with strict care that the tone and language shall be such as can give personal offence to none. With regard to those questions of British and European politics which principally excite the public attention at home, such articles will be extracted from the leading organs of every political party as may present to the reader a comprehensive view of the opinions and feelings of each.[9]

Brenan did not, unfortunately, get an opportunity to translate his thoughts into action, for his life was cut short at the age of 36 in 1839. His death from cholera unexpectedly hampered the progress of the newspaper. William Henderson of Elphinstone College and Richard C. Knight of the Bengal Medical Service successively tried their hands at editing the paper, published every Wednesday and Saturday, but ultimately the choice of the proprietors fell on Buist. The fact that the latter was a 'very dear' friend of James Calder Stewart, one of the original shareholders of the *Bombay Times*, must have influenced the choice (Buist 1846: xxv).

Buist (ibid.: xii) describes the changes that he brought about on arrival:

> I immediately took charge of our paper, and found my duties in all respects considerably more onerous than I had anticipated. I had then the most liberal and gentleman like set of employers to deal with, the dividends proving for a time illusory, my salary was increased—the circulation of the paper was advancing rapidly and everything going on well. The publication of a Magazine of Selections, discontinued the year subsequent, was begun a few months after my arrival; the Monthly Summary, speedily destined to attain so conspicuous a position, and be productive of so much wealth, was commenced on the 1st Oct [1840]—its original circulation was about 500, in less than two years it had a circulation of nearly 3,000—yielding a profit of upwards 1,000 a year.

Hard work, however, affected his health. Within a year, in June 1841, he was down with a serious brain fever, a malady that doctors ascribed to excessive labour. During his eighteen years in Mumbai, seventeen as editor of the *Bombay Times*, Buist probably never forgot his role as preacher and lecturer, which had been his original calling. Like the self-appointed Messiah of a defeated and demoralised nation, he ran the newspaper with devotion and made it both a successful commercial venture and an influential organ of public opinion. Indeed, the total despatch of newspapers from India to England rose from 77,000 in

1841 to 106,830, of which 39,983, or nearly two-fifths, were sent from the *Bombay Times* office.[10] During the first ten years, his administration returned tenfold the money originally invested by the proprietors; in February 1845 the dividend on the paper's shares was declared at 43 per cent (ibid.: 16)!

Buist entered into a new arrangement of five years with his employers during which time he came to enjoy great personal influence and command respect both from the elites of western India and from the earliest generations of those who received Western education, by his criticism of government policies, as well as of the personal behaviour of civil servants. He made the *Bombay Times* a force to be reckoned with: first to break the news, fearless in comments, healthy in approach to civic problems and eager to advance scientific knowledge in India. In fact, the qualifications that the *Bombay Times* acquired were those brought to it by Buist himself. J.M. Stocqueler (1800 to 1865), Editor of the Calcutta-based *Englishman* (previously called *John Bull*), recounted succinctly in his memoirs how difficult it was to compete with the *Bombay Times*, even in the latter's infancy:

> after a while, came a new rival more formidable than any of the mofussil papers, two of which "shut up". The *Bombay Times* started into [*sic*] existence. Well-written, audacious, good paper and so forth, it began by an assertion that Bombay was practically about to become the capital of India, for a steam communication with England via the Red Sea was on the point of being established, and of course Bombay would be the "port of all India". The commercial interests of Calcutta took the alarm, and not a little perturbation seized the hearts of the newspaper editors. We were "tarred on" to a furious controversy and really, . . . "there was much throwing about of brains". To my horror, a steamer did actually arrive at Bombay with late news from England. The papers of the Presidency immediately issued extras and supplied them to the North-West Provinces long before we could get the intelligence at Calcutta and distribute it to our subscribers. How the *Bombay Times* did crow! I saw that the danger to the *Englishman* was imminent and resolved at any cost to avert a repetition of such disasters. It was only to be done by establishing an agent at Bombay who would, upon the arrival of a mail from England, immediately print all the news and forward the copies of the *Englishman Extra* to my mofussil subscribers. This proved a "happy thought" but, still, the *Bombay Times* was generally a day ahead, for my agent could not get out his edition quite so early as a paper with large printing resources. . . .[11]

Buist went all out to score points over his competitors, and generally succeeded.[12] A man of strong likes and dislikes, he even charged 'many of his competitors, including the *Times*, London, with "pilferage"'.[13] He did not think twice before entering into mud-slinging matches with his detractors. This at times landed him in trouble: during his editorship he had to face two libel suits, the first known as the Grant Contempt Case (1840), the other as the Smith Libel Case (1843).

Buist had views on every subject, and they were usually expressed with force. As a journalist his reputation was at its height by the close of the First Afghan War, when he, with uncanny journalistic sense, foretold the disastrous results of invading Sind and Punjab. His dauntless attacks on Charles Napier

(1782-1853) remain unique in the history of Anglo-Indian journalism as the battles of a strong journalist with that of an equally strong, if not stronger, statesman. Through hard-hitting editorials, Buist condemned British policy in Afghanistan, Sind and Punjab in the 1840s.[14] Charles Napier, who had initially been an admirer of the *Bombay Times*, instantly became its bitterest enemy. However, the more he fought back the more virulent became the Editor's attacks. The latter were mentioned by many biographers of the British 'hero'. For example, in his eight-volume *magnum opus* on his brother, William Napier (1857) poured the choicest abuse on Buist 'the miserable wretch' and 'blatant beast' and his paper, 'the vilest of the Bombay journals'. This prompted Buist to issue a point by point rebuttal of Napier's charges, in an open letter (Buist 1857), in which he sought to defend his stance.

The crux of Napier's arguments was that Buist was the mouthpiece of James Outram (1803–63), with the Chief Secretary of the Bombay Government, John Pollard Willoughby as their go-between. Outram was an adversary of Charles Napier, called by the latter 'the Bayard of India', an epithet which stuck to him for the rest of his life. Meanwhile William Napier styled the three allies 'the Bombay intriguers'. However, Buist not only refuted these allegations in his open letter, but also argued that his writings (Buist 1843) were 'indeed, momentous revelations, and they came before the world at a most momentous crisis' (Buist 1857: 60). For, according to him,

> the 6,000,000 pounds sterling the swamps and sands of the Indus valley have absorbed since 1844, doubled by the amount of interest since then accruing on it, is exactly the sum required for the redemption of the dividends, and the rescue of India from that position of extreme insecurity she at present occupies. The sum would have given us just over two thousand miles of railway, anticipated the wants of Lancashire, diminished the drain on Europe for specie, and rendered a mutiny impossible.[15]

These attacks and counterattacks helped project Buist's image as a fearless journalist in the pages of the *Bombay Times*. He himself wrote about his vocation thus:

> as a journalist I have endeavoured to discharge my duties of that high office with honesty, fearlessness and independence; censuring freely as I praised abundantly, when praise or censure seemed due, without relation to the office or position of the individual, to personal interest, or bias from private feeling. (Buist 1857: ii)

Buist's journalistic success was further enhanced when he married Miss Hunter from St. Andrew's, 'the love of his early life and a lady of the highest order of intellect and accomplishments, with a heart as warm and a hand as open to melting charity as her mind was ample and well-stored'.[16] The youthful pair must have been the darlings of the Anglo-Indian and Indian elite of Mumbai. He had been so deeply engaged in journalistic activity, as well as in the intellectual life of the city, that his lady-love might well have had to stay at home. Certainly, what little public spirit existed in Mumbai at the time was largely prompted by Buist. He was the moving spirit behind the scientific and literary societies of his time and, despite his heavy workload, gave the benefit of his knowledge on these subjects to all who sought it. As the (unpaid) Inspector of Observatories, from October 1842 onwards, he is said to have initiated the study of meteorology in India by establishing a number of observatories. While holding this charge, he had, in May 1844, conducted for the officers of the Indian Navy a course of lectures on natural philosophy, chemistry and natural history, to which the general public was also admitted free of cost.[17] He was first (from the moment of his arrival in India), a member and then, from 1842, the Secretary of the *Bombay Geographical Society*, established in 1834. He remained so until 1859 and also edited the Society's *Journal*, contributing articles on meteorology, geology and antiquities.

When he was thus endearing himself to the educated and earning the respect of Anglo-Indians all over western India, Buist was distressed by a domestic tragedy. His beloved wife, when pregnant, contracted dysentery and died. Her benevolent influence on Buist is best summed up in the *Bombay Times* of 6 September 1845:

> Dr Buist has often been blamed, and perhaps justly, for the passionate violence of expression in which he occasionally indulged and the persevering and obstinate inveteracy with which he hunted down a person or subject to which he was opposed. It was well-known in the Presidency how incessantly his wife, who in most matters had unbounded influence over him, strove in these things to mitigate or restrain his intemperance, and how grieved she felt when anything calculated to give pain to anyone appeared in the columns of the *Times*.

Having found it impossible to continue his work, Buist decided to retire, at least temporarily, to England. He left Mumbai 'homeless and houseless' on 21 May 1845, and after many agonizing days reached England (Buist 1846: xvii). He was to be absent from Mumbai for nine months, during which time his editorial duties were assumed by one Scott of the Bombay Chamber of Commerce.

At home Buist renewed his intimacy with scientific agriculture which, as Secretary of the Bombay Agri-Horticulture Society (founded in 1840), he was later to apply to improving cultivation in western India. He had also agreed to provide a collection of geological specimens for the museum of the Elphinstone College, for which he was given requisite funds. While in England, he completed the collection and shipped it to India (Buist 1846: xxii). He also prepared the Bombay Observatory Report for 1844, comprising the results of about 170,000 observations (ibid.: xxiv). He also conducted there a series of experiments on the clays and argillaceous earth from the region around Mumbai, with a view to improving the conditions of pottery manufacturers.

Buist is credited with introducing the art of glazing to Mumbai, as well as wood-cut engraving, having for a long time cut, with his own hands, the blocks required to illustrate the events of the First Afghan War for the *Bombay Times.* In the charity schools of Byculla, which were in a bad state due to the want of employment for their pupils who then fell back into bad habits, Buist devised a plan for instructing the pupils in letter-press and lithographic printing, wood-cut engraving and other arts. He was the first to introduce the printing machine—that on which the *Bombay Times* was then printed. It was the only one in operation in India.[18] Few men devoted to literary avocations have employed their leisure time to better advantage than Buist. Therefore, when he found it difficult to continue in Mumbai owing to the loss of his wife, and decided to return home, he was entitled to a large share of public gratitude.

Buist returned to India on 8 January 1846, with no strings attached, and began his work again at the *Bombay Times*, and at various Societies, most of which aimed to educate and enlighten his brethren and work for the uplift of the people of his chosen country. An encouraging letter from J.C. Stewart in Calcutta must have acted as a booster to him, as it informed him that 'We now have a press—fulfilling its high mission—and you are the deliverer and interpreter of the public mind by general acclaim' (Buist 1846: xxvi). In the same year, in recognition perhaps of his services, he was made Sheriff of Mumbai, a position that gave him further opportunities for working for the people of the city. He also developed, at Sewri, the first Botanical Garden of the city. It was also at Sewri that he built, in 1846, a fairly large house, adjoining the sea and adjacent to Sewri Fort.[19] Although he travelled 10 miles to his place of work everyday, he never failed to first visit the plants in the Garden, on which now stands the Sewri Cemetery.

Sewri, now a suburb of Mumbai, was also known for the Reformatory School for Industry, which Buist started in 1849, with the help of the Parsee philanthropist Jamshetjee Jejeebhoy (1783 to 1859). It was hoped to transform juvenile offenders into the useful artisans that a developing industrial centre like Mumbai needed.[20] A visitor to the School in 1852 recorded his satisfaction with its useful work: 'That excellent Institution will remain a monument to his zeal for the welfare of his fellow creatures—of that portion of them, too, who are in general so sadly neglected.'[21] Along with these labours, Buist spent nearly his entire fortune for the development of the School. In 1854 he was appointed the Secretary of the Western India Canal and Irrigation Company. There he became the first to project and carry out the construction of irrigation canals by private enterprise in India, 'without a guarantee or any sort of assistance from the Government' (Buist 1857: ii; Priyolkar 1971: 512-13). In September 1855, when the government decided to establish a central museum 'for the illustration of general economic processes, and the development of the commercial and industrial resources of Western India', he was appointed its Secretary and first Curator. He was also one of the promoters of The Bombay Paper Manufacturing Company; indeed, scarcely was there a society or a public enterprise in Mumbai with which he was not associated.

A person who thus devoted himself 'with earnestness to pursuits tending to extend the field of human knowledge and the happiness and welfare of the natives of the East' (Buist 1857: i) deserved retirement with all honour and respect. That, however, was not his destiny. To be sure, he was doing well at the *Bombay Times:*

The undertaking was a small one in those days; but for all that we learn from a paper published in 1850, when the *Bombay Times* changed its proprietors, that during the previous ten years Buist had earned as a renumeration or free profit the sum of Rupees 3.3 lakhs in cash, besides meeting all the charges of the establishment and extending its strength and efficiency. The paper, in fact, flourished so much, yielding 30-40% annually on the amount originally invested, that many of the most distinguished Government officials became shareholders, as soon as the Court of Directors passed the order allowing its civil and military servants to be connected with the Press.[22]

In 1847, among the chief proprietors of the *Bombay Times*, besides the editor, were the Puisne Judge of the Suddar Adawlut, the Collector of Customs, the Deputy Quartermaster-General of the Bombay Army, the Secretary to the Medical Board who afterwards became Physician-General and the Medical Storekeeper who later became Superintending Surgeon of the Presidency.

The close connection which government servants maintained with the *Bombay Times* in those days is also evident in the subscription list. At the beginning of 1852, of every 1,000 subscribers 123 were civil servants, 179 messes of regimental libraries, 317 military men, 52 British merchants, 36 banks and public corporations, 26 'natives', 243 private individuals, uncovenanted servants, tradesmen and so on, and the rest clergymen, lawyers and princes.[23] The paper had become a daily on 2 September 1850. In announcing that change, a reminder was given to readers that 'those of them who take in a paper without objection are liable in conscience and may be compelled by law to pay for it even if it should never had been ordered by them'. A strange notice, but how characteristic of Buist, the editor!

Of his services to the public during the first twelve years of his editorship, Buist (1852) said that he

> not only devoted the columns of the *Bombay Times* to the advancement of good Government, to the spread of education, of improvement and economy, to the denunciation of those bloody and superfluous wars, which within these twelve years have cost us 30 million sterling, and that policy which under the name of expediency disregards the principles of truth and justice and sets up a standard of morals for statesmen opposed to the principles of Christianity, and the evils of which to our name and characters, as Wellington has so well remarked, cannot be compensated by the most brilliant victories, but has, as far as circumstances permitted, endeavoured in his private capacity to promote the improvements he as an editor recommended—a circumstance to which numerous letters of acknowledgement received from the Government bear ample testimony.

Buist continued to be Editor even after the change of proprietorship in 1850, when many Indian merchants bought shares in the paper, which thus came under their control until 1860. This decade was to prove a stormy one in the history of the *Bombay Times*, due mostly to its Editor. In May 1857, the Sepoys of Meerut rebelled against the British Raj. Echoes of their rebellion—which some historians prefer to call the First Indian War of Independence—were heard in Delhi, Agra, Oudh and a large part of central India. The heat and dust created by the rebellion resulted in merciless killings of Anglo-Indians and Indians. The Anglo-Indian press in the country was, for the most part, 'teeming with statements of a highly provocative nature, inflammatory incitements to revenge appeared in both the editorials and the correspondence columns of the Anglo-Indian newspapers' (Barns 1940: 249). During the months of crisis Buist was in England, having gone there on leave in January 1856. When he returned in October 1857, the worst was already over, although even in Mumbai rumours of an uprising of the 'native' population were afoot between May and September. Men of such eminence as Jagannath Shankersheth (1804–65) were said to have only narrowly escaped arrest for treason (Edward 1923: 45), but the city was saved from cruelty by the extreme precautions adopted by Charles Forjett, the Police Superintendent. However, the scars left in the wake of events in north India could never be completely healed, and the fissure created between rulers and ruled was impossible to bridge.

Readers of the *Bombay Times* saw a totally different Buist on his return. He joined the fray with the cry of 'blood for blood', and shocked his readers. The shock increased along with the virulence of his attacks day by day. He began to denounce Indians of all castes and creed and to ridicule their institutions. Coming from the pen of one who had, just a few years ago, striven hard for the advancement of the 'natives', these attacks were unexpected and inexplicable. The *Bombay Times* had among its shareholders many educated Indians, who naturally resented these intemperate outbursts, and the rift between them and the Editor widened by the day. *The Madras Examiner* observed that Buist

> fell in with the cry for vengeance, and his writings were of a character to damage very considerably the cause of the natives, it could not therefore be expected that the proprietors, unless they were lost to every feeling of regard for their countrymen, would consent to have their paper converted to an anti-native organ.[24]

It was obvious that the situation could not last for long. On 23 December, at the instance of Nawrojee Furdoonjee, a meeting of the proprietors was convened to discuss the situation in the presence of Buist. Furdoonjee declared that a journalist whose aim and object ought to be the happiness and welfare of the great mass of people of the country, ought to be the last person to cast unfounded and sweeping imputations on their character; or to accuse the whole population of treachery and cruelties committed by a particular class or section of it, or to call the whole population 'ferocious tigers', 'treacherous barbarians', and 'cruel savages'.[25] The motion of Nawrojee was carried by a majority of 60, and it was resolved

> that the proprietors of the *Bombay Times* newspaper are of the opinion that the recent articles therein published by the present editor, Dr Buist, regarding the character and conduct of the natives of India in general, and the opinions and sentiments which the editor has therein expressed on the subject of the policy which should be adopted by Government towards the natives generally, and the treatment of which they are deserving at the hands of Government and of Europeans, are illiberal, impolite and unjust, and tend to alienate the native chiefs and Her Majesty's subjects from the British Government, and to excite discontent and disaffection throughout British India, and are, therefore, distinctly in violation of Act No. XV of 1857. The proprietors therefore distinctly direct

that Dr Buist forthwith desist from the course which he is pursuing, and entirely change the tone and tenor of his editorial writings in these respects, to bring them into accordance with the general views and feeling of the proprietors as above expressed. And further, that he be called upon at this meeting to pledge himself in distinct terms so to do.

Had Buist relented and given the pledge, one of the stormiest dismissals of an editor in the history of Indian journalism could have been averted. But Buist considered this directive an interference in editorial policy, and refused to oblige. As a result, the meeting further resolved

that Dr Buist, having declined to pledge himself to follow the directions contained in the foregoing resolution, and the meeting having reason he has hitherto pursued, which is contrary to his engagement with his proprietors, in opposition to their views, and detrimental to the interests of the country at large, determined that Dr Buist is forthwith dismissed from the situation of editor of the *Bombay Times*, and that the committee of directors be authorised to secure the services of another gentleman to fill the post.

The dismissal sent shock waves through journalist circles. Many Anglo-Indian newspapers commented strongly on the drastic step of the proprietors. The Editor of the *Bombay Telegraph* felt that

Whatever may be the shortcomings or faults of the philosopher of Sewree, he did not deserve the arbitrary treatment he has received from the native proprietors in whose service he has grown grey.[26]

By contrast, the *Madras Examiner* remarked:

It is the business of an editor before entering into engagements with proprietors, to ascertain for himself what are the principles which the paper is to advocate, and then if he cannot conscientiously write up those principles, he should refuse to enter into any engagement. In like manner, if, having changed his views the Editor should find himself unable to advocate the policy for the support of which the paper had been established, resignation is the only honourable course left for him. The proprietors of the *Bombay Times* acted very properly in dismissing their Editor, when the latter endeavoured to use the paper against themselves; they did just what most English proprietors would have done under similar circumstances, and we see no reason why they should be censured except it is because they are natives. . . .[27]

However, all editors were equivocal in accepting the change of opinion in Buist. If the words of the *Bombay Telegraph* can be taken as representative, his crusades against all educated natives were 'senseless'[28] and exhibited 'extreme bad taste'.[29]

That Buist's dismissal would evoke considerable reaction was anticipated by the proprietors of the *Bombay Times*, for they soon mitigated their stand, saying:

The proprietors of this journal are quite conscious of the fact that Dr. Buist carried with him the sympathy of a considerable part of the community. They pledge themselves to the subscribers that their columns should show conclusively the falsehood of the charge that they wished to fetter their Editor. . . . Their Editor, whoever he may be, shall be free to utter all his mind, and they have sufficient confidence in Englishmen generally to believe, that few amongst them could be found ungenerous enough to abuse that freedom in the way that Dr. Buist did, and which it remains to be seen whether his countrymen will generally approve.[30]

The Committee of Directors, who presented the views of the proprietors, cited many examples to prove that there was reason to believe that Buist was 'an engine to minister to the suppression of truth, or the indulgence of private animosities'.[31] They asked

whether Dr. Buist sought the public good, or indulged in private resentment in his recent disingenuous attacks on Dr. Fraser; whether he expressed the public opinion in his attempts to screen the P & O Steam Navigation Company from the exposures of his predecessor, or ministered to the gratification of his well-known personal friendship towards the gentleman who represents the company in Bombay; whether the incessant attacks on Mr. Leeke, prolonged even until quite recently, were suggested by resentment of certain proceedings at the Board of Conservancy or by a watchful concern for the public well-being; whether the attacks upon the Committee of the Government Central Museum were for the gratification of his own fancied wrong at their hands, or for the interest of the community.[32]

The Directors did not fail to mention the change of heart in Buist, who had begun to attack by name two of its members because they happened to be members of the Bombay Association, an organization established around 1850 to promote the Indian cause. Buist, a close friend of Bhau Daji (1824-74), who, in the initial years, was the spirit behind the Association, was himself an advocate of the latter and had written in support of it. Buist and Bhau Daji were, in fact, associates in many projects of public interest.

Due to the heat generated by Buist's dismissal, the proprietors were compelled to publish, in a four-page supplement on 6 January 1858, complete transactions of their meeting of 23 December 1857. This included the speech of Furdoonjee, which gave excerpts of Buist's writings in the *Bombay Times* after his return to India in 1857.[33] Only two quotations will suffice to illustrate the latter's *volte face*. On 10 October he wrote:

The past 6 months have laid before the eyes of men the fruits of those religions which desire to be perpetuated in the East, and from them the tree whose blossoms are murder, whose leaves are incarnadined with innocent blood, may be known.

In the same issue, he described the 'Natives of India' as worse than ferocious animals and wild beasts:

It is one of the most dreadful things connected with the Rebellion that it has disclosed to us all at once the facts, that we have for a century been living in a den of wild beasts, without having tamed one atom of their ferocity, and that the feline is absolutely a less treacherous and more animal than the human tiger.

This whole episode makes for sad reading. For a person who strove hard for the amelioration of a city's civic and intellectual life, this sort of ignominious exit was the undoing of a decade and a half's good work. That he was no respecter of facts when it came to dealing with adversaries and friends alike is clearly evident in Buist's writings. As the paper observed on 4 October 1860, 'the rock on which Buist split was his personal friendships and resentments'. Concerning the aftermath of the sepoy rebellion, his judgement was clouded by the waves of emotionalism, agony and despair of his self-appointed Messianism. 'Had he been less comprehensive—had his imagination been less ardent and his prudence less assured—he might long ere this have retired to England to enjoy in learned ease the fruits of his toil', said the same paper the day before, breaking the news of his death from dysentery, which occurred just after his arrival in Calcutta from Allahabad where he had gone to assume charge as Superintendent of the Government Press. (By then he had made an unsuccessful attempt at starting *Buist's Bombay Times*, as well as taking a stab at editing a rival paper, the *Bombay Standard*, which merged with the *Bombay Times* on 31 December 1859. For a brief period he was also appointed the Municipal Commissioner in Mumbai, a singular honour for one who had already occupied the Sheriff's chair earlier.)

The death of Buist preceded the cotton boom in Mumbai due to the starvation of Lancashire, and the subsequent prosperity that left a distinct mark on the city for years to come. Buist did not live to see the new face of the city, or the new generation of inhabitants coming out of the portals of a newly established university. Had he done so, perhaps he would have changed his opinions about the educated 'natives' of the city.

Buist's life and work thus reveal contradictions in the character of a self-proclaimed Messiah. A strong conviction about British superiority found its expression after the rebellion. Buist's behaviour betrays irrationality not only in the prejudices and preferences that mark his earlier journalistic writings, but also in whatever he did. His Messianism assumed the genuflection of the 'natives', in whose cause he claimed to have served so ably. Else it is difficult to explain and justify his vitriolic attacks on Indians. His characterization of Indians as beasts shows how deeply within him was embedded the assumption of a pusillanimous acceptance by the 'natives' of the cultural superiority of Victorian Britain. It may be fair to say that his behaviour was far from rational—unlike that of conservative 'liberal' administrators like Elphinstone who believed as early as the 1820s that British rule would be short-lived,[34] or the ideologue of empire, Stanley Reed (1872-1954) who as Editor of the *Times of India* saw clearly, in the 1920s, that the days of the British in India were numbered. Indeed, Buist's Messianism was marred by an emotionalism, and therein lay the seeds of his failure.

NOTES

1. The term 'Anglo-Indian' is used in this paper to denote the English community in India. Although the term has been officially used since 1916 for persons of mixed English and Indian parentage, the original usage remained equally prominent until India gained its independence in 1947.
2. Buist himself records that he 'was born at Tannadice, in Forfarshire on 17 November

1803, being the second oldest of a family which at one time consisted of five sons and four daughters' (Buist 1846: vi). Buckland's *Dictionary of Indian Biography* mentions 22 August 1905 as his date of birth. *Dictionary of National Biography* (*DNB*) (ed. by Leslie Stephen and Sydney Lee, vol. III, 1908: 288) corroborates the date. The entry written by S. Lane-Pool on Buist in the *DNB* has a foot note: 'the date of birth is misprinted as 1803' in Buist's own *Memoirs*.

3. He was called 'India's foremost man of letters' (Buckland 1905: 60, also the obituary notice in the *Bombay Gazette* on 4 October 1860).
4. His contributions brought him the honour of being described as 'the life of the scientific and literary societies of the place [viz., Bombay]' in the *Bombay Times*, editorial of 4 October 1860.
5. In contrast to the above notices he was also dubbed 'Bloody Buist' (Sanyal 1980: 103).
6. Origins of the concept of the 'Chosen People', of course, date back to the Persians and Jews of antiquity who both claimed supernatural powers for themselves. The Arabs arrogated the same role in the Middle Ages. However, it was the mystic Polish philosopher Hoene Wronski who coined the term 'national Messianism' (Schenk 1966: 189). Messianism, as used in this paper, denotes what Fichte claimed the German nation did to Prussia to sustain the morale of a defeated people after their humiliation at the hands of Napoleon.
7. *Bombay Times*, editorial of 4 October 1860.
8. *The Times of India, 1838-1938*. Centenary Supplement, 7 June 1938: 5.
9. Ibid.
10. Ibid., 6.
11. J.M. Stocqueler, Memoirs of a Journalist. Serialized in the *Times of India* intermittently during July and August of 1872.
12. 'The *Bombay Times*, we believe, was the first journal in India to give authentic accounts of the Russian designs upon Khive, so far back as December 1839, and has ever been since quoted by its English and Indian contemporaries as an early authority on this all-important subject'. The *Bombay Times*, 13 May 1840.
13. In an editorial comment, titled *Borrowing our Leaders*, Buist wrote: 'We are not only plundered, but we are abused; our columns are first mercilessly pilfered, and then we are told that we are a parcel of pitiful fellows, not worthy of the notice of the gentlemen who have robbed us. . . . The *Times*, while it affects to patronise us, inflicts on us a double injury; it quotes its correspondent who has already pilfered from us by the yard, and, after pronouncing a sort of general eulogy on the Indian Press at large it seizes on the *Bombay Times* without saying a word about it, and thence clips out an editorial bodily and adopts it as its own. . . .' *Bombay Times*, 22 December 1841.
14. For example, the missing figure—Deficit due to occupation in Punjab. *Bombay Times* 8 December 1841. What is to be done with Afghanistan? *Bombay Times*, 22 December 1841. The Ladies of the Amir's zenana. *Bombay Times*, 6 May 1842.
15. This refers to the mutiny in Sir Charles' own army and not to the events of 1857-8.
16. Bombay Correspondence in *Morning Post*. See *Bombay Times*, 6 September 1845.
17. *Bombay Times*, 9 August 1845.
18. *Bombay Times*, 9 August 1845.
19. It stands even today, and is the residential quarter of a high official of the Bombay Port Trust.
20. Cf. 'Schools of Industry', in Buist 1848: Appendix: lxxxiii-lxxxv.
21. 'The School of Industry' *Bombay Times*, 28 February 1852.
22. 'Sixty years of the *Times of India*', in *Calcutta Review*, 1899: 95.
23. Ibid.
24. *The Madras Examiner*, 5 January 1858, quoted in the *Bombay Times*, 14 January 1858.

25. Supplement on Dr. Buist. *Bombay Times,* 6 January 1858.
26. Quoted in the *Bombay Times,* 4 January 1858.
27. *The Madras Examiner,* 5 January 1858.-
28. *Bombay Times,* 4 January 1858.
29. Ibid.
30. *Bombay Times,* 30 December 1857.
31. Ibid.
32. Ibid.
33. Dated 3, 6, 9, 10, 11, 16, 17, 19, 24 and 26 October and 5, 6, 13 and 18 November 1857.
34. When Governor of Mumbai (1820-7), Elphinstone wrote to his friend Mackintosh thus: 'the belief that our Indian Empire will not be long-lived is reason, and not prejudice. It is difficult to guess the death it may die. . . . The most desirable death for us to die of should be the improvement of the natives reaching such a pitch as would render it impossible for a foreign nation to retain the government, but this seems at an immeasurable distance. . . . A time of separation must come, and it is our interest to have an early separation from a civilised people. . . .' Quoted in Cotton, 1892: 185.

REFERENCES

Publications of George Buist

BOOKS

1843, *Outline of the Operations of the British Troops in Scinde and Afghanistan betwixt Nov. 1838 and Nov. 1841.* With remarks on the Policy of the War. Printed and published at the 'Times' office.

1844?, *Tracing of the Wind-guage [sic] for 1842 and 1843,* Made at the Bombay Government Observatory.

1844, *Provisional Report on the Meteorological Observations made at Colaba, Bombay, from the 1st of September to the 31st of December, 1842.* With a general notice of the weather for the year 1842. Mumbai.

1844, *Provisional Report on the Meteorological Observations Made at Colaba, Bombay, from the 1st of January to the 31st of December, 1843.* With a general notice of the weather for the year 1843. Mumbai.

1846, *Memoirs with Testimonials, & Co. of George Buist, LL.D.* . . . Addressed to his friends. (Cupar: G.S. Tullis).

1849, *Annals of India for the Year 1848* : An outline of the principal events which have occurred in the British Dominions in India. From 1 January 1848 to the end of the Second Sikh War in March 1849, with a prefatory notice of the circumstances which led to our connection with the Punjab. Mumbai: Printed at the Times Press by James Chesson.

1851, *Memoirs of Sir Alexander Burnes, C.B.* (See J. Burnes, Notes on his name and family.)

1852, *Notes on India,* Booklet #3 of the *India Reform,* London: Saunders & Stanford.

1852, *Petition Complaining of the Evidence Given Before the Select Committee of this House on the Government of India Territories on the Subject of Newspapers in India,* Mumbai.

1852, *Index to Books and Papers on the Physical Geography, Antiquities and Statistics of India,* Mumbai: Bombay Education Society's Press.

1852, *Manual of Physical Research Adopted to India*, Pt. 1, Mumbai.

1857, *Corrections of a Few of the Errors Contained in Sir Wm Napier's Life of His Brother, Sir Charles Napier, so far as They Affect the Press in India, in a Letter Addressed to the Author.* London: Smith, Elder & Co.

ARTICLES

n.d., 'On the saltiness of the Red Sea', *The Transactions of the Bombay Geographical Society*, IX: 38ff.

n.d., 'A Catalogue of the most remarkable hailstroms which have occurred in India between 1822 and 1850', *The Transactions of the Bombay Geographical Society*, IX: 184ff.

n.d., 'Notices of the most remarkable meteors in India of the fall of which accounts have been published', *The Transactions of the Bombay Geographical Society*, IX: 197ff.

n.d., 'The volcanoes of India', *The Transactions of the Bombay Geographical Society*, X: 139ff.

n.d., 'Geology of Bombay', *The Transactions of the Bombay Geographical Society*, X: 167ff.

n.d., 'On the principal depression on the surface of the globe', *The Transactions of the Bombay Geographical Society*, XII: 7ff.

n.d., 'Remarkable hailstroms of India from March 1851 to May 1855', *The Transactions of the Bombay Geographical Society*, XII: 1.

n.d., 'A short account of the principal Arctic expeditions undertaken in England by sea and land between 1853 & 1854', *The Transactions of the Bombay Geographical Society*, XII: 26.

n.d., 'Notes on the lotus or the sacred Bean of India', *The Transactions of the Bombay Geographical Society*, XIII: 1.

n.d., 'Notes on a journey through part of Kathiwar and Guzerat in January 1855', *The Transactions of the Bombay Geographical Society*, XIII: 11.

n.d., 'Notes on certain discoloured appearances met with on the surface Sea in Warm latitudes', *The Transactions of the Bombay Geographical Society*, XII: 108.

n.d., 'Globulare lightning, fireballs of the Glow Discharge of Electricity Contre distinguished from the Meteorolites or fireballs usually composed of solid matter', *The Transactions of the Bombay Geographical Society*, XIII: 148.

n.d., 'Physical geography of the Red Sea', *The Transactions of the Bombay Geographical Society*, XIV: 1.

n.d., 'On the geology of the Rock of Gibraltar', *The Transactions of the Bombay Geographical Society*, XIV: 46.

n.d., 'On Prof. Owen & Mr Horner's views of the Age of Man upon the Earth as laid before the British Association, September 1858', *The Transactions of the Bombay Geographical Society*, XIV: 50.

n.d., 'Geology of Lower Egypt, Esp. of the portions between Alexandria & Cairo and Cairo & Suez', *The Transactions of the Bombay Geographical Society*, XV: 1.

n.d., 'Hurricanes in the Eastern Seas', *The Transactions of the Bombay Geographical Society*, XV: 19.

PUBLICATIONS OF OTHER AUTHORS

Barnes, M., 1940, *The Indian Press—A History of the Growth of Public Opinion in India*, London: George Allen & Unwin.

Buckland, C.E. (ed.), 1905, *Dictionary of Indian Biography.*

Cotton, J.S., 1892, *Montstuart Elphinstone* (Rulers of India Series).
Edwardes, S.M., 1923, *The Bombay City Police—A Historical Sketch 1872-1916*, Mumbai.
Jejeebhoy, J.R.B., 1932, Historical survey of Mumbai journalism, *Jame Jamshed Centenary Volume*, Mumbai.
Natarajan, S., 1962, *History of the Press in India*, Mumbai: Asia Publishing House.
Napier, Sir W., 1857, *Life and Opinions of Sir Charles Napier.*
Phadke, Y.D., 1975, *Social Reformers of Maharashtra*, New Delhi: Maharashtra Information Centre.
Priyolkar, A.K., 1971, *Dr Bhau-Daji—Vyakti kaal va kartutva,* Mumbai: Mumbai Marathi Sahitya Sangh.
Sanyal, R. (ed.) 1894, *Reminiscences and Anecdotes of Great Men in India*, Calcutta: Riddhi (rpt., 1980).
Sathe, Tarabai, 1975, *Aparajita Rama*, Pune.
Schenk, H.G., 1966, *The Mind of the European Romantics—An Essay in Cultural History*, London: Constable.
Senagupta, Padmini, 1970, *Pandita Ramabai Saraswati: Her Life and Work,* Mumbai: Asia Publishing House.
Tilak, A.D. (ed.). 1973, *Smriti Chitre of Laxmibai Tilak 1934-35*, 4 vols., Nasik: Nagarik Prakashan.
Times of India, 1899, 'Sixty Years of the Times of India', in *History of the Anglo-Indian Press* (*Calcutta Review* of 1899).
———, 1938, '*The Times of India*, 1838-1938', in *One Hundred Years in India* (7 June 1938).
Umakant, 1925, *Kai Shri Ramabai Ranade*, Mumbai: Hind Mahila Pustakamala, Book 1.
Vaidya, Sarojini, 1985, *Ek samajik shokantikechi nayika, sankraman,* Pune: Shrividya Prakashan.
Varde, Mohini, 1982, *Dr. Rakhmabai: ek artha,* Mumbai: Popular Prakashan.
Vividhajnanavistar (Marathi magazine), Mumbai.

The Discourse from the Other Side: Perceptions of Science and Technology in Western India in the Nineteenth Century

J. MASSELOS

The coming of European knowledge, its science and arts, as well as its tangible technological artefacts and inventions, evoked complex responses within Indian society. In western India the parameters of the interaction began to be apparent from the second decade of the nineteenth century when Indians of the region first confronted the products of the new century's science and technology. People were faced, consciously and unconsciously, with the problem of accommodating the new tangible and intangible artefacts of the day into their perceptual and intellectual universes. The appearance of new knowledge and strange objects introduced a novel subject-matter into daily discussion. But it did more than merely provide new talking points; it questioned the nature of the perception of the alien material, whether and how it was to be incorporated within existing social structures and thought patterns. There was, inevitably, another underlying context, that of race and nation—the discourse about the relationship between ruler and ruled; involved were ideas of inferiority and superiority and of the lack of power and possession of knowledge.[1] Questions of polarity and opposition emerged in an especially acute way because of the form of British domination and the colonial context.

Increasingly confident of their political and military domination, the British had, from the 1820s, begun to talk to Indians in the city of Mumbai and Bombay Presidency in a different way, and by introducing subject-matter that did not, as previously, concentrate only on matters like trade, commerce and administrative regulations. The dialogue between alien and local acquired new overtones which paralleled the formation of different structures of relationship.

The British spoke with the self-assurance of victors, conscious of their domination of the region after the recent conquest of the Maratha state. What they said inevitably related back to British paramountcy and what was to be done with their gains in the succession to power. The discussion assumed a variety of forms and covered a range of topics, some of which the Governor of Bombay, Mountstuart Elphinstone, detailed in an 1824 Minute on Education that has rightly become famous (Elphinstone 1824: 77-117).

Elphinstone noted that much greater effort was needed in western India than on the eastern side to promote education because 'the number of Europeans here is so small and our connection with the natives so recent' (Elphinstone

1824: 83). A consequence of the recent 'connection' was likely to be that 'the present abundance of people of education' who had been needed to administer the Maratha government was likely to disappear, unless efforts were made to maintain and spread education (ibid.). Elphinstone was careful not to confine his observation only

> to what is called learning, which, in its present form, must unavoidably fall off under us, but to humbler acts of reading and writing, which, if left to themselves, will decline among the Brahmins without increasing among the other castes. (Elphinstone 1824:83)

Elphinstone's strategy to promote literacy and diffuse knowledge involved close cooperation with an education society, the establishment of village and district schools, the publication of translations in Indian languages, the provision of prizes, stipends and salaries to those who displayed achievement in education, the spread of English, and the furtherance of higher education. While he advocated the continuation of the Peshwa patronage of Hindu learning in Pune by using the Dakshina Fund to pay for the salaries of Hindu professors, some of whom would teach Hindu divinity and mythology, Elphinstone did not see the arrangement as permanent. Once the Poona College had become an established place for Brahmans, he intended progressively to 'improve' its system of education over time and so make it 'a powerful instrument for the diffusion of our civilisation' (Elphinstone 1824: 110).

Although Elphinstone distinguished 'European knowledge' from 'Hindu learning'[2] he did not make the separation complete: Europe and India were not, for him, polarized entities. He was, for instance, prepared to concede that Hindu learning had some 'more useful branches' (Elphinstone 1924: 97). His view that Western science was a superior and more highly evolved form of what existed in India also meant that the two were neither conceptually distinct nor in opposed categories. The learning of the Brahman pandits, he contended,

> may have been obscure and degenerate, but still it bore some affinity to real science, into which it might in time have been improved. They were not, perhaps, inferior to those monks among whom the seeds of European learning were long kept alive; and their extinction, if it did not occasion the loss of much present wisdom, would have cut off all hope for the future. (Elphinstone 1824: 108)

Whatever its past merits, such learning was to be tolerated only for as long was expedient: the teachings of Hindu mythology and divinity he considered 'unprofitable' and justified only in a society ' where knowledge has always been in the hands of the priesthood, and where science itself is considered as a branch of religion. (Elphinstone 1824: 108)

From his position of authority, Elphinstone thus outlined a strategy which sought to subvert Hindu learning and replace it with Western arts and science. His approach was formulated in a way which emphasized that European learning was superior: but it reflected more the perceived realities of political and military victory than notions of ascribed hierarchy. He did not present a view which correlated British success with a concept of the innate superiority of the British people as signified by the possession of an equally superior learning. Nor did he postulate a view of British supremacy as being derived from possession of a superior knowledge. The various elements present in his writings—military and political British supremacy, superior European knowledge, a distinct nation and people—were not gathered together into an equation for the purposes of explaining innate difference or affirming national superiority. His realization of the extent and spread of learning under the preceding Maratha state effectively inhibited any unambiguous formulation of such views. Similarly, his desire to share Western learning and science and spread it among Indians went beyond the limited functional need to provide qualified personnel for the bureaucracy (Elphinstone 1824: 96). There were other beneficial consequences. His reference to medicine highlights the point: there are few sciences, Elphinstone wrote, 'in which the natives have so little to preserve, or in which we have so much to teach, and so much facility in teaching' (Elphinstone 1824: 92).

Elphinstone did not seek to appropriate what existed in India, but rather to replace it with what Britain had produced. He did so on the basis of the British achievement of sovereignty and the ability to exercise force, and in order to spread and promote knowledge. Such knowledge was not yet articulated as synonymous with British power, or inextricably interlinked with it.

In the following two or three decades, the tenor of Elphinstone's views was repeated in a range of face to face situations between rulers and ruled. Select audiences of wealthy Indian merchants, bankers and traders, as well as Western educated Indians and others in the professions or bureaucracy, were subjected at a variety of public meetings and formal situations to numerous speeches and addresses about the nature and benefits of Western culture, its arts and sciences. The ostensible subjects of such gatherings covered a diverse range of topics, but the discourse was about the British presence, and British civilization. The annual general meetings of the Bombay Native School Book and School Society (from 1824) and of its successor, the Bombay Native Education Society (between 1825 and 1839), provide prime examples of the discourse in such set situations. Under Elphinstone's inspiration, the Society had been founded to diffuse 'the benefits of intellectual and moral improvement to the natives, and . . . introduce them to a knowledge of the arts and sciences of Europe' specifically by setting up schools and by promoting the translation and publication of Western works into Marathi and other regional languages (*BNSB c.* 1824: n.p.).

Many of the early British speakers at the Society maintained a sensitivity to some Indian achievements and, therefore, like Elphinstone, did not choose to establish a formulation which completed the equation between political, scientific and national supremacy. John Malcolm, Elphinstone's successor, told his audience at the March 1828 meeting that

> the inhabitants of India . . . were not behind us in many of the useful arts of life, and in their domestic conduct; . . . We were undoubtedly more advanced in literature and in some sciences, which, while they gave energy and dignity to the mind, promoted the comfort and happiness of the human race. (*BNES* 1828: 8)

William Newnham, a member of the Bombay Council and Vice-President of the Native Education Society, maintained in 1831 that it was an 'undisputed fact'

> that knowledge came from the East; and it was the principal, as it was the fairest object of an Institution like this, to convey it back to its original source and spread it over a land from which Europe had borrowed the first fruits of all science and literature. (*BNES* 1831: 5)

It was, therefore, not difficult for Indian audiences to receive back from their 'European Brethren' an improved version of what had gone out from India: 'the knowledge so borrowed from the East had been considerably polished and refined in Europe', commented Manuckjee Cursetjee, a wealthy Bombay Parsi, at the 1833 general meeting, while

> here . . . in India, every thing as it appears was kept in ignorance and instead of being brought to light, it was concealed in darkness. However, those days are now no more. . . . Europe has not only faithfully returned what she had borrowed first, but a great deal more by way of compensation or interest. (*BNES* 1833: 8–9)

The use of commercial terminology to explain what was happening was particularly appropriate at a meeting whose Indian audience had consisted largely of prosperous merchants and bankers, and held in a city with a heavy business orientation. The terminology, however, did not merely serve as a convenient metaphor for the speaker, but also reflected a view of Western knowledge, its arts and sciences, as a commodity, easily transported and, when acquired, easily adopted for use like any other material good. As a commodity, rather than a new paradigm, Western learning would not conflict with what already existed in India, would bring about improvement and not disruption. 'Within a few years', pointed out Bombay's leading Hindu banker, Jagannath Sunkersett, 'our children [will be] enriched with the knowledge, and conversant with the Arts and Sciences of Europe, and yet retaining all that we consider sacred in the religious peculiarities of our several Tribes' (12 April 1831, *BNES* 1831: 8).

Initially, doubts were expressed in the printed reports of the Society concerning the extent to which European knowledge might be transported to alien environments. European ideas were so dissimilar and so rich in their variety, while English words had such a multiplicity of meanings, that it was considered difficult for any Indian to comprehend the range of concepts and their nuances. How much less likely was it that they would be able to translate the concepts into Indian languages, where the difficulties would be compounded by the lack of an equivalent terminology (*BNSB* 1825: 12). Here surfaced momentarily the view that ideas represented not an easily transportable commodity but a different way of thinking, a new and alien paradigm. But the commodity view of knowledge prevailed, given that the objections ran counter to the Society's objectives, the translation of scientific works into Marathi and Gujarati. Not surprisingly, therefore, three years later, the Annual Report noted the appearance of excellent translations of mathematics and algebra texts, whose quality disproved the arguments regarding the 'hopelessness of rendering English works of science intelligible to the natives of this country (8 March 1828, *BNES* 1828: 14–15).

If Western knowledge, its science and arts, was perceived as a commodity, what then was its worth? The prominent Indians who involved themselves with the Society attached a value to its functioning. They funded much of its activity and put considerable effort into ensuring its success; they were zealous in attending meetings and other important occasions. There they might enjoy the occasional novelties offered: at the end of the 1825 General Meeting there was a display of the working of lithography 'at which, the numerous native gentlemen present expressed their surprise and entire satisfaction' (*BNSB* 1825: 8). Entertainment aside, such gatherings provided opportunities to mix with one another and, perhaps of greater importance, to fraternize with the powerful of the land, with 'our English friends' (Jagannath Sunkersett in *BNES* 1831: 8), 'our European Brethren' (Manuckjee Cursetjee in *BNES* 1833: 9), opportunities that were to recur later when other scientific bodies were formed in the Presidency. The effect was to bring both social groups together in apparent shared control of the commodity and in the dialogue about it.

But what use was Western knowledge and the education by which it was purveyed? For Malcolm, in 1828, it was the path to employment and the maintenance of excellence ('of establishing and supporting distinction in the community', *BNES* 1828: 6); literature and sciences, moreover, 'gave energy and dignity to the mind, [and] promised the comfort and happiness of the human race' (*BNSB* 1828: 8). By the late 1830s, with the appearance of a more pronounced Christian and evangelical strand in British officialdom, the accent was placed on individual morality and social stasis. Sir Robert Grant saw the value of Western knowledge as enabling the individual to achieve 'mental discipline and high moral feeling' (Speech of 2 January 1836 in *BNES* 1836: 7). His sentiments were echoed three years later by another Governor, James Farish, when he proclaimed that 'literature and science itself were but the means and ornaments, they were the branches which support', both would produce a moral result which would enable people to 'fulfil their duties well and adorn their station in life' (15 January 1839, *BNES* 1839: 10).

Contemporary Indian assessment was less lyrical. The authors of a Marathi abridgment of an English grammar accepted the justification that learning English was a way to obtain employment but it was also a way into 'thousands of books on the sciences, arts and every other subject, which it is of the greatest import to study'. In any case, the writers seemed to imply, it did not matter what that knowledge was, only that it belonged to India's masters: 'The Government of this country, having passed for the present into the hands of the English nation, it is of great importance to know its language, habit and customs' (Janaradhan and Bal Gungadhar Shastree 1837: n.p.).

What had begun to surface was a perception that British power and scientific achievement were interlinked and that in such an equation the one, either one, explained the other. The movement of thinking in this direction had already been signposted in the contents of the first Anglo-Marathi newspaper, the *Bombay Durpun*. Under the editorship of the brilliant young scholar and teacher, Bal

Shastri Jambhekar, it had been founded in 1832 to promote the study of European literature and to diffuse European knowledge (Prospectus, *BD* 6 January 1832 in Jambhekar 1950: II, 2). Jambhekar thereafter consistently put forward the view that British rule was good for India because it improved the moral and intellectual condition of the people; by permitting them to acquire 'a superior knowledge of the Arts and Sciences of Europe' the 'gloom of ignorance' would vanish. Sometime in the future, Indians would come to vie with Europeans in scientific achievement (*BD* in Jambhekar 1950: II, 8).

More than most of his Mumbai contemporaries, Jambhekar saw science as something other than a commodity to which attached financial rewards. Science required a dedication unfamiliar in the world of commerce; research should be pursued in a disinterested manner, and for its own sake. Europeans he admired for the way they were 'voluntarily subjecting themselves to privations, and exposing themselves to dangers, purely out of a desire to advance the objects of Science, and add to the information of mankind'. Disinterested research produced tangible benefits through discoveries and inventions which enlarged the powers of man and furthered his usefulness (*BD* 13 July 1832 in Jambhekar 1950: II, 48).

In another way, also, Jambhekar was beginning to make the distinction between science as a commodity and science as a paradigm, by representing it as an alien thought system and one productive of significant and unique material and social consequences. For that reason, he argued, scientific methods and scientific knowledge were at the root of the difference between India and Europe. Disinterested scientific research was

> one cause, at least, and that a principal one, of the pre-eminent superiority of the inhabitants of Europe over the rest of the world, in almost every department of Science, and the wonderful perfection to which they have attained in most of the Arts. (*BD* 13 July 1832 in Jambhekar 1950: II, 48)

In a later essay, which borrowed its title of *Knowledge is Power* from Bacon, Bal Shastri Jambhekar wrestled with the problem of Asian backwardness. He could not understand why this had happened since knowledge originated in the East and moved West. Why had the maxim not applied equally between the two regions? Why is it, he asked, that 'the advantages of knowledge have not been appreciated in this country in their proper light?' His only answer was that Asian philosophers had concentrated on obtruse branches of knowledge like Metaphysics and Logic and had 'regarded all knowledge as useful only in religion, or as a means of gaining victory in argument, and in no way connected with the common purposes of life' (*BD* 24 August 1832 in Jambhekar 1950: II, 52). Perhaps Jambhekar's functional, utilitarian approach inhibited his understanding of the different kinds of power which the philosophers were seeking, but what it did do was to highlight the polarization that had developed in perceptions of East and West as mediated through scientific achievement. For him this was only attainment and not innate difference: 'knowledge is not confined to a particular country, and ... human nature is the same everywhere' ('Remarks suggested by the account of the steam engine', *BD* 21 March 1832 in Jambhekar 1950: II, 28).

That Indians were expected to perceive science (and the British connection) in utilitarian terms is evident in the answers offered by college students in 1839 to an examination question on the advantages of a literary and scientific education. (The question did not need to specify that the education was European.) The examination scripts serve as a guide to the kind of thinking, the parameters of the discourse, prevalent within the dominant institutions of the day and give some indication of the range of attitudes expected of students and Indians. The framing of the question itself prompted a functional approach in the answers. Nanabhoy Morojee, for instance, saw three advantages in such an education: to the mind which, when uncultivated, made man 'nothing more than a beast'; to mankind as demonstrated in the achievements of James Watt who had 'added greatly to the happiness of mankind'; and, finally, to the Deity and to the world to come (The United Institution of the Elphinstone College and School of the Native Education Society 1840: 18–19).

Another student, Vedadri Sadasan from Elphinstone College, was more pragmatic. Such education enabled an individual to become known to his countrymen and enabled him to do good for them; he was useful to his country and to all surrounding nations. Sadasan went on to examine the impact of science upon a nation and its people: it is almost as if he viewed science as a *mantra* which ensured superiority and power:

> Look at the English, how barbarous they were some years ago, and how much refined they are at present. When the Romans first visited them, they were little better than brutes.... But now they are the most civilised nation on the face of the Earth; the finest cloth comes from their country; their food consists of excellent things; they have seen the greater part of the world; they daily invent and discover something new that is of advantage to them; they try their utmost to do good to other people; and in short they are the best and most powerful nation in the world. To what are we to attribute this great and wonderful change? Why, to nothing else but their knowledge of science. (The United Institution of the Elphinstone College and School of the Native Education Society 1840: 18)

Science thus explained to Indians what they were not and also how they might change. It explained foreign superiority while it rationalized local undevelopment. It mediated values of utility and service and in some cases its proponents even used it as a vehicle for morality and religion. It was perceived as a commodity, as a *mantra*, as a paradigm. Whichever, it was considered to be available and accessible to the upper strata of Indian society, to the wealthy, the educated and those to be educated from the higher castes and caste-type groups. It distinguished them from the lower who were not permitted access to education or to the world of science and learning.

Not all, of course, initially wanted the new education or the avenues which it opened. The old style teachers, the *pantojis*, continued to promote Sanskrit and the study of grammar, much to the annoyance of young firebrands like

Gopal Hari Deshmukh who, as Lokahitvadi, denounced the uselessness of such traditional learning.[3] Everyone should acquire British science, he argued; it had made the British wise and prosperous and it had made them great conquerors and knowledgeable people.[4] Lokahitvadi also gave the study of science another justification. God had made men rational so that they could do good to others and make them happy; to make others happy men should acquire knowledge in order to use the properties of everything that God had created; man should therefore learn to make machines. Physics was the science of machines and hence it was necessary to study physics (Deshmukh 1850: 225-6).

Lokahitvadi was concerned that his fellow countrymen should develop their minds by intellectual exercise: by reading, travelling around the world, and mixing with learned people.[5] But there were probably far more pragmatic reasons to study science in the first half of the nineteenth century and for meeting learned people. Science enabled the upper groups to develop a degree of identification with the 'superior' alien by establishing points of contact. It provided a meeting-place for them that was not only metaphorical but, as was the case with the Native Education Society in the 1820s and 30s, a physical fact. It should be emphasized that the Society had been about the promotion of learning, about how to implement an approach, rather than about the discussion or interchange of ideas. It had been about the achievement of change and the wielding of power, rather than about the consideration of scientific concepts. It was, therefore, a meeting place for the powerful of the land.

Concurrently, other kinds of forums had emerged which did give space for the discussion of ideas. In them, the people who came together continued in some way or other to feel that they were still students. Such, for example, was the Students' Literary and Scientific Society founded in 1848 in order to enable students, ex-students and staff of Elphinstone College to keep abreast of what was happening in the world of ideas (see the Annual Reports of the Society as well as its history, Students Literary and Scientific Society 1950; also Masselos 1974). Similar was the Bombay Natural History Society whose origins can be traced to 1833 and to eight founding members, two of whom were Indian (Bombay Natural History Society 1933: 1). Likewise, an Agri-Horticultural Society had been established in 1830, again with European and Indian members (Agri-Horticultural Society of Western India 1861: 3-4). The new arenas provided for considerable interchange between Europeans and Indians, but it was interchange about the content of ideas as much as it was about the place of Western knowledge in an Indian context. The sub-text, however, remained the achievement of equality and the attainment of a renascent national greatness, even if the specific terminology of *swaraj* was still largely an anachronism. It was a sub-text that was being articulated with careful clarity by one of the city's most powerful intellects at the end of the 1850s:

If . . . by the advance of civilisation in my country, it shall be her fitting task to undertake her own Government, I shall have sufficient faith in the progress of humanity to believe, that England will come to recognise the fact, and generously disencumber herself of the gift of Empire; she will remain content with the glory of having educated my people into a nation of free men. (Bhau Daji Lad, 10 October 1859 in Mainkar 1974: 374)

The perceptions of the impact of Western learning that have constituted the bulk of the discussion were, of course, limited to a relatively select section of society. It is unclear how far other sectors were then aware of the inroads of modern science although accounts of the first appearance of modern scientific artefacts in western India invariably stress the wonder and excitement of the spectators—and their numbers. The first steamboat on Mumbai waters was considered 'something marvellous by the wondering natives',[6] while the first sight of a steam locomotive in operation in Mumbai in 1853 provoked immense enthusiasm among an audience estimated at over a hundred thousand.[7] The enthusiasm was only surpassed by the first display of ballooning by a Mr Kyte:

> Flight in the air! . . . All Bombay and its wife in their hundreds and thousands had turned out from all points of the compass to view this new fairylike thing. . . . It was the wonder of wonders and the talk of every unit for many a day. Some versifier of the day commemorated in Rhyme the praise of the valiant Kyte who soared like the eagle upwards to reach the heavens. (Wacha 1920: 432-4)

The inventions of science and technology swiftly moved from objects of wonder to objects of use; they became part of the daily round of living. Neither social constraints nor the force of custom inhibited significant use of the achievements of the nineteenth-century world. In 1834, a group of Purvoes had hired a steamboat for a weekend excursion down the coast from Mumbai and, as the first such trip, it had been of sufficient importance to be noted in the local press (*BD*, 14 March 1834 in Jambhekar 1950: II, 90-2). By the 1850s, passenger traffic by steamboat along the coast of Mumbai had become so common as to be barely noticed. Similarly with the railways; within a few weeks of their being opened, Indians were using them 'as calmly as if they had been shigrams or Bullock hackeries' (Bhau Daji, 10 October 1859 in Mainkar 1974: 374). The moral was clear: value systems did not necessarily inhibit the acceptance of new approaches and, as the same paper noted, 'Surely European writers are wrong when they say that natives are the slaves of custom, and prejudiced against all reform' (ibid.).

It would be wrong, nevertheless, to assume the universal and widespread acceptance of all scientific and technological products. 'The old Native School Masters' (*BNES* 1831: 11) had opposed the mode of instruction introduced by the Native Education Society at the beginning of the 1830s, probably as much in objection to the competition they were made to face as in dislike of new systems of thought. After an initial breathing space, there had, however, been little difficulty in attracting upper class students to the new learning in numbers sufficient for the capacity of the schools.

Presumably, where issues of ritual pollution were involved there was an orthodox reaction against new technologies and learning. High caste students were apparently initially unwilling to undergo medical training, since it involved handling the polluting matter of bodily fluids. However, from at least the 1830s some leading Indians had been demanding Western medicine. Their wishes were partly met by the setting up of the Medical and Physical Society of Bombay in the 1830s in order to encourage a spirit of scientific enquiry. In the early 1840s, the Presidency Government went further and decided not to allow 'prejudice. . . to stand in the way of . . . amelioration' of existing medical practice (Grant Medical College 1849: 2). Not long after, in 1845, the Grant Medical College was established in Mumbai. Of the twenty-nine students who presented themselves for the first intake, twelve were found to be qualified. Nine of the original applicants were Portuguese, six were Shenvi (Saraswat Brahmans), and there were three Parsis, five Purbhoos (Prabhus), and six others from lower castes ('First report of the Grant Medical College', ibid., 10). Although there were no representatives from castes at the very apex of the ritual hierarchy, the intake subsequently included men from higher groups. The pattern largely continued into the third year when there were twenty-two students: three Portuguese, nine Parsis and ten Hindus. The latter now included three Shenvis, one Brahman (of unspecified *jati*) and three Pulsyas (Palshikar Brahmans, a local *jati* from the neighbouring Thane region) ('Annual Report of the Grant Medical College, Bombay. Third Year. Session 1848-49', ibid., 1).

Six years later, the Grant Medical College Society was founded to maintain habits of systematic thought and spirit of professional cooperation among College graduates (Proceedings, cited in Mainkar 1974: 343). Again, as had been the case with the city's other scientific and learned societies, the arena enabled Europeans and Indians to meet and discuss their work: collectively they shared control of the discipline.

A frequent speaker at the Society's meetings was the early and brilliant graduate of the College, the Shenvi Dr Bhau Daji Lad. His great curiosity of mind is reflected in the range of papers he delivered; the topics are a profile of his approach to Western medicine and of his attempts to understand its relationship with the Indian environment. One paper analysed the diet of Indians in the region, and others began a survey of local plants to find out if they had medicinal value (Mainkar 1974: 346-9).[8] The papers followed the investigative procedures of Western medical science and were not statements about the relative merits of European or Asian medical systems—or of their respective nations. Bhau Daji did not in any case accept that one was necessarily inferior or superior to the other: in the specific example of snake bite he insisted that Indian remedies be given a fair trial before they be rejected.[9] He was, therefore, not willing to concede without proof that the West had the monopoly of all medical knowledge; in this sense, the thrust of his work was in the direction of independence, away from uncritical acceptance of the hegemony of Western medicine. Significantly, of course, he was only able to develop such a position by using the methodology of Western science. Through one, specifically Western methodology, the other Indian remedies, might be legitimated. He adopted Western methods of proof to justify the methodological polarity which derived from the different learning of an alien nation. He was thus enabled at the same time and in seeming contradiction to deny inherent correctness in the treatments of one continent or the other.

Most of the time, however, Bhau Daji purveyed the techniques of Western medicine and did so skillfully and with considerable success. In 1853, with his physician brother Narayan Daji, he opened a charitable medical dispensary in Nagdevi, a heavily populated Indian section of Mumbai. The dispensary was soon handling over a hundred patients a day,[10] a sign of its acceptance in the community. The extent of acceptance is suggested, but of course only suggested, in the six people discussed by Bhau Daji in his paper on stones in the bladder: there were two Banias, a Parsi priest, a Hindu Lohana, and two Muslims whom he treated and operated upon. The account mentions that four of the six had used local medical remedies for the condition—opium, presumably as a pain-killer—before going to Bhau Daji ('Cases of Lithotomy' in Mainkar 1974: 350-4). In other words, when local medicine proved ineffective, when the threshold of pain reached a certain level and no remedy seemed in sight, then some Indians were prepared to accept that there was little option but the surgical procedures of Western medicine. Interestingly, while two of the patients were men of forty-seven and fifty, and presumably made their own decisions, the other four cases were of boys under the age of ten, brought to the dispensary by their parents.

While Western medical techniques may have achieved a degree of acceptance in the city, particularly where the results were patently effective or no alternatives existed, a strand of suspicion was also present as a major current in the popular psyche for at least the following half century or even thereafter. People continued to seek comfort in the old and familiar; and local doctors, including *hakims* and *vaids*, continued to hold sway. They were often preferred—even when they were unable to produce satisfactory results. As late as 1895, a Dr M.J. Sanjagiri noted the tendency in his paper presented to the College Medical Society on 'The Extraction of Piles as Practised by Native Hakims'. After discussing the *hakim's* method of treatment he maintained that it was

> the duty of every [Western] medical man to expose such impostures with a view to save people from being duped, and subjected to hardship. These so-called cures of Piles not only screw money from people but inflict such untold misery on their victims, that sometimes the patients are either rendered miserable for life, or die from the effects of the treatment. (July 1895 in Grant Medical College Society 1895: 3)

Apart from the specific efficacy of the 'remedies' proposed by the two forms of medicine, the paper highlights the polarization and hostility present between their practitioners; the tone is far removed from the enquiring approach of Bhau Daji and his consensual attitude towards alternative systems.

Equally, Sanjagiri's comments underscore the continued reliance on traditional medicine by the population and their loyalty to it. Some sense of the extent of the attachment may also be gauged negatively through occasional outbreaks of violent antagonism against Western medicine or its practices. Such incidents related to medical control over people's bodies. In 1875, a stable hand was kicked in the head by a horse and died a couple of days later. Immediately after the inquest, students from Grant Medical College were given reluctant permission by the educated members of the boy's caste-group, the Mughals, to conduct a post-mortem on his body. The boy's friends, however, peered over the shutters of the dissecting room and saw him being cut up. They went to nearby Bhendy Bazaar, collected a group of fifty others and rushed into the dissecting room

> with a terrific shout. The [medical] students were panic-stricken and fled in all directions. The enraged Moguls had nothing to fling at the fugitives, but seizing hold of the scalp, the liver, the disjointed limb, etc. [of the dead body], they used these freely as missiles. (*Bombay Gazette* 7 December 1874)

The incident is replete with symbolism. Although it has parallels with anti-dissection riots in Britain in that it encapsulates the conflict between personal and scientific values, the incident is also about styles of medicine, about an intensified intersection between East and West, and about the tyrannies of control of those with knowledge and power.

In a more dramatic manner, the same undercurrents again surfaced during the Mumbai plague of the late 1890s. The polarity between styles of medicine then became clear, as also the popular preference for *hakims* and *vaids* over Western style medical personnel. Both styles were initially ineffective in coping with the epidemic, until Haffkine developed his inoculation. Western treatments were, nevertheless, imposed on the city and were disruptive and intrusive, demanding what was considered to be objectionable access to the living and removal of the sick and the dead. In October 1896, for instance, mill hands stoned the Municipal Infectious Hospital at Jacob Circle in what the *Times of India* (30 October 1896) thought was probably the first riot in India directed at hospital treatment. There was only 'trifling damage'[11] to the hospital but some policemen were later assaulted by crowds elsewhere.

Of particular interest in terms of the present discussion are the rumours which surrounded the attack on the hospital: sick people who did not have the plague, it was said, were being taken to the hospital, given poison and killed, so that they would not return home and spread illness (*Rast Goftar* 29 October extract in *TI* 3 November 1896). This was the rumour that seems to have had the strongest impact in sparking off the riot and highlights the considerable fear that existed towards the handling of the plague, as well as a continuing fear of Western techniques and the power that went with it. The underlying fear is apparent in two other rumours associated with the riot. The first connects police power with pollution through a story that glass bangles worn by women in the city were being coloured with cow's blood. This may have referred back to the onset of the epidemic when women were stopped in the streets (according to some accounts, by policemen) and their bangles broken. The second rumour was that the brains, heart and liver of people taken to hospital were removed and were to be used in the foundations of bridges that were being rebuilt after recent floods (*TI* 31 October 1896). Medicine thus had overtones of magic about it: it functioned much like a *mantra* that might be seen either as benign or malign, beneficient or malevolent, but a *mantra* nevertheless.

In the fearsome time of the plague, it was inevitable that other incidents should occur: five months later, a crowd of over two thousand people attacked the military guard and municipal servants who had come to take away a plague victim (*TI* 22 and 25 March 1897). The most potent opposition to plague medicine and enforced public health measures occurred the following year. In January and late February, there were a number of relatively minor incidents in which crowds had attacked the police and the military guards on house to house searches for plague victims (*TI* 11 and 13 January, and 3 March 1898). The largest outbreak occurred on 9 March, when crowds attacked a plague search party that had come to take away a twelve-year-old Muslim girl. The armed police escort fired and wounded some of the crowd. The disturbance spread throughout the Indian part of the city: plague ambulances were seized and burnt, at least two hospitals were attacked and partially burnt; two English soldiers wandering around the city were killed and there were other beatings and stabbings of solitary Europeans as well as attacks on European police officers (*inter alia TI* 10 March 1898). Crowd violence was very much directed against Europeans, something unprecedented in the history of street violence in Mumbai.

Involved in the antagonisms were people from the major communities in the city even though the riot had begun amongst a specific group, the Julhai Muslims. Earlier they had succeeded in obtaining the right to be treated by their own *hakim* in their own hospital; this intervention, however, had not been enough to persuade them to accept the removal of the girl (*TI* 10 March 1898). The ensuing incidents were sparked off by Muslims, but Hindus were not far behind in participating, and in one locality 'they seemed to have sallied forth from lanes and gullies mostly to attack passing Europeans'.[12] The widespread antagonism to the plague measures and to their underlying medical philosophy surfaced clearly in the days immediately following the riots, when Hindu and Muslim shopkeepers closed their shops, the dockworkers and the bullock cart drivers went on strike as did coolies and cartmen in the Railway Goods Yards—all in support of the general thrust of what the riots had expressed in violent form. Part of what was being expressed was opposition to government fiat and administrative implementation of control over people's bodies in a literal sense and that, in turn, was an opposition to Western forms of medicine which permitted and legitimated the exercise of such power. That Western medicine was seen specifically as antagonistic is evident from the recourse to indigenous doctors on the part of the Julhais—and, indeed, of other communities—while the attack on Europeans was the recognition of the nexus of government power and national origin. The published Government Resolution on the riots captured the polarities of the situation when it noted that attacks against Europeans were

> not unnatural, as, in the eyes of the ignorant masses, the European members of the community are identified with the authority that had imposed the obnoxious measures. (*TI* 8 June 1898)

In a different manner from the savants who had sought Western learning and science in the early decades of the century, the city's street population by the end of the century had nevertheless also reached much the same kind of perception of polarities. They made similar connections between race/nation, power, and scientific learning/application. The paths differed but the end point of correlation was much the same. The equation explained some of the features of the realities of the day. Although science as a body of knowledge and as a methodology of research had been adopted by the new Western educated Indian, and so in part permitted some identification with the British rulers and a limited share in the power that went with that knowledge, the share was indeed limited. It did little to modify the perceived polarity between Indian and Briton. If anything, it furthered it with its epithets of advance, progress and achievement. Urban rioters, when they attacked Englishmen with shouts of *maro, maro*, presumably had other epithets in mind as well, but in their profound disapproval they were expressing much the same polarity between themselves and their British rulers.

Both groups, though in different ways, had comparable responses to the new knowledge as commodity, *mantra* and paradigm, even if the emotion, the *rasa*, which attached to such responses varied according to circumstance. Just as a *mantra* might be benign or malign, so too, for example, were the effects of Western medicine in its imposition over the body and its effects upon it. The test of the *mantra* was its utility, its effectiveness, and in that sense it was much like a commodity designed to ensure well-being and profit. How far the new learning was perceived as a different and new means of control over the physical universe, a different understanding of that universe rather than a superior or alien form of *mantra*, is another matter. In the long run, perhaps, the context of colonial power inhibited awareness of new intellectual paradigms and delayed effective understanding of innovative thought structures. The paramount discourse was that of domination, not of knowledge.

NOTES

1. The thrust of the discussion that follows has been influenced by Foucault 1980. Some of the research on which this paper has been based was financed by an Australian Research Grant Scheme Award between 1977 and 1980. I am grateful for comments on earlier versions of the paper when it was presented at research seminars at the Universities of Sydney and New England.
2. The terms are used throughout the Minute and are most clearly juxtaposed on Elphinstone 1824: 97. Other terms used in the text to describe European systems of thought include 'European sciences' (90), 'Useful science' (91), 'European learning' (109).
3. See, for example, G.H. Deshmukh, 1849, *Bhatanchya vidyecha nirupayog* ('The uselessness of the knowledge of the Brahmins'), Letter No. 71, 12 August 1849; G.H. Deshmukh, 1864, *Vidwan konas mhanave?* ('Who is to be called learned?'), Letter No. 142, 10 June 1864; and *Sushiksha wa pantoji ani Sanskrit wa Ingreji bhasha* ('Good education and teachers and Sanskrit and English language') in Priyolkar, 1967: 175-8, 244-5, 396. I am grateful to Rajendra Vora for his help in translating the material by G.H. Deshmukh.
4. See also Lokahitvadi's article, *Sanskrut ani ingrej vidya* ('Sanskrit and English learning'), Letter Nos. 29, 69, 19 July 1849 in Priyolkar 1967: 172-3.

5. See Lokahitvadi, *Vidwan konas mhanave?* ('Who is to be called learned?'), Letter No.142, 10 June 1864, in Priyolkar, 1967: 396.
6. 'How natives appreciate modern invention'. *Oriental News*, 11 December 1853, rpt. in (Mumbai) *Telelegraph and Courier*, 13 December 1853.
7. Ibid.
8. See, 'The diet of the natives of West India', 15 August 1856; 'Notes on some of the native medicinal drugs used in the Nagdevi Charitable Dispensary', 14 August 1855; 'Vegetable biters in the Flora of the Bombay Presidency', 10 April 1858, and an untitled paper on two plants commonly known as Bach-Nag, 9 October 1858, in Mainkar, 1974: 346-9.
9. On the native remedies used in the treatment of poisoning by venomous serpents, in Mainkar, 1974: 348.
10. Secretary of the Medical and Physical Society of Bombay, cited in T.G. Mainkar (ed.), 1974: 350, fn. 2. G.M. Laud (1974: 35) states that eight thousand people attended the Dispensary for medical consultation in its first year of operation, while the *Annual Report of the Grant Medical College for 1855-56:* 15: claimed a total annual attendance of about ten thousand as cited in Mainkar, 1974: 347.
11. Telegram of Commissioner of Police, Bombay, to Governor of Bombay, Mahableshwar, 29 October 1896, Proceedings No. 1761 in *Government of Maharashtra State Archives, Judicial Department*, vol. 205, 1896: n.p.
12. R.H. Vincent to Heaton, n.d. (*c.* 10 March 1898) in *Maharashtra State Archives, Judicial Department*, vol. 217, 1898: 46.

REFERENCES

Agri-Horticultural Society of Western India, 1861. *Annual Report.* Mumbai: Exchange Press.

Bombay Durpun (*BD*).

Bombay Gazette.

Bombay Native Education Society (*BNES*), 1828, *The Fourth Report of the Proceedings of the Bombay Native Education Society*, 1827, Mumbai: n.p.

———, 1831, *The Sixth Report of the Proceedings of the Bombay Native Education Society: 1830,* Mumbai: Messenger Press.

———, 1833, *The Seventh Report of the Proceedings of the Bombay Native Education Society: 1832*, Mumbai: Samachar Press.

———, c. 1836, *The Ninth Report of the Proceedings of the Bombay Native Education Society: 1836*; Mumbai: n.p.

———, 1839, *The Eleventh Report of the Proceedings of the Bombay Native Education Society: 1838,* Mumbai: Journal of Commerce Press.

Bombay Native School Book and School Society (*BNSB*), 1824, *First Report, 1823-1824*, Mumbai: n.p. (Mumbai University Library typescript copy).

———, 1825, *Second Report*, Mumbai: n.p.

Mumbai Telegraph and Courier.

Deshmukh, G.H., 1850, *Yantradnyan* ['Physics'], Pune: Dnyan Prakash Press, rpt. in Parikh and Parikh, 1988: vol. I.

Elphinstone, M., 1824, Minute in *Selections From the Minutes and Other Official Writings of the Honourable Mountstuart Elphinstone, Governor of Bombay,* ed. by G.W. Forrest, London: Richard Bentley, 77-117.

Foucault, M., 1980, *Power/Knowledge: Selected Interviews and Other Writings 1972-1977*, New York: Pantheon Books.

Grant Medical College Society (*GMCS*), 1895, *Annual address delivered on the 26th February 1895 by Balchandra Krishna (Bhatawadekar)*, Mumbai: Subodh Prakashan Press.

Grant Medical College, 1849, *Reports of the Grant Medical College for the Years 1845-6, 1846-7, 1847-8*, Mumbai: Education Society's Press.

Jambhekar, G.G. (ed.), 1950, *Memoirs and Writings of Acharya Bal Gangadhar Shastri (1812-1846), Pioneer of the Renaissance in Western India and Father of Modern Maharashtra*, vol. 2, Pune: Author.

Janardhan, R., 1837, Preface, *Abridgement of Murray's English Grammar, with a Marathi Translation, Compiled for the use of Native Students*, revised by B.G. Shastree, Mumbai: Jaggonnath Canoba, Durpun Press.

Laud, G.M., 1974, *Dr Bhau Daji Lad Parsekar 1821-1874*, Panaji: Government of Goa, Daman and Diu.

Mainkar, T.G. (ed.), 1974, *Writings and Speeches of Dr Bhau Daji*, Mumbai: University Press.

Masselos, J.C., 1974, *Towards Nationalism, Group Affiliations and the Politics of Public Associations in Nineteenth Century Western India*, Mumbai: Popular Prakashan.

Parikh, G. and I. Parikh (eds.), 1988, *Lokahitvadi samagraha wangmaya*, vol, 1, Mumbai: Maharashtra Rajya Sahitya Sanskriti Mandal.

Priyolkar, A.K. (ed.), 1967, *Lokahitavadikrit nibandhsangraha*, Mumbai: Popular Prakashan.

Students' Literary and Scientific Society, 1950, *Students' Scientific and Literary Society (1848-49 to 1947-48)*, Mumbai: Students' Literary and Scientific Society.

The Bombay Natural History Society, 1933, *The Bombay Natural History Society, 1883-1933, printed in Commemoration of the Golden Jubilee of the Society*, Mumbai.

Times of India (*TI*).

The United Institution of the Elphinstone College and the School of the Native Education Society, 1840, *The Twelfth Report of the Proceedings of The United Institution of the Elphinstone College and the School of the Native Education Society, 1839*, Mumbai: Imperial Press.

Wacha, D.E., 1920, *Shells From the Sands of Bombay: Being My Recollections and Reminiscences—1860-1875*, Mumbai: K.T. Anklesaria.

Ramakrishna Gopal Bhandarkar and the Academic Renaissance in Maharashtra

R. N. DANDEKAR

THE BACKGROUND

Mahadev Govind Ranade has described the last years of the *Peshwai* as a period characterized by moral degradation, decadence of virtue, rampant self-seeking, and mutual jealousies. Citing the example of the *daxina*, he says:

> The Daxina charity, started with a view to encourage learning, became a grant generally to all Brahmins and Poona became the centre of a large pauper population. As many as 30 to 40 thousand Brahmins were fed for days together at state expense at the great festivals with the costliest viands. All these distinguishing features of purely sacerdotal or class ascendancy characterized the close of the 18th century, and introduced a demoralization of which few people have any correct idea.

It is interesting to note that, in another context, Elphinstone had reported in 1821 that the Daxina fund was not always utilized for the laudable purpose for which it was instituted, but *did* help—albeit indirectly and to a limited extent—to keep ancient learning in India alive. He admitted that this learning was barren and useless from the practical point of view, but asserted that the Brahmans who were the bearers of it were in no way inferior to the clergy of mediaeval Europe. He therefore strongly advocated the continuance of the institution. Anyway, the first quarter of the nineteenth century saw the country, particularly Maharashtra, woefully overcome by stagnation and cultural degeneration. Later (in 1901) in his *Social History of India*, R.G. Bhandarkar diagnosed this state of things as the result of 'a threefold tyranny to which we have been subject—political tyranny, priestly tyranny, and a social tyranny or tyranny of caste'.

The years immediately following the fall of the *Peshwai* were marked by the rapid consolidation of British power through the East India Company. Its early officers, who were responsible for such consolidation like Bentinck, Munroe, Elphinstone, were generally liberal-minded. They actively promoted the awakening of the subject population through new education. The beneficiaries of this education began to compare wistfully the conditions in their own country with those in the West, particularly in the context of social and religious regeneration. The best representative of this trend was Raja Rammohun Roy. Such was the background to which Ramakrishna Gopal Bhandarkar was born on 6 July 1837.

SYSTEM OF EDUCATION

Sufficient historical evidence is available to show that the state in ancient India freely patronized educational establishments, but left them to develop on their own lines, without interference or control. Indeed, Indian education may be said to have had a continuous tradition from the ancient to the most recent times. In the course of this long period, changes were no doubt inevitable, but the general pattern and its salient features, such as the *gurukula* ideal, oral instruction, insistence on moral discipline and character-building, freedom in the matter of the courses of study, absence of external controls, and consciousness on the part of the state—and, what is perhaps more important, on the part of the general public—that education was one of its basic responsibilities, had remained essentially the same. Buddhism and Jainism may have, in the early stages, brought in new influences, but they soon adapted themselves to the mainstream, orthodox, pattern. The advent of the Muslim conquerors also does not seem to have affected the indigenous system of education to any appreciable extent. It was contact with Europeans, particularly the British, which first created an intellectual ferment among Indians. This contact became responsible for a re-orientation of educational ideals and methods.

The pattern of indigenous education in the seventeenth, eighteenth and early nineteenth centuries was something like this: there existed two types of schools, both privately run. In the elementary schools the three 'R's were taught through the mother tongue. So-called higher learning was restricted to the study of Sanskrit in *pathasalas* and *tols*. The *madrasahs* for the teaching of Arabic and Persian may also be mentioned here. Generally, students who desired to learn Sanskrit did not attend the elementary schools at all, but directly joined *pathasalas*. The latter, usually held in the teachers' houses or in temples, depended largely on the financial assistance of rulers, landlords, rich merchants, and the religiously minded public. The name of the pundit under whom one learnt was the only guarantee and qualification, but the emphasis was more on sanctification than on dynamic knowledge. In its early years, the East India Company, which was after all a body of merchants, was wholly indifferent to indigenous education. However, in 1781 Warren Hastings started the Calcutta Madrasah, mainly 'to conciliate the Mahomedans of Calcutta'. His example was followed by his successor, Lord Cornwallis, who, at the instance of Jonathan Duncan, started at Varanasi, in 1791, the Benares Pathasala or Hindu College, which later came to be called the Sanskrit College. The two purposes of the East India Company in starting the Sanskrit College were officially stated to be to endear itself to the Hindus, and to rear a group of scholars who could assist it in administration and the law. About the time of the establishment of the Sanskrit College, another tendency in the educational policy was becoming evident. Charles Grant, who had been the Secretary of the Board of Trade created by Hastings, wrote in 1792 a tract called *Observations on the State of Society among the Asiatic Subjects of Great Britain, particularly with respect to Morals and on the Means of improving it*. In it, Grant proposed that the panacea for the moral degradation of the Indians was 'the communication of knowledge . . . by the medium of our language'. Since that time, 'Western knowledge through the medium of English' became a popular slogan even among some educated Indians. One outcome of all these circumstances was that by the Charter Act of 1813 the East India Company was forced to recognize the education of Indians as one of its foremost duties. In 1823, a General Committee of Public Instruction was set up in Calcutta to carry out the proposals embodied in that Charter Act. In spite of the new ideal of Indian education, which was sponsored by Grant and which was becoming popular day by day, the Committee, in its initial stages, showed its preference for Oriental studies. This started the famous controversy between Orientalists and Anglicists. There emerged an ironical spectacle: while leading Indians were agitating for instruction in European literature and science, and were protesting against the continuance of the prevailing Orientalism, a body of English gentlemen was found to be insisting on the retention of Oriental learning to the practical exclusion of the former. But the influence of the Orientalists soon waned, and the popularity of English education grew fast, culminating in the tirade of Trevelyan against Sanskrit literature, and in Macaulay's minute of 1835 which sought to produce 'a class of persons, Indian in blood and colour, but English in taste, in opinions, in morals and in intellect'. Finally, Wood's educational Despatch of 1854 resulted in the establishment of a Department of Education in each province, the encouragement of local efforts in the field of education, and the impetus to the founding of three universities in 1857.

The credit for the reorganization of education in the Mumbai Province goes mainly to Elphinstone who became Governor in 1819. He did not disturb the basic pattern of the two existing types of educational institutions, but increased the number of such institutions and transformed some of them into government schools by supporting them financially, and by insisting on their periodical inspection by District Collectors. In 1821, Elphinstone revived the Daxina which had been discontinued in another form: he diverted a part of its resources towards the establishment of a Sanskrit College in Pune. In 1828, an English school was started in Mumbai, and in 1837 English and other modern subjects were included in the curriculum of the Poona Sanskrit College. In course of time English schools were established in other big towns of the Bombay Presidency. According to the 1842 Report, the number of government Primary Schools in the Presidency was 120, and the number of government English Schools was four—one of those being located in Ratnagiri.

BHANDARKAR AS A STUDENT

Bhandarkar had his initial schooling in private primary schools at Malvan and Rajapur, places where his father was employed. In 1847 he was sent to the English School at Ratnagiri, which must indeed have been a bold decision on the part of his father. Having spent six years there, Bhandarkar shifted to the Elphinstone Institute in Mumbai, and passed the final examination in the School Section in 1854. Incidentally, the Director of Education, Howard, in his report of 1855, has made a special mention of Bhandarkar as the only pupil who had shown satisfactory progress—even in Bhandarkar's later career as student and teacher the same Howard acted almost as his godfather.

Four years later, in 1858, Bhandarkar passed the final examination of the College Section of the Elphinstone Institute. His favourite subject was mathematics, but he also paid adequate attention to the study of English, history and science. In 1858, Howard proposed to the government that a portion of the old Daxina fund be utilized towards the institution of six Daxina Fellowships to be granted to promising young scholars for higher studies. Accordingly, Bhandarkar was appointed a Daxina Fellow in January 1859. He served in that capacity in Mumbai for one and a half years, and in Pune for four years. This period proved to be the most crucial in his career, for it was then that he devoted himself to an intensive study of Sanskrit, and thereby laid the firm foundation of what was to become his life's mission. It is noteworthy that Bhandarkar was not required to study Sanskrit at any stage in his education. His teachers in Sanskrit were Pandit Govind Shastri Lele and Pandit Appa Shastri Khadilkar in Mumbai, and Pandit Bal Shastri Dev and Pandit Anant Shastri Pendharkar at Pune. He also profited from active contact with European teachers of Sanskrit in those cities.

Curiously enough, after the establishment of the University of Bombay in 1857, Bhandarkar, already a Daxina Fellow, was required to appear for the various examinations of that University. Accordingly, he passed the Matriculation examination in 1859, the B.A. in 1862 and the M.A. (with Sanskrit as his second language) in 1864.

BHANDARKAR AS A TEACHER

Bhandarkar began his teaching career as a Daxina Fellow in Poona College (now Deccan College) in 1860. There he taught philosophy, logic and English up to 1864. He also taught Sanskrit during the leave vacancy of Martin Haug. In 1864, he relinquished the Daxina Fellowship, and, still in two minds as to whether he should take to the study of law, was appointed by Howard headmaster of the Government High School in Hyderabad, Sind. When he returned to Mumbai thence during the summer vacation, he began thinking about joining the revenue department where the service prospects appeared perhaps more attractive. It was again Howard who resolutely dissuaded him from such a step, and fortunately for the future of Indology in India, he succeeded in convincing Bhandarkar that higher study and research were the most suitable fields of activity for a gifted young Sanskrit scholar. He transferred Bhandarkar to the headmastership of the Government High School at Ratnagiri, which post he held for about three and a half years.

In the beginning of 1869 there came about a propitious break in Bhandarkar's career. Bühler, who had been Professor of Sanskrit in Elphinstone College, went on leave and, on his special recommendation, Bhandarkar was appointed Acting Professor. After his leave Bühler was appointed to a higher post in the

Education Department, and Bhandarkar continued in his appointment up to 1872. Then Peterson, who in every sense was less qualified, was appointed in Bühler's substantive vacancy, and Bhandarkar was made an Assistant Professor under him. For a short time—1879-80—Bhandarkar was transferred to Deccan College, Pune, as Professor of Sanskrit in the leave vacancy of Kielhorn. When the latter retired, the government began considering the appointment of another European scholar in his place, which gave rise to a public controversy. Ultimately, wise counsel prevailed, and Bhandarkar was appointed a permanent Professor of Sanskrit at Deccan College. The first Indian to occupy that distinguished chair, he served in that capacity from 1882 to 1893, when he retired from government service.

BHANDARKAR'S RESEARCH ACTIVITY AND THE ACADEMIC RENAISSANCE

Bhandarkar's research activity was truly prodigious, as is amply testified by four volumes of his *Collected Works*, published by the research institute that now bears his name. However, I shall only refer to such of his writings as have a relevance to what I have termed the 'Academic Renaissance'. In Bhandarkar's time the conditions for such a revival were becoming increasingly favourable. For one thing the attitude of British officers was encouraging. Elphinstone, to whom Bombay Presidency owes much of its progress during the consolidation of British power, had warned his compatriots that it would be an idle dream to believe that British rule might continue for all time. Therefore, he urged the government to help the natives in all possible ways, particularly education, so that they could obtain the competence to manage their own affairs and thereby contribute to the welfare of their country and of the world. In his Bombay University convocation address of 1882 Governor Lord Reay had said:

> I am not aware that for a British subject there is a more honourable profession than that of holding an appointment in the Department of Higher Education in India. England must give India a due proportion of its best men. Unless Indian Universities receive the best representatives of English learning, they must fail, and failure in this instance entails positive and not merely negative results.

Responsible Englishmen of the time such as Wedderburn and Wordsworth vouched for the fact that, by and large, Western education had proved to be highly salutary in the case of newly educated young men in the Presidency. Principal Wordsworth further argued that the British needed to give up their superior attitude, and not grudge this new awakening among Indians.

Bhandarkar, on his part, had ever been explicitly conscious of the immense debt he and his contemporaries owed to Western education and Western teachers, though elsewhere he had written that

> the European Professors and teachers that come out regard themselves as exiles in this country and have got no permanent stake in it.... Hence it is that, though we have had European professors and teachers here for more than half a century, not a single work of

a nature to make its mark in the world has been published by any one of them, except the German professors of Oriental Languages.

Anyway, Bhandarkar keenly felt that it was a momentous period in the history of India. In his Bombay University convocation address of 1894, he said (perhaps with some exaggeration in places):

Upon our conduct at this period depends the future of our country. The Indian intellect has been dormant for centuries. Original thought had disappeared with the old Rishis; the fermentation of philosophical and religious ideas ceased with the decline of Buddhism; philosophy became verbose and wasted itself in trifling subtleties; poetry assumed an artificial character; religion degenerated into forms, ceremonies and superstitions; and custom became a hideous tyrant . . . there was no moral force in the land to do battle with the evils (generated by custom). It was reserved for the foreigner to put some of them down with the strong arm of the law; but in the cases in which the foreigner will not interfere they still flourish. The intellect and the moral sense of the country must now wake up under the influence of European civilization, and the task and heavy responsibility of regenerating her has devolved upon ourselves, who have felt that influence. Thought on every subject of interest to humanity must be stimulated, literature and philosophy have a fresh start, our vernaculars be improved, and a desire for knowledge propagated.

But Bhandarkar did not lose sight of the rapidly changing world situation. Speaking about his impressions of his extensive travels in Europe on the occasion of the International Congress of Orientalists in Vienna in 1886, he said:

I believe the vigorous civilization of Europe is on its trial, and the war between the French and the Germans which must come some day, and the socialistic and nihilistic movements, if they make further progress, will determine whether it is not one-sided and its ideals have not been chiefly, if not exclusively, material. And in this respect we should by no means be very anxious to realise it among ourselves.

On the other hand, Bhandarkar has elsewhere referred to Principal Wordsworth's view that there had started a renaissance in Europe due to the study of Buddhist and Brahmanic literature. When the religious and philosophical ideas of the Hindus had been influencing Europe, a neglect of them on the part of Indians was sure to be attended by melancholy results. Bhandarkar has succinctly enunciated his objectives in the following words: 'What we are trying to reach is the more healthy condition of the past—minus the corruption of the later ages.'

The strongest motivation for Bhandarkar's research activity came from a feeling later picturesquely articulated by one of his distinguished pupils in the following words: 'We do not till the soil which we own; others come, toil hard on it, and reap away the harvest.' The discipline of scientific Indology may be said to have begun when European scholars became acquainted with Sanskrit in the truly academic sense. The foundation at Calcutta, in 1784, of the Asiatic Society may be regarded as the most significant starting-point in this context. Twenty years later, the Bombay Asiatic Society was instituted by James Macintosh, and similar institutions were subsequently established at other places—the Asiatic

Society at Chennai in 1818, the Société Asiatique in Paris in 1822, the Royal Asiatic Society of Great Britain in London in 1823, the American Oriental Society in Boston in 1842 and the Deutsche Morgenländische Gesellschaft in 1844. In the meantime, Indological studies also came to be introduced in some Western universities in one form or another. It must be noted that, initially, the Asiatic Societies in India were almost exclusively non-Indian. For instance, it was only in 1840, thirty-six years after its foundation, that the Asiatic Society of Bombay admitted its first Indian member, Manekji Cursetji. However, the promoters of these societies soon realized that their work could not make substantial headway without the collaboration of Indian scholars, and they opened their doors to them. A new wave of enthusiasm for scientific Indology became evident, and Bhandarkar emerged as one of the most ardent votaries of that discipline.

Bhandarkar had been an avid student—and later, teacher—of history. He often spoke reverentially of the salutary influence of Sydney Owen, Professor of History at the Elphinstone Institute, on him. He was also quick to realize that a correct understanding of the political, social and religious history of a country was a basic condition for its renaissance. His *Early History of the Deccan down to the Mahomedan Conquest* (1896), indeed, constitutes the earliest comprehensive work on the history of Maharashtra or, for that matter, of any major region of India. Beginning with the Aryan settlement, Bhandarkar expertly deals with the reigns of successive dynasties from the Satavahanas to the Silaharas. He has ably discussed the political, religious, social and economic conditions of their times, discreetly utilizing all the available sources—particularly literary and epigraphic. It is to Bhandarkar's credit that most of the views he expressed in that work have been corroborated by later researches.

In *A Peep into the Early History of India from the Foundation of the Maurya Dynasty to the Downfall of the Imperial Gupta Dynasty—BC 322 to ca. 500 AD* (1900) Bhandarkar has chosen to portray one of the most eventful and glorious periods of Indian history, so that later generations might become aware of the excellence of their forebears which should be emulated, and of their defects which should be made good. From among his numerous papers on historical subjects, attention may be especially drawn to 'A Sanskrit Inscription from Central Java' (1887), the conclusion of which deserves to be quoted here in full:

> If from the first century of the Saka era to about the twelfth, Brahmanas and other Hindu castes set at naught the prohibition of the Shastras against crossing the sea, and went on voyages lasting 90 days and more, there is no reason why they should not do so in this 19th century. . . . The amount of energy and enterprise that the Hindus of those days displayed, in thus keeping a constant intercourse with Cambodia and the islands of the Archipelago, establishing colonies there and imparting to the native Polynesians their own civilization, ought, in the midst of a great deal in our present condition which is very discouraging, to fill us with hope as to the innate capacities of our race. If, according to the interpretation I have ventured to put forward of the Javanese tradition, it was in consequence of their contact with the Sakas that the Indian Aryas first showed these qualities, we have by our side at the present day the sturdy Anglo-Saxon to spur us

on. Let us accept his guidance and leadership with a willing heart, and move on in all fields of human activity. . . .

It will thus be seen that it was always Bhandarkar's endeavour to relate history to the contemporary situation.

In his various writings relating to social life, Bhandarkar dealt with such topics as the complexities of the caste system, the age of marriage for girls, and the incorporation of foreigners into the Hindu social organization. Treating the last of these in some detail, he showed how the Yavanas, Sakas, Abhiras, Turuksas, Magas, Hunas and Gurjaras—who came into India in different periods—became absorbed into Hindu society. But the focus in all his writings is evidently the necessity of social reform. His *Vaishnavism, Saivism and Minor Religious Systems*, which was published through the prestigious *Grundriss der Indo-arischen Philologie* series in 1913, represents a landmark in the study of the religious history of India. Later writers on the subject have mostly followed in his trail. Significantly, in the first part of this book, Bhandarkar has dealt, among other subjects, with the contributions of the saints of Maharashtra like Namdev and Tukaram, emphasizing their central teaching (*bhakti* serves as the most efficacious rallying point for all). This closely conforms to Bhandarkar's own creed as reflected in the activities of the Prarthana Samaj.

Bhandarkar lays great store by adequate methodology which, according to him, would be the hallmark of a true academic renaissance. At one place, he seems to suggest that such a methodology in Indology should reflect, on the one hand, a deep and sound study of the original texts relating to different branches of Sanskrit learning like *nyaya* and *vyakarana*, and on the other, the critical, comparative and historical method of inquiry. He has discussed this topic at length in a paper entitled 'The critical, comparative and historical method of inquiry, as applied to Sanskrit scholarship, philology and Indian archaeology' (1888). He also emphasizes the importance of the complete mastery and judicious utilization of all available original sources. His own keenness in this respect becomes evident from his numerous epigraphical studies, such as 'The Nasik cave inscriptions'. His paper on 'The work done by the Bombay Branch of the Royal Asiatic Society towards the elucidation of Indian history by the study of inscriptions' may also be mentioned in this connection. Bhandarkar admits that Western scholars experience inherent difficulties as far as an adequate exploitation of original sources is concerned, and also points to certain deep-rooted misconceptions in indigenous scholarship. For instance, the Indian scholar is generally prone to 'reject any foreign influence on the development of his country's civilization and to claim high antiquity for some of the occurrences in its history.' On the other hand, the European scholar is inclined 'to trace Greek, Roman or Christian influence at work in the evolution of new points, and to modernize the Indian historical and literary events.' Nevertheless, Bhandarkar asserts that 'when the evidence is irrefutable, it is unscholarlike to deny foreign influence'. He points out in this connection that Indian astronomical works contain several Greek terms, the names of the twelve signs of the zodiac being translations of Greek names. He heartily commends the declaration of Garga, quoted by Varahamihira:

> *mleccha hi yavanas tesu sastram etat pratisthitam/*
> *rsivat te 'pi sampujyah*

Bhandarkar may be said to have belonged to the Ranke school of historiography. Ranke laid great stress on eschewing all romantic elements—all invention and imagination—from historical writings and rigorously sticking to the facts. He wanted the study of the past to be divorced from the passions of the present. Bhandarkar almost echoes the views of Ranke when he compares the critical method of research to the method pursued by the judge who impartially weighs all aspects of the evidence and then pronounces his verdict. Further, as a seeker of truth, the historian must possess candour and honesty to revise his judgement, if necessary, in the light of newly furnished evidence. Bhandarkar himself exemplified this enviable trait, as, for instance, in connection with the dates in the grants of the Maitrakas of Valabhi, a number of which he had edited. Originally he thought that those dates referred to the Saka era of AD 78, but, in a later paper, he modified his earlier view and correctly identified the era used by the Valabhi kings with the Gupta era beginning in AD 319.

Promotion of the study of Sanskrit was, in Bhandarkar's view, another *sine qua non* for academic renaissance. It may be recalled that he himself took to a serious study of Sanskrit at a very late stage in his career—at the age of nearly twenty-four years—but within the next six years attained remarkable proficiency in it. By way of giving an impetus to others, he produced two very useful text-books, and it would not be an exaggeration to say that they served generations of students not only in Maharashtra, but also elsewhere. In the preface to the *First Book of Sanskrit* (1st edn., 1864) Bhandarkar says:

> The study of Sanskrit has but recently risen in the estimation of the educated natives of this Presidency and of our educational authorities. The old Sanskrit College of Pune owed its existence and continuance rather to a spirit of conciliation and toleration in our rulers than to their conviction of the utility of Sanskrit as a branch of general education. The modern critical and progressive spirit was not brought to bear upon it. . . . The newly-awakened and more enlightened zeal in favour of Sanskrit cannot last, or produce extensive results, unless books are produced to facilitate the general study of the language.

And he concludes the preface to the *Second Book of Sanskrit* (3rd edn., 1873) with the words:

> I am very happy to perceive that this book has also met with favour and that, along with the first, it has become the means, however humble, of facilitating and promoting the study of the language of the ancient Rishis among their modern descendants.

Incidentally, it may be pointed out that much was achieved in the direction of the promotion of Sanskrit in western India also after the newly constituted University of Bombay had made a second language compulsory at its matriculation examination. For, in the case of a majority of students, irrespective of caste or creed, this second language happened to be Sanskrit.

Sanskrit literature is like an iceberg whose tip alone is presently visible, a larger portion being submerged in the manuscripts scattered over the country. A planned programme for the resurrection of this rich treasure must constitute an essential feature of the academic renaissance in India. Happily, the government of the Bombay Presidency took a lead in this matter and organized a regular search for Sanskrit manuscripts. Bhandarkar himself worked on this project for ten years and produced four monumental reports (between 1882 and 1891). As Bühler has rightly said, these reports are veritable mines of information regarding the hitherto dark aspects of Sanskrit literature and Indian history.

Bhandarkar stressed the need for critical editions of Sanskrit texts, and set forth a model through his critical edition of Bhavabhuti's *Malatimadhava*. He insisted that the Indians have every reason to be proud of the signal service of the pundits and shastris who kept the tradition of Sanskrit learning alive. In this connection he refers, among other things, to the modes of Vedic recitation as practised in various parts of the country. At one place, he betrays some touchiness about an attempt made at equating the Shimga among the festivals and the Puranas among the literary works.

Yet, promotion of Sanskrit at the expense of the spoken languages did not find a place in Bhandarkar's vision of renaissance. Actually, Bhandarkar is known to have realized the necessity of studying Sanskrit while he had been reading the works of Marathi poets like Moropant andVaman Pandit. In his *Wilson Philological Lectures on Sanskrit and the Derived Languages* (1877). He pointed out that the presumption of the artificial nature of Sanskrit and of the Prakrits was unwarranted and current languages, though different from the Prakrits in their general appearance and phonetic and grammatical structure, were really nothing other than their evolved forms.

Bhandarkar worked assiduously throughout his long life on the 'tilling of the soil which we own', but was ever conscious of what little had been accomplished in relation to the enormity of the task. He continued to guide his fellow-men both by example and precept. Two papers, entitled 'The ideal of an Indian scholar' (1893) and 'Lines for fresh research in Sanskrit literature and Indian antiquities' (1905), are particularly instructive in this regard. In his evidence before the Education Commission of 1904, Bhandarkar emphasized the need for active government sponsorship of higher study and research by competent graduates. But he also insisted that research must become a living interest for such scholars. He once stated (in 1889) that 'It is very much to be wished that more of us devoted ourselves to learning and research.' About the middle of the nineteenth century, Sir Henry Maine had prophesied that Sanskrit studies in India would die out within fifty years and, if they at all survived, it would be due only to the efforts of European scholars. Thanks to the vision and inspiration of Bhandarkar, and fortunately for the academic renaissance, Maine's prophecy did not come to fruition!

Vishnu Moreshwar Mahajani and Nineteenth-Century Antecedents to Keshavsut

PHILIP ENGBLOM

It is generally agreed that in the last decade of the nineteenth century, Keshavsut wrote the first Marathi poetry that can be defined without serious qualification as modern. By the turn of the century a significant number of Keshavsut's prominent contemporaries had adopted the style if not the entire substance of the kind of modernity Keshavsut propounded and exemplified; and it rapidly came to define 'serious' poetry as understood by the Marathi elite at least up to 1920.

To fully gauge the extent of Keshavsutian 'revolution' in Marathi poetry, it is essential first to understand the context, historical and literary, in which it took place and out of which it emerged. At least seven decades of British colonial rule preceded the poetry of Keshavsut and his fellow moderns. The purpose of this paper is to examine the culture of elite Marathi poetry during this incubatory period and especially the ways in which it prefigured modernity and conditioned it.

The chief inheritance of nineteenth-century elite Marathi poetry came from the tradition of the pundit poets. As M.V. Rajadyaksha points out in *Panca Kavi*, a veritable literary caste system—a microcosm of the larger society—existed within the recognized canon of Marathi literature, in which the work of the pundits assumed preeminence over the 'Sudra' poetry of the *santas* and *shahirs* (Rajadyaksha 1946: 13). During the *Peshwai,* Maharashtrian culture was marked to an extraordinary degree by Brahman dominance. The Peshwas themselves have taken an active part in supporting specifically Brahman institutions and in encouraging Brahmanical culture (Kumar 1968: 39ff). The natural consequence of this emphasis, as G.M. Kulkarni (1965: 16-17) has pointed out, was that Maharashtrian culture and particularly Marathi literary culture became heavily Sanskritized. This was the environment in which Moropant and the pundit poets had come to define the norms of elite Marathi poetry.

With the advent of the British, in spite of their policy 'to conciliate literate groups and to disturb as little as possible the social order of the region' (Mcdonald 1968: 594), the system of Brahman patronage under the Peshwas was largely dismantled. As a class, the dispossessed Brahmans lost access to their traditional prerogatives, and they were forced to turn to other means to regain some of what they had lost. The chief means of advancement under the British was the new system of education that they began to establish as early as the 1820s. Traditionally the primary literate caste, Brahmans pursued the new educational means in hugely disproportionate numbers. Consequently, after a period of adjustment, this same class of dispossessed 'Chitpavan administrator families, with little wealth but with education and firm social status . . . provided a large percentage of the political and educational leaders of Maharashtra until well into the present century' (Tucker 1977: 7). The new literate and literary elite that developed in nineteenth-century Maharashtra under the British turned out to be in large measure the old elite, but set in wholly different circumstances, as subjects of alien rule.

As a sign of good faith and benevolent intentions toward Brahman society in Pune, the British reinstituted the Dakshina fund, which had been such an important part of Peshwa patronage, in 1821. It was greatly reduced from the days of the Peshwas and served primarily to support the officially sanctioned Pune Pathshala where a traditional mode of education could continue, the expectation being that it would gradually develop a more Western curriculum. In 1851, however, the government felt obliged to hasten this process by joining the Pathshala with the Government English School. The new Pune College that emerged from this odd marriage served to prepare a class of scholars who were equally versed in Sanskrit and English. These *shastris,* as they were titled, were to have a profound influence on the development of Marathi literary culture. They were drafted in large numbers into the government education department where they filled a variety of functions: to develop Marathi as an educational medium, to create Marathi schoolbooks, and to translate selected specimens of Sanskrit and English literature into Marathi (Pandit 1965: 231; Bhate 1939: 99). The books and educational materials they produced provided the literary education of several generations of Marathi students. Moreover, their peculiar Brahmanical and Sanskritized linguistic and literary culture, as epitomized in their style of writing, left an indelible impression on literary and, especially, poetic style and taste throughout the remainder of the century. As Kulkarni (1965: 35) puts it, 'This is what is known as the Pune style (*valan*).' That it received the encouragement and actual sponsorship of the government assured that the style had the most widespread influence.

The *de facto* dean of the *shastris*, the oldest and in some ways the most accomplished of them all, was Parshuram Ballal Godbole (1799–1874). The work for which he has been justly immortalized was his compilation of an anthology of Marathi poetry from the pre-British era entitled *Navnit,* published in 1854 at the behest of the education department. This particular book served as the standard text of Marathi literature in all government schools for many generations (Bhate 1939: 82). It went through numerous reprints well into the twentieth century. Every student who passed through the new system of primary and secondary education was required to memorize large portions of the poetry in *Navnit.*

Godbole made his selections from seventeen of the principal Marathi poets, beginning with Dnyaneshwar. He included a fairly representative selection from the saint-poet tradition besides Dnyaneshwar; but he gave disproportionately large space to Waman Pandit and Moropant. Their poetry together occupies nearly half the book. This emphatic approbation of the pundits was hardly coincidental. For Godbole, Waman Pandit and especially Moropant represented the indisputable culmination of Marathi poetry. Besides the testimony of *Navnit*, he made his admiration for Moropant abundantly clear in his essay 'Kekadarsha', which he wrote in criticism of Moropant's poem, 'Kekavali'. He himself wrote verse in the so-called 'Moropanti arya' metre, which he based explicitly on Moropant's model (Pandit 1965: 232). In *Navnit* his editorial intention was clear: to foster the pundit style of poetry as the standard of excellence. The effect on many generations of Marathi students, who had dutifully to memorize hundreds of lines of Waman and Moropant, including 300 lines from 'Kekavali' (Gumpertz 1965: 307), was profound. Perhaps more than any other factor, it formed the poetic taste and understanding of the new educated elite of Maharashtra.

Godbole's *Navnit* was by no means the only volume dedicated to the publication of pre-British Marathi poetry. Out of the 230 printed Marathi books in verse through 1864, 197 were the works of poets of the pre-British era (Ranade 1915: 8). Godbole and the other *shastris* played a major role in editing and publishing these works (Pandit 1965: 232). These editions, along with *Navnit*, represented almost the sole means of transmission of traditional Marathi poetry to the generations educated in the new English system that followed Godbole and the *shastris*.

Godbole's other major contribution to Marathi literature were his translations, again at the behest of the education department, of several Sanskrit plays. His translation of *Venisamhara* in 1857 was the first such attempt in Marathi. He followed this with the translation of the *Uttararamacarita* (1859), *Sakuntala* (1861), *Mrcchakatika* (1862), *Nagananda* (1865) and, finally, *Parvatiparinaya* (1870) (Sardar 1971: 786). In these translations he rendered prose as prose and verse as verse, often retaining the original Sanskrit metre, though occasionally he also ventured to substitute the native Marathi *saki* or *dindi* moric metres or even a *lavani* or *abhanga* (Pandit 1965: 233).

Several other *shastris* assisted Godbole in the task of translating selected specimens of Sanskrit drama and *mahakavya*. Some of the plays they published included *Ratnavali* (1864), *Malvikagnimitra* (1867), *Mudrarakshasa* (1867), two more translations of *Sakuntala* (1869, 1870), and two of *Vikramorvasiya* (1872, 1874) (Sardar 1971: 786). Krishnashastri Chiplunkar (1844-78) made an important contribution, not by translating plays, but rather with a much admired translation of Kalidasa's *Meghaduta*, and with a free adaptation of Jaganathapundit's *Bhaminivilasa*. He also wrote his own Marathi poem, *Padyaratnavali*, a series of 20 allegories based on Sanskrit models. Following his example, a number of his contemporaries either translated Sanskrit *mahakavyas*, or more or less freely used Sanskrit models to write their own Marathi poems. Ganeshashastri Lele, for example, translated Kalidasa's *Raghuvamsa* and also attempted his own long Marathi poems based on Sanskrit models, *Gangavarnana* and *Sivajicaritra*.

The creation of the *dakshina* competition in 1867, with the express purpose of stimulating the production of original Marathi poetry, added impetus to this incipient trend toward original poems. The committee in charge of the competition would select a topic for the given year (Shivaji, the Ganga, the seasons of the year, the Hindu festivals, and so on), and would reward the winning entry with a sum of money. They then submitted the poem to the education department for publication. Numbers of the losing entries were also published by other means. Many poets, predominantly *shastris*, participated in the competitions. So although it constituted a wholly artificial stimulus, the Dakshina prize competition resulted over the years in the publication of a sizeable body of contemporary Marathi poems.

None of the poems were masterpieces, but they represented an important stage historically in the development of Marathi poetry toward its modern form. By and large the poems reflected the character of the *shastri* class that took such a large part in writing them: they show a clear debt to Sanskrit poetry on the one hand, while on the other they bore the impress of Moropant and the pundit poets. Their style was learned, Sanskritized and consciously ornamented with the standard figures of speech. The metres used were either the Sanskrit *aksaragana* metres or the Moropant-style *arya* and *giti*, and more rarely the Marathi *saki* and *dindi*. For the most part they were long poems of a narrative character. These poems represented, in short, a continuation of the pundit tradition. Their chief novelty was the great expansion of subject-matter, out of the confines of the epic stories that had occupied Waman and Moropant.

The *shastris* contributed many significant things to nineteenth-century Marathi poetry. Their work in editing and publishing the pre-British poets was essential for the preservation of the prior Marathi tradition. Their translations of Sanskrit literature helped substantially to diversify the taste and understanding of Marathi literary culture. Though it lacked originality, their own verse demonstrated how something new could be written in Marathi after a general hiatus of several decades and how it could be published through a printed rather than an oral medium.

Although the *shastris* themselves made their major contributions during the decades of the 1850s to the 1870s, their style and understanding of poetry survived long after them. A major line of poets, who largely maintained the norms the *shastris* established, continued well into the twentieth century. Even the first 'modern' poets such as Keshavsut and Narayan Waman Tilak, especially in their early work, show clear evidence of the style. Modern poetry, as Keshavsut in particular came eventually to define it, might in many respects be defined negatively by its degree of reaction to or abandonment of the norms and conventions of the *shastri* style.

As a counterpart to the *shastris* and their heavily Sanskritized literary culture, there emerged in the 1860s and 1870s another class of Marathi writers, among the first university graduates, who were heavily imbued with English culture and English literary values. Quite understandably, they sought to enrich Marathi by adapting or imitating English poetry. By 1899, Bombay University had granted a total of 4007 degrees; approximately 15,000 students had enrolled at the various affiliated colleges for some period of time; and perhaps as many as 60,000 had passed through the Anglo-vernacular secondary schools (Gumpertz 1965: 186). Clearly, a quite sizeable (at least potential) constituency was being created, during the last four decades of the nineteenth century, for a new, English-influenced poetry.

In 'A note on the growth of Marathi literature' (1898) Justice Ranade complained, however, that the new, university-educated elite in Maharashtra had not contributed their full share in the development of modern Marathi literature. He pointed to the statistics he had compiled from the *Catalogue of Native Publications*, which showed that at the turn of the century hardly ten per cent of the published Marathi writers were graduates. Using this evidence, he inveighed against the decision in 1865 to exclude Marathi from the university curriculum, to which he attributed the loss of all incentive for the university-educated to cultivate Marathi (Ranade 1898: 26).

During the last third of the nineteenth century, Marathi literature had to grow in a large measure as one removed from the University. Except for the token incentive of the Dakshina prize, official encouragement of vernacular literature, which had characterized the earlier decades, was withdrawn and the emphasis placed on classical languages, Persian and Sanskrit, as well as on English. The fact that Ranade himself chose to write only in English illustrates his point about the devaluation of Marathi among the university-educated elite. On the other hand, the publication of Marathi literature during this very period was rapidly acquiring momentum of its own. Non-graduates filled the ranks of writers to a large extent, especially in the popular new genres of prose fiction and drama (Ranade 1898: 43). Even in the case of Marathi poetry, out of all the significant poets of Keshavsut's generation, (that is, the first acknowledged as modern poets) only one or two were university graduates. These first modern poets represented, in effect, a kind of secondary Maharashtrian elite, whose chief intellectual resource and medium of discourse was neither Sanskrit nor English but Marathi.

But to return to the 1860s–1880s: Ranade's lament obscures the real situation to some degree, by ignoring other relevant factors. A large number of the university-educated who wrote in Marathi made their mark in journalism and might, therefore, not have been reflected in Ranade's sample. They contributed very importantly nevertheless to the formation of a new type of literary culture, which propagated itself through journals and periodicals of every kind. Moreover, what they did contribute to Marathi tended to have a disproportionate influence—one need only mention Chiplunkar, Agarkar and Tilak by way of illustration. The same holds true, to a lesser extent, for the group of university-educated poets in the generation that preceded Keshavsut. Ranade himself recognized the special contribution these poets made, citing them and the poems for which he commended them by name (Ranade 1898: 25).

Since English poetry constituted a major part of the school and college curriculum, poets of this intermediate generation came to be imbued with the values of English poetry, and understandably began to regard English poets as models for emulation.[1] Like the *shastris* before them, who had relied on Sankrit models so heavily, the university-educated poets sought to enrich Marathi from English sources. They set about their task by quite deliberately adapting poems from English. Their poetry was consequently as little original as that of the *shastris*. But it was the first Marathi poetry to show the explicit effects of English, and as such it served as an important bridge between the conservative style of the *shastris* and the modern style associated with Keshavsut's generation.

While adapting Sanskrit poetry to Marathi, the *shastris* did not have to stretch the conventions of Marathi poetry very much to accommodate it, owing to the kinship of the two languages. They had, moreover, the examples of Waman and Moropant and the other pundit poets to serve as guide. Adapting English poetry to Marathi represented a much more difficult undertaking in many respects because of the stark differences between the two traditions and because there were no precedents. The university-educated poets proceeded with their task as a whole with marked circumspection: 'This adapted literature began to be spread gradually through the periodicals of that time. It created its own special class of readers. With the passage of time, the character of this verse became more firmly established' (Pandit 1965: 248).

The aspect of English poetry that appears to have left the deepest impression was its seeming simplicity. That 'serious' poetry could be, from their perspective, so shorn of the formal embellishments of style and figures of speech, so seemingly straightforward in its meaning, came as a revelation. The traditional norms of Marathi poetry had included the laboured elaboration of scores upon scores of figures of speech of both sense and sound. Their conspicuous absence in English poetry made it very difficult for many who had been educated in the elaborate style of Moropant, to accept English poetry seriously, at least at first.

What happened with the first attempt at direct adaptation of English poetry into Marathi is an instructive example. As early as 1860, the Education Department commissioned one of its *shastris*, Mahadev Govind Kolhatkar (1822–62), to translate the poems in the *First Book of English Poetry* to serve as a school textbook. As it was an anthology intended for the instruction of children, the *First Book* contained little 'serious' English poetry, although it did include pieces by Wordsworth, Scott and Longfellow. It could hardly be expected to stand up to intensive comparison with the existing Marathi poetic tradition. But its Marathi adaptation was roundly ridiculed in its own time for its 'insignificant subjects, childish sermonizing, childishly simple language and prosaic style' (Pandit 1965: 252). Kolhatkar's manner of translating these simple English poems could only make their acceptance still more problematical. For at least half of them he used the metres (*arya* and various Sanskrit *aksaragana* metres) and the concomitant style of the pundit poets. For the remainder he used the *abhanga* and *ovi* forms that unavoidably had associations with the great saint-poets. The discrepancy between the expectations raised by the forms and the actual poems could only lead to grave misapprehensions. But the book did have its effect. It was taught in schools as part of the curriculum, and it shaped the perception of poetry of the following generation.

The university-educated poets in the generation before Keshavsut's approached their task somewhat differently, if only voluntarily. They chose for their adaptations the poems to which they were exposed in college. Bajaba Ramchandra Pradhan (1838-86) established the precedent with his free adaptation of the first and final cantos of Scott's *Lady of the Lake*, which he published as *Daivaseni*. *Lady of the Lake* had been, not coincidentally, part of the English curriculum when Pradhan was in college (Pandit 1965: 250). Years later (1878), he was also to make a prose translation of Shakespeare's *Comedy of Errors* (*Bhrantikrta camatkara*), to which he had also probably first been exposed during his college career. *Daivaseni* is in parts quite a straightforward translation, but as a whole it is more accurately described as an adaptation. Pradhan Indianized his version to the extent that he transformed the Scottish Highlanders of Scott's poems into Rajput nobility. The poem was acclaimed in its time by no less a critic than Vishnushastri Chiplunkar, and it must have had relative popularity because it went through three printings (Deshpande 1954: 84). Metre and style are particularly noteworthy features of the poem. It has 235 stanzas altogether, all of which are in metres traditional to the pundit-shastri style—Sanskrit *aksaragana* metres interspersed with various *arya*-related metres as well as the *saki* and *dindi*. And the style is entirely congruent with this traditional metrical medium—to the extent, indeed, that A.N. Deshpande sees distinct affinities between Pradhan's style and that of Raghunathapundit (Deshpande 1954: 84). Clearly then, Pradhan had Indianized *Lady of the Lake* in more ways than one. He had addressed the new without in any significant way disturbing the conventions of old.

At the opposite end of the spectrum, we find the somewhat ill-starred and ill-famed poem, *Raja Shivaji*, by Mahadev Moreshwar Kunte (1835-88). It is an adaptation not of any particular English poem, but of a genre, the heroic epic. When Kunte undertook to write it for the first Dakshina prize competition of 1867-8, he held the models of *Paradise Lost* and Pope's English versions of the *Iliad* and the *Odyssey* before him (this according to his own testimony), and it is clear that he emulated them with the greatest care. He intentionally steered clear of the Sanskrit epic conventions, very conscious all the while that he was doing something altogether new.

When the English department published the first three cantos of *Raja Shivaji* in 1869, after it had shared the Dakshina prize with another poem on the same subject, Kunte added a preface in English explaining what he had undertaken. He intended, quite simply, to revolutionize Marathi poetry. He evoked the precedent of Wordsworth's preface to *Lyrical Ballads* to legitimize his own preface, and he attempted something of what Wordsworth had done in writing a critique of tradition and a manifesto for a new style. Kunte excoriated the tradition of the pundit poets and especially Waman and Moropant as 'degenerate Sanskrit-Marathi poets'. He espoused, as had Wordsworth, a natural, native idiom that reflects the spoken language; and he deplored the continued bondage of Marathi poets to the conventions of the Sanskrit tradition and the pundit poets. As an example of the natural idiom that would give Marathi its due respect as a poetic language in its own right, he offered his own poem.

While Kunte's preface has been honoured by present-day critics as one of the most significant critiques of Marathi poetry in the pre-modern era and as the first important harbinger of modernity, the reputation of the poem itself has been very different. In spite of winning the Dakshina prize, *Raja Shivaji* was subjected to intense ridicule in its own time, and even modern critics, though less harsh, have agreed that it is an ambitious experiment that failed as a poem.[1] B.S. Pandit qualifies his criticism of the poem somewhat by suggesting that Kunte was ahead of his time and that part of the reason for the failure of the poem was due to the hidebound literary conventions of his time, which instinctively rejected anything new (Pandit 1965: 256). It was Vishnushastri Chiplunkar again who established the pattern of subsequent criticism of *Raja Shivaji* with comments so venomous, that they smack of personal animosity (Deshpande 1954: 88). Kunte himself became so dispirited by the adverse reception given to his poem that he published only six of a proposed twelve cantos, and nothing more in Marathi verse for almost fifteen years.

The principal criticism of *Raja Shivaji* has been that Kunte applied his reform too obsessively and, in the absence of sufficient countervailing poetic ability, produced a poem most notable for the awkwardness and harshness of its language. On the one hand, he deliberately included many rustic (*gavthi*) turns of speech as examples of the kind of authentic Marathi speech he held as the new norm for poetic diction. On the other hand he found it as impossible as Wordsworth had to write only the common language of the common man, so that Sanskritized usages mingle with the more rustic elements of speech in a strange hodgepodge. Similarly, his choice of the *bhujangaprayata* metre, on the grounds that it bore some resemblance to the English iambic line, went directly against the associations that metre had, in the minds of most of his readers, with Ramdas' *Manace sloka:* it had renunciatory, not heroic, resonances.

Raja Shivaji left its mark on Marathi poetry nevertheless in a number of significant ways. Its unabashed espousal of English norms of poetry presaged the way modern Marathi poetry would eventually develop. Its repudiation of established poetic idiom had a discernible effect on later poets in their attempt to write a simpler and more natural Marathi. Kunte also introduced English punctuation to Marathi poetry for the first time in *Raja Shivaji* (Pandit 1965: 257), which allowed him the unprecedented liberty to place stops where he chose rather than necessarily at the line's end as tradition dictated. This in turn allowed him to enjam his lines vigorously. If Kunte was roundly abused in his time for this travesty of tradition, it at least made Keshavsut's predilection for doing the same thing a generation later seem a somewhat less radical.

Some of the innovations Kunte pioneered are encountered again a few years later—in a more pleasing and therefore better accepted way—in another Dakshina prize-winning poem, Panduranga Vyankatesh Chintamanipethkar's

Gangavarnana. It consists of a description of the Ganga river in 332 elegant *slokas* in selected *aksaragana* metres, and it thereby indicates its affinities with tradition. But the way in which Chintamanipethkar used his traditional medium is what makes his poem unique. In the manner of Kunte, he eschewed the stylized conventions of Sanskrit nature poetry (e.g. the beautiful but elaborate figurative elegancies of Kalidasa's *Meghaduta*) and turned instead to the more directly descriptive mode of English poets. He innovated significantly also, like Kunte, by allowing the rhetoric rather than the metre to dictate the periods. He also broke the traditional confinement of the *sloka*, in each of which only one complete thought was to be expressed. This freedom to violate the *sloka* container bore important implications, for example, for the later development of the sonnet, especially of the Petrarchan form with its octave and sestet.

Another significant adaptation of a specific English poem appeared in print in 1884. This was Kanhoba Ranchodas Kirtikar's *Indira*, a free adaptation of Tennyson's *Princess*. Kirtikar (1849-1917) was a doctor who went to England for advanced medical training—something rare in those days. His experiences in England and his education made of him a strong social progressive, especially with regard to improving the position of women. He wrote *Indira* under such a persuasion. The original poem provided primarily the narrative framework, of a quite fanciful kind, upon which Kirtikar constructed his own poem in an 'independent manner' (Pandit 1965: 263). He Indianized the characters and the setting, but his theme reflects the debate on the equality of the sexes prevalent in Victorian England and manifested in such diverse ways as John Stuart Mill's *Subjection of Women* and Tennyson's own *Princess*. Kirtikar embellished his adaptation freely with denunciations of the particular injustices borne by Indian womanhood. *Indira* is still cited with admiration (Deshpande 1954: 85) as the first Marathi poem to express this essentially modern social viewpoint.

In terms of technique, *Indira* remained essentially conservative in that Kirtikar maintained the use of the Sanskrit *aksaragana* metres. In two cases, he introduced changes from their established patterns, but it remains a matter of some doubt whether he did so in experiment or by mistake. *Indira* also showed the effects of *Raja Shivaji* in the occasional use of rustic turns of speech. But this poem was favourably received and Kirtikar lived to acquire great honour within the Marathi literary community, including the presidency of the Baroda Sahitya Sammelan in 1909.

Govind Vasudev Kanitkar (1854-1918) was Kirtikar's close contemporary, and he shared with him a progressive social viewpoint. He translated Mill's *Subjection of Women* into Marathi, in fact, as a token of his commitment to the cause of social progress. His actions spoke as loud as his words: he encouraged his wife to become the first published woman novelist in Marathi. Kanitkar wrote a number of poems that show the effects of his wide reading in English literature. He is best known for the long reflective poem he wrote while still in college in 1873, entitled *Sammohalahari*, the revised edition of which he published in 1900. The poem is a meditation on nature, God and religion, and it shows Kanitkar's deep debt to the English philosophers. Stylistically, however,

Kanitkar modelled his poem very deliberately on Moropant's *Kekavali*, as is evident in part by his use of the same *aksaragana* metre, the *prthvi*, throughout the poem. His style is less elaborate than Moropant's, but R.S. Jog (1951: 128) at least compares it favourably with the older work.

Kanitkar's combination of new intellectual matter with an old stylistic mould epitomizes the transitional nature of the verse written by his generation of university-educated poets. Their education prompted them to say something new and different, but the only recognized poetic medium they had already at hand was the learned style they inherited from the pundit and *shastri* poets. With the exception of Kunte, theirs was largely a matter of putting 'new wine into old containers' (Kulkarni 1965: 66). They did introduce some important stylistic innovations: English punctuation, an 'English' lack of figurative ornamentation, some freedom to transgress the containment of line-end and stanza. But their very retention of the *aksaragana* metres and much of the related style those metres had inherited from the pundit poets symptomizes the incongruity of what they had attempted. That they chose to write (even in adaptation from English) long narrative and didactic poems demonstrates also the bondage of their understanding of poetry to that tradition.

The wealth of short lyrical poems in English had remarkably little visible effect on Marathi poetry until late in the nineteenth century. Mahadevshastri Kolhatkar's ill-starred adaptation of the *First Book of English Poetry* notwithstanding, Marathi poets consistently overlooked English lyrics as a suitable model. The limitations of the English curriculum in school and college contributed to the neglect of the lyric, no doubt; but there was a preexisting bias already, inherited from the pundit tradition, in favour of long narrative and didactic verse.

The publication of Palgrave's *Golden Treasury* in 1861 was chiefly responsible for changing this state of affairs. The anthology was published too late in the century to affect the English education of the first generation of university-students, which may explain why they overlooked English lyric poetry (Pandit 1968: 146). The *Golden Treasury* was actually never a part of the English curriculum; but by the early 1880s it had arrived in India and English-educated Maharashtrians were reading it avidly. Their exposure to the 'best original Lyrical pieces and Songs' in English as they found them in the *Treasury* brought about a major sea-change within Marathi poetry.

The first direct fruits the *Golden Treasury* bore in Marathi were the lyrical poems of Vishnu Moreshwar Mahajani (1851–1923), published serially in the monthly *Vividhajnanavistara* between 1883 and 1885. Nineteen of these forty-one poems were adaptations of poems in the *Golden Treasury*. Among the remaining poems, three were Mahajani's own, others included short 'lyrical' selections from *Paradise Lost*, Cowper's *The Task*, and Tennyson's *In Memoriam*. The final poem of the collection was an adaptation of Longfellow's *A Psalm of Life*. Mahajani based the largest number of his adaptations on the Romantic poets, Scott, Burns, Wordsworth, Coleridge, Byron, Shelley and Keats, who were represented prominently in the fourth book of the *Treasury*.

Mahajani published a collected edition of these poems in 1886 under the title *Kusumanjali* (Flower Offering). In his preface he acknowledged the novelty of what he had done: 'These flowers are different from our own—their form is different—their colour is different—their fragrance also is different. I am uncertain whether our bees will like them or not.' Although his materials were certainly new and different, Mahajani avoided picking a quarrel with tradition over technique and form. He adhered strictly to the conventions of Marathi versification as they were understood in the nineteenth century, so that many of his adaptations show only a rough equivalence with their originals in length and sense; and with the exception of one instance of crossed rhymes (probably the first in Marathi) he made no attempt at correspondence between stanzaic forms or rhyme schemes. He used the standard metres of his day—*aksaraganas* metres and the *dindi*, *saki*, and *arya*—and his style as a consequence also followed the learned and Sanskritized pattern to that extent. But his use of these conventional means was so skilled that his adaptations to this date elicit sincere praise. B.S. Pandit (1968: 110) writes of them, for instance: 'The skill of Mahajani's adaptations was unequalled. His style overall is mature and affecting.' They were also very well received in Mahajani's own time and given considerable exposure—appearing as they did first in the prestigious *Vividhajnanavistara* and subsequently going through two editions in the span of about five years. Moreover, they had a discernible and indeed seminal effect on the culture of poetry in those days. In subsequent years, right up to the turn of the century, many others followed Mahajani's example and translated English lyrics into Marathi. Some of these can be found in the pages of *Vividhajnanavistara*, but there is a much larger number in *Kavyaratnavali* (founded in 1887), which became the leading journal of poetry in the last decade of the nineteenth century.

Much more important than this fad for translations, however, is the effect Mahajani's adaptations had on the early development of Keshavsut. It is virtually certain that Keshavsut as a student at the New English School in Pune had read the poems in *Kusumanjali*, when they first appeared in *Vividhajnanavistara* (Engblom 1988). One can point out many parallels and affinities of style and technique between the early works of Keshavsut and the poems of Mahajani, especially in the very similar kinds of translations Keshavsut did, even of the same poems in a couple of cases.

It is instructive in this context to examine how Mahajani dealt with a very specific type of English lyric poem, the sonnet, three instances of which appear in *Kusumanjali*. The sonnet form was later on, of course, to be taken up and championed by Keshavsut. Indeed, it was his efforts that chiefly legitimized it and established the pattern it would take in Marathi. But the inception of the Marathi sonnet we find in Mahajani's words.

The first of Mahajani's sonnet adaptations is based on Wordsworth's well-known sonnet, 'It is a beauteous evening, calm and free', which he apparently found in Book 4 of the *Golden Treasury* (see Appendix A, No.1). The original is a Petrarchan sonnet containing two slight anomalies in the rhyme scheme but in all other respects true to the form. As in all his adaptations, Mahajani adapted this sonnet very freely. He made no attempt to preserve the fourteen-line length of the original, even if that had happened to strike him as a significant defining feature of the poem. Instead, having settled on the *sardulavikridita* as his metre (and its gravity is not a bad choice for the subject of the poem), it followed from established convention that he would write quatrains—the multiples of which are either twelve or sixteen lines—rhymed *aabb, ccdd*, etc. The *sardulavikridita* itself is one of the longer *aksaragana* metres, having nineteen syllables to a line or thirty morae when scanned – – – U U – U – U U U – /– – U – – U–. It is a much longer line than the iambic pentametre of the original poem, and it provided, therefore, a much more expansive canvas upon which to convey the sense. But since Mahajani was not attempting a literal rendering, this was not an important discrepancy for him. By making his adaptation a twelve-line poem in three quatrains he compensated in a sense for the length of his lines.

Mahajani diverged from Wordsworth's original sonnet in another important respect also in that he introduced imagery of his own, particularly in the first quatrain. The following line-by-line rendering should illustrate the differences:

How beautiful this quiet evening feels! How it calms the mind!
Truly like a *yogini* it seems, sitting absorbed in contemplation!
The sun, Aditya, has descended to the sea, to take his evening bath;
Repeating his mantra and free of all passion he dips under—
who enraptures the day

These quiet waves of the sea seem like saintly men—
My mind also steadies, though its movements carry on unhindered!
Listen to this deep thunderous sound! It never wanes or ceases;
An everlasting image it is, reminding us of the very image of God we love!

Watching the sea my mind immerses in immeasurable depths of joy;
My eyes half close with bliss as the years waste and fade away in my mind!
O Child! Even if your nature does not seem like this, still who—
undeniable brute—
Would dare say, 'The Lord does not dwell in your heart'?

The strongly Indian images have changed the atmosphere of the poem substantially from the original sonnet. The octave, moreover, has shown in the adaptation much expansion and elaboration; while the sestet has been crowded into the last two lines and truncated severely in sense, perhaps owing to the difficulty of conveying the meaning of the Judeo-Christian symbol of 'Abraham's bosom'. The way Mahajani managed it, the poem appears in Marathi as nothing radically new.

Mahajani turned to Shakespeare for his next sonnet adaptations. These are two of Shakespeare's most anthologized poems, and they appear in successive order in the first book of the *Golden Treasury* (see Appendix A, No. 2). Thematically, the poems are closely related, and they develop a common argument. Mahajani thought them related enough to join them together as one poem of five quatrains, with the two original sonnets divided in sense between the first three and last two quatrains respectively. As an inevitable result, the structure of the original sonnets has been significantly distorted in the adaptation. The first sonnet finds ample room in the first three *sardulavikridita* quatrains to create a reasonable correspondence of the lines. But even by capitalizing on the length of the *sardulavikridita* Mahajani could not squeeze the second sonnet into the last two quatrains without resorting to a large measure of paraphrase:

Great temples of the gods, palaces of kings, have gone to ruin;
Idols have been shattered to bits and moved from their own places;
Kings have built great unconquerable forts, have expended their wealth;
All have fallen and gone to dust! Everything yields to decay!

Here the sea forever eats away the shore, the earth wastes away;
The Ganga, the Sindhu, the Mahanadi, see, reach the ocean here;
Where water once, there now the earth; the water now where before was the shore!
By one's growth the other's decay increases, one's decay causes the other's growth;—such is life's way!

When each moment I see this continuing decline and decay
My heart feels fear: the wave of time will take away my love;
When such a thought enters my heart, I fall into dejection;
That which, when it leaves, gives grief, when actually gotten makes me weep.

If this decay will leave neither the stones nor the earth nor the sea,
Tell me—how will a flower-soft lass not feel its fear?
Can the continual blows of time leave untouched the realm of flowers?—
Whose hammers make dust of stones and demolish iron!

Where can this beautiful jewel be hidden? Where is the chest,
In which, if hidden, the jewel will not be found by the eyes of time?
Who will drag back his foot, which tramples the flowers of beauty?
In what is this power, I do not know, if it be not in poetry!

Here, as in the adaptation from Wordsworth, Mahajani has been careful to maintain all the established conventions of Marathi versification. The sonnets have lost their character as sonnets in the conversion; but the resulting Marathi poem, in spite of its conventional medium, must have seemed striking and bold within the context of its time.

From the evidence of his adaptations it appears that Mahajani failed really to grasp the peculiar genius of the sonnet form. The sonnets were to him evidently just two more short lyrics among the hundreds in the *Golden Treasury*. If he did sense the special nature of the structure, he remained in practice loyal to the traditional dictates of Marathi verse form. He was the first in Marathi nevertheless to try his hand at coming to terms with the sonnet; and it was he who, for better or worse, first brought together the *sardulavikridita* and the sonnet form. Keshavsut was to continue to use the *sardulavikridita* for all his sonnets—indeed he made it one of the dominant conventions of the form in Marathi. His early experiments with the sonnet, which include several translations from English all rendered faithfully in the *sardulavikridita*, especially suggest that Keshavsut was very much conscious of Mahajani's precedent. He very soon went much farther than Mahajani in establishing the separate identity of the Marathi sonnet and, in the larger perspective, in creating a new and distinctive poetic voice and technique. But his debt to Mahajani and the kind of poetic culture his poems embodied is clear. He could not have done what he did in realizing the almost quantum change his poetry represents (and in the process defining the very terms of modernity in Marathi poetry) outside the specific context, conventions and values which his predecessors had established.

The poetry produced by Mahajani and the intermediate generation of university-educated poets in fact gave much maturity to Marathi poetry and expanded its possibilities. They helped gradually wean it away from the tried and true formulas it had inherited from its past, and prepared it for its modern *avatar*. Their heavy reliance on explicit English models, however, greatly diminished their originality of their own role as poets. They were to a large degree dilettantes, occasional poets. Their verse had a 'largely bookish character' (Pandit 1965: 274) and the innovations they introduced were more superimposed than intrinsic. Only in the following generation—of Keshavsut and his peers, poets 'born to be poets'—could these innovations be assimilated in a new, original, and organic way.

APPENDIX A

1. William Wordsworth, 1936, 'It is a beauteous evening, calm and free', in T. Hutchinson, (ed.), *Wordsworth: Poetical Works*, Oxford: Oxford University Press (2nd edn. revised by Earnest de Selincourt), p. 205.

It is a beauteous evening calm and free,
The holy time is quiet as a Nun
Breathless with adoration; the broad sun
Is sinking down in its tranquillity;
The gentleness of heaven broods o'er the Sea:
Listen! the mighty Being is awake
That doth with his eternal motion make
A sound like thunder—everlastingly.
Dear Child! dear Girl! that walkest with me here,
If thou appear untouched by solemn thought,
Thy nature is not therefore less divine:
Thou liest in Abraham's bosom all the year;
And worshipp'st at the Temple's inner shrine,
God being with thee when we know it not.

2. William Shakespeare, 1967, Nos. 64 and 65, in J. Dover Wilson (ed.), *The Sonnets*. Cambridge: Cambridge University Press (2nd edn.), pp. 34-5.

When I have seen by Time's fell hand defaced
The rich-proud cost of outworn buried age,
When sometimes lofty towers I see down-raised,
And brass eternal slave to mortal rage.
When I have seen the hungry ocean gain
And the firm soil win of the watery main
Increasing store with loss, and loss with store.
When I have seen such interchange of state,
Or state it self confounded, to decay,
Ruin hath taught me thus to ruminate
That Time will come and take my love away.
This thought is as a death which cannot choose
But weep to have, that which it fears to lose

Since brass, nor stone, nor earth, nor boundless sea,
But sad mortality o'ersways their power
How with this rage shall beauty hold a plea,
Whose action is no stronger than a flower?
O how shall summer's honey breath hold out,
Against the wrackful siege of batt'ring days,
When rocks impregnable are not so stout,
Nor gates of steel so strong but time decays?
O fearful meditation, where alack,
Shall Time's best jewel from Time's chest lie hid?
Or what strong hand can hold his swift foot back,
Or who his spoil or beauty can forbid?
O none, unless this miracle have might,
That in black ink my love may still shine bright.

NOTE

1. Vishnushastri Chiplunkar, in an essay published in 1875 in *Salapatrika* [*Marathi kavita* reprinted in S.N. Banhatti (ed.), 1974, *Vishnupadi*, Pune: Suvichar Prakashan, 63-6] describes the unfortunate effect that the reading of English poetry had on the attitude of contemporary university graduates. He laments that for most it created a strong prejudice against Marathi poetry. In his own graphic way, he describes their minds as being made *dusita* by their exposure to English poetry.

REFERENCES

Bhate, G.C., 1939, *History of Modern Marathi Literature: 1800-1938*, Mahad: n.p.

Chiplunkar, V.S., 1875, *Marathi kavita, Salapatrika*, reprinted in S.N. Banhatti (ed.), 1974, *Visnupadi*, Pune: Suvichar Prakashan.

Deshpande, A.N., 1954, *Adhunika Marathi vangmayaca itihasa, bhaga pahila*, Pune: Venus.

Engblom, P., 1988, 'Keshavsut and Early Modernist Strategies for Indigenizing the Sonnet in Marathi', *Journal of South Asian Literature* 23.1.

Gumpertz, E.M., 1965, *English Education and Social Change in Late Nineteenth Century Bombay, 1858-1898*, Ph.D. dissertation, University of California at Berkeley.

Jog, R.S., 1951, *Arvacina Marathi kavya: Kesavasuta ani nantara*, Mumbai: Mumbai Marathi Sahitya Sangha (2nd edn.).

Kulkarni, G.M., 1965, 'Rajkiya sthityantar va tyace vangmayin parinam', in *Marathi vangmayaca itihas: khand cautha (1800-1874)*, R.S. Jog (ed.), Pune: Maharashtra Sahitya Parishad Prakashan.

Kumar, R., 1968, *Western India in the Nineteenth Century*, London: Routledge and Kegan Paul.

McDonald, E.E., 1968, 'The Modernizing of Communication: Vernacular Publishing in Nineteenth Century Maharashtra', *Asian Survey* 8.

Mahajani, V.M., 1892, 'Prastavana', *Kusumanjali*, Mumbai: n.p.

Pandit, B.S., 1965, 'Kavya', *Marathi vangmayaca itihas: khand cautha (1800-1874)*, R.S. Jog (ed.), Pune: Maharashtra Sahitya Parishad Prakashan.

———., 1968, *Adhunika Marathi kavita*, Nagpur: Suvichar Prakashan (2nd edn.).

Rajadyaksha, M.V., 1946, *Panca kavi*, Mumbai: Karnatak Prakashan.

Ranade, M.G., 1898, 'A Note on the Growth of Marathi Literature', in *Journal of the Asiatic Society of Bombay* 20, reprinted in *The Miscellaneous Writings of the Late Hon'ble Mr. Justice M.G. Ranade*, Mumbai: The Manoranjan Press.

———., 1915, 'Remarks on the Marathi Portion of the Catalogue', in *The Miscellaneous Writings of the Late Hon'ble Mr. Justice M.G. Ranade*, Mumbai: The Manoranjan Press.

Sardar, G.B., 1971, *Arvacina Marathi gadyaci purvapithika (1800-1874)*, Pune: Modern Book Depot (rpt. of the 3rd edn.).

Todmal, H.K., 1963, *Arvacina Marathitila khandakavya: 1850-1950*, Pune: Continental Prakashan.

Tucker, R.P., 1977, *Ranade and the Roots of Indian Nationalism*, Mumbai: Popular Prakashan.

Agarkar, Apte, and the Kanitkars

I. M. P. RAESIDE

Accounts of western India in the 1880s those that are written in English at least, focus on the hey-day of Ranade and the rise of Tilak and Gokhale. Agarkar is mentioned only briefly and almost exclusively for his opposition to Tilak, for he was unlucky to die young.[1] The only Apte we ever hear about is Vamanrao (V.S. Apte) the Sanskritist and first Superintendent of the New English School, but for every Maharashtrian *the* Apte of the 1880s, and the following two decades as well, is Hari Narayan, the first major Marathi novelist whose early work played an immensely important role in the spreading of liberal, reformist ideas.[2] In this paper, I aim to describe the relationship between these two and the Kanitkars, husband and wife, who influenced and inspired a whole generation of Maharashtrian reformers especially in the field of women's education and the question of the treatment of women in Hindu society.

Gopal Ganesh Agarkar was born in 1856 at Tembu near Karhad in Satara District, of a once prosperous but then impoverished Karhad Brahman family. He was bright and industrious and, supported by his better-off relations, became a fellow-student of Tilak's at Deccan College. In 1879, while Tilak was studying for the LL.B. degree there, Agarkar was starting his M.A. with a fellowship more or less as a gift of Principal Selby, who approved of him.[3] As two senior and idealistic students they formed for a time a close friendship in spite of their different characters and very different backgrounds, for Tilak came from a wealthy family and was strong and tough, with something of the inherent self-satisfaction of the well-favoured, whereas Agarkar had not only had to struggle with poverty all his life but was weak and unhealthy. With others they were founder members of the New English School on the significantly un-Hindu auspicious date of 1 January 1880 and later of the Deccan Education Society (24 October 1884) and of Fergusson College (2 January 1885). Together they founded and ran the two papers *Kesari* and *Mahratta* from the beginning of 1881 and together they went to gaol, as responsible Editors, over the Barve libel case of 1882. From now on, however, they became increasingly enstranged and Agarkar found himself holding a minority view which was constantly attacked not only in *Mahratta* but by most of the articles in *Kesari* of which he was the declared Editor. In October 1887 he was forced to resign, and a year later with his younger disciple Gokhale founded his own paper, *Sudharaka* (The Reformer).[4] Tilak and Agarkar's quarrels, probably all the more bitter because of their earlier friendship, went on inside the Deccan Education Society over financial and organizational matters and here it was Tilak who was worsted and resigned in

1890. Two years later, Agarkar became the Principal of Fergusson College, and in 1895 he died. He and Gokhale after him consistently headed the party of reformists who believed and constantly wrote that Hindu society must first purge itself of its injustices, in particular its injustices towards women and towards lower castes, before India would be fit to govern itself. Agarkar himself was almost entirely secular and agnostic in outlook, an attitude that he may well have learned from his guru at Deccan College.[5] All this is fairly well known.[6]

About Hari Narayan Apte there is very little in English,[7] nor have any of his novels and other writings been translated into any European language.[8] He was born in 1864. His mother died when he was four and he was brought up largely under the care of his successful lawyer-uncle, Mahadev Chimnaji, whose only son died young, and who lived a distinctly pleasure-loving life in Mumbai and mixed with many of the Westernized reformers of the city. In 1878 the young Hari moved to Pune to live with his aunt and grandmother but it was still mainly his uncle's money that kept the family going and paid for Hari's schooling, his thread-ceremony, his wedding in 1879, and continued to support him throughout his undistinguished student career at Deccan College, with a brief interlude at Fergusson, from 1883 to 1888. Through these five years, Apte managed to get stuck in Class 1, consistently failing his maths examination so that he never achieved the Previous Certificate. On the other hand, he spent all those years in talk, in voracious reading of English and Sanskrit literature, in learning to read French and a little German, and more and more in writing. As a somewhat aged schoolboy he had contributed juvenile literary criticism to the newly-founded *Kesari*[9] and a year later, on the death of Vishnushastri Chiplunkar, he dashed off a eulogy of 90 Sanskrit *slokas* which, after some judicious metrical emendation by the editor of the erratically published *Natyakatharnava*, was printed. A thousand copies are said, on what evidence I do not know, to have been sold out in two days and Agarkar read excerpts from the poem at the Chiplunkar Memorial meeting.[10] He contributed more articles to yet another Marathi monthly, *Nibandhacandrika*, founded in 1882 specifically in memory of Vishnushastri and to promote his ideas, and in 1885, the year that he spent at Fergusson College (just founded), his first novel *Madhalisthiti* began to appear serially in the journal *Punevaibhava*. It was now, while still nominally a student and working hard to please his uncle, to get a B.A. and obtain the well-paid government job that fell almost automatically in those early days to anyone with a degree, that Apte began to develop his relationship with the Kanitkars, whom he had met first in 1882 as members of his uncle's reformist set in Mumbai.

The Kanitkars are practically unknown outside Marathi writing.[11] Govind Vasudev Kanitkar (1854-1918), who came from a rich educated Pune family, married Kashibai in 1870, when she was nine and he sixteen. He obtained his B.A. at Elphinstone College and graduated at the same time as Tilak, receiving his LL.B. also at the same degree ceremony as Tilak in January 1880,[12] but he stayed with the law and Kelkar and others always referred to him as the *munasupha*—'a civil judge of the lowest grade' as Molesworth puts it. In 1886, he was stationed at Nevasa, north of Ahmadnagar on the Pravara. Govind Vasudev wrote rather old-fashioned poetry and like many educated young men of his day, had become enthused at college by the writings of Mill and Spencer to the extent that sometime in the mid-1880s he embarked on a translation of Mill's last work, *The Subjection of Women*.

What is most remarkable about Kanitkar, however, is that he set out to do, and did, what most reformers of the time only dreamed about—that is to educate his wife into becoming an intellectual companion instead of the usual domestic slave. We have no real information on how he was so successful in this where so many failed, but presumably it was partly due to his own persistence and to the fact that as soon as he took up his appointment he was able to remove his wife from the barriers that the joint family throws up against women's education, but mainly due to the innate intelligence and determination of Kashibai herself.

Around 1885, Hari Narayan Apte was drawn into the education process when Kanitkar told him that on reading the first chapters of *Madhalisthiti*,[13] Kashibai had been so impressed that she was inclined to abandon her own first attempt at a Marathi novel, which was already called *Rangarava*. Clearly, this was little more than a piece of flattery to induce the rising young writer to contribute his exhortations and extensive knowledge of European literature, to Kashibai's intellectual development. There followed the famous correspondence from Apte to Kashibai and Govind Vasudev between 1886 and 1899; famous because it was almost unique in the history of Marathi literature up to 1900.[14] With Kanitkar providing the money and Apte a good deal of the material, together with some editorial supervision and a lot of leg-work, they started the monthly *Manoranjana* in 1886.[15] For this Apte wrote his second novel, *Ganapatarava*, as well as essays and one-act plays based on plots taken from Molière; Kashibai contributed *Rangarava*; and Govind Vasudev, from the first number, began his translation of Mill under the title *Striyanci paravasata* in the first issue. Sadly, the magazine died in 1892, soon after Apte had started his long-lasting monthly *Karamanuka*—the two events are probably not unconnected—and the correspondence, too, sem to have withered and died at the same time. There are only three letters for the whole period from 1893 to 1899. Kashibai's own replies are lost but she went on to produce several more books and died only in 1948.

As far as I know, the Kanitkars' sole appearance in English is in Ramabai Ranade's biography of her husband where they are the unnamed couple who held out nearly to the end against accepting the Shankaracharya's penance over the famous affair of the Panch Howd Mission tea-party.[16] The identification is made by N.C. Kelkar in his work on the life of Tilak.[17]

Apte's first novel had not been noticeably reformist in theme. It started life as a *rupantara*, a recreation in Marathi and in terms of Indian culture of *The Mysteries of Old London* by G.W.M. Reynolds, the Chartist and novelist whose name was once mentioned in the same breath as Scott and Dickens, but is now so forgotten outside India that it appears only in the most compendious histories of English literature. The somewhat lurid plot with its double-dyed villains and its heroine's virtue under constant siege is typical Reynolds[18] and the drunkenness and debauchery of London stews which Apte transposes to a nest of licentious 'reformers' in Rasta Peth was taken as an attack on those who had abandoned orthodoxy and traditional values for the temptations of western vice. However, *Madhalisthiti* came out between 1885 and 86 and this was precisely the time when Malabari was pushing forward his campaign against child-marriage and the maltreatment of Hindu widows[19] and the controversy over the *Dadaji* v. *Rakhamabai* case was at its height.[20] It was the pressure of these events which widened the split between Agarkar and Tilak. As early as in the thirty-first number of *Kesari*, early August 1881, Agarkar had attacked child-marriage as in some respects worse than *sati*,[21] and it was his belief that only the introduction of a government-imposed law would be effective against it that was ultimately anathema to Tilak. Later, in *Sudharaka* Agarkar would demand such government intervention quite explicitly.[22]

The biographers of Apte are usually at pains to point out that he was not an out-and-out reformist, not a keen follower of Agarkar, but always maintained a cautious post well to the rear. In many ways this is true but in his letters to Kashibai Kanitkar at this time and to a certain extent in *Ganapatarava* he displayed a greater commitment. No doubt this was partly due to the influence of Kanitkar, to his patronage and the example he had shown in turning his ignorant nine-year-old bride into Marathi's first lady novelist. Apte's first letters to Govindrav and Kashibai are ingratiating to the point of sycophancy. In part though his more forthcoming views on women's rights must have been in response to the English literature that formed part of his curriculum at Deccan College, to the inevitable Mill and Spencer, and also to the European literature he encountered in his attempts to learn French and German with Father Rivington of the Panch Howd Mission. It has often been remarked that nearly all the books that he mentions in his correspondence, those that he has read and those that he sends or recommends to Kashibai, are English or Sanskrit. Kanitkar's translation of *The Subjection of Women* began, as we have seen, in the first number of *Manoranjana* together with the beginning of *Ganapatrava,* and it is interesting to note how many themes of reform and women's liberation appear in the first chapter.[23]

Two young men are strolling along the road between Deccan College and Bund Gardens, each reading a book. They are in their early twenties—Apte was 22. One is sturdy, well-nourished and confident-looking; the other thin, darker and retiring, obviously much poorer. One feels that Apte may be describing Tilak and Agarkar themselves as far as physical appearance goes, though not, as it turns out, in sentiment. The author has already intervened in one of his typical asides, after describing the topiwalas and memsahebs as they walk hand in hand by the roadside in the cool of the evening, behind them trotting their faithful colleys, spaniels or terriers, to say 'Seeing them no young student could help but feel how blessed were these creatures (*dhanya he prani*—the English couples, not the dogs) and wonder whether such a delightful custom would ever arise amongst our people. But straightaway as the present social climate came to mind the little sprouting hope died almost as it was born.'[24] What are the books that these young men are reading? Ganpatrav, the larger, dominant character, is reaching the end of a small red-bound volume which is none other than Mill's *The Subjection of Women* and several times he tries to interest his friend in the contents, exhorting him to read it for himself and give up for the time his thick, black book which turns out to be Bacon's *Essays*. 'Is there a single marriage like this amongst us?' he asks and proceeds to read the following passage:

Both are equal in virtues, in learning and in powers of appreciation; and so if in one matter one is skilled then the other is in another; in one concern if the opinion of only one is of use then in another nothing would be done without the advice of the other. I do not say what happiness there would be in the marriage of such a man and such a woman because there is no need to describe it to those who can form any idea of that happiness, and to those who cannot it will seem like a mirage however often one describes it.[25]

Apte calls this a summary (*saramsa*) of the original which is this:

What marriage may be in the case of two persons of cultivated faculties, identical in opinions and purposes, between whom there exists that best kind of equality, similarity in powers and capacities with reciprocal superiority in them—so that each can enjoy the luxury of looking up to the other, and can have alternatively the pleasure of leading and of being led in the path of development—I will not attempt to describe. To those who can conceive it there is no need; to those who cannot it would appear to be the dream of an enthusiast.[26]

I have quoted the two passages in full because I suspect that Apte's might well be a direct quote from Kanitkar's translation.[27] If so, it strikes me as rather well done—a simplification that is much more effective in Marathi than any attempt to translate every clause of Mill's elaborate structure.

The other student responds to this effusion by saying that it is better to achieve something little by little than to express grandiloquent sentiments 'and, by the way,' he adds sharply, 'have you taught your wife to read and write yet?' Ganpatrav replies that he is really going to take his wife's education in hand as soon as he has passed his B.A. examination. The exchange lights up one of the main problems of women's education in the 1880s where the husband, be he ever so enlightened, had in any attempt to educate his wife to fight against the united opposition of all the other women in the joint family. Ramabai Ranade has described her own experience in this.[28] Kashibai herself has described equal if not worse opposition, but the extent of her triumph over it no doubt explains why Apte was so fascinated by her and so assiduous in his correspondence. His letters give more than a glimpse of his own efforts in this direction. On 25 September 1885, he ends a mainly literary letter by telling of his difficulties in getting his wife—who it must be remembered he saw only once a week at the most when he paid a ritual visit home from Deccan College—to try to write a short letter to Kashibai whom he asks to write a few encouraging lines.[29] In mid-October it is the same story. He describes in distinctly unfeeling terms how he could not help laughing aloud at his wife's few scrawled lines and awful spelling and how he could not possibly send her efforts to a cultivated lady like Kashibai.[30] Clearly educational psychology played no part in the make up of the most cultivated of Maharashtrian males of that period.

In March 1887, Apte writes:

Your young sister-in-law (meaning his wife) learns nothing. I am doing my best to see that I shall not be accused of leaving her uneducated. Would you just try giving her a good telling off? We don't expect several languages but it's not right that one shouldn't even know one's own and moreover have no desire to learn. Still this is the nineteenth century and we have no independent opinions and independent desires and there's is nothing to be done about it.[31]

I wish I could be sure that this was written tongue-in-cheek. In spite of being fully aware of these difficulties, Apte has just expressed to Kashibai what his biographer[32] calls unrealistic ideas of having women educated exactly the same as men, saying that women are just as fit as men to benefit from higher education. He even declares himself prepared to defend against Mill the view that women are not necessarily the physically weaker sex.[33] Of course, here he is largely flattering the egos of his correspondent, and her husband. It is sad to recall that Apte's poor wife, having lost a baby at some unspecified date at the beginning of 1888, died producing a second in 1891. The child only lived for six weeks. It is well known, too, that Apte, like Ranade before him, succumbed to family pressure and took a second wife, a girl of eleven, a year later, and then more or less refused to acknowledge her existence for the following nine years. It is possible that the self-disgust inspired by his feebleness may have something to do with the withering away of the Kanitkar correspondence in the 90s but there are probably other, more practical reasons: the replacement of *Manoranjana* by *Karamanuka* as already mentioned and the increasing duties devolved on Apte from his position as director of the *Anandasrama*, yet another favour he owed his generous uncle.[34]

Until his uncle died in 1894, Apte had to remain a closet reformer. The opinions that he expresses to the Kanitkars are much stronger than those emerging from *Ganapatarava* which began life anonymously, as being by 'the author of *Ajakalacya gosti*.

It was Agarkar, welcoming the new monthly *Manoranjana* in *Kesari*, who revealed its authorship and Apte was, or at least professed to be, extremely annoyed by this.[35] The character of Ganpatrav is in many respects himself. He is at college and married and wishes to do something about educating his wife. Later on in the book, he writes a letter to his friend Nana and after once again recommending him to read *The Subjection of Women* says:

I am struggling constantly to teach your Vahini and try to get into her head all our plans and all our thoughts for the future, but she is so stupid! Nothing at all goes into her head. . . . She will tell you (some time) in her hen-scratching dog's paw writing. It's true. When she starts to write I have to laugh. It seems to be much harder for women to write than to read—I don't know what other people's experience is.[36]

The circumstances are exactly those of his letters to Kashibai.

After posting the letter to Nana, Ganpat walks by the river at night letting his mind play over all the reforms he wants to see in Hindu society: remarriage for widows, prohibition of child marriage, women's education, the eradication of caste differences. He wants them all straight away. There is no place in his schemes for caution, for the idea of advancing step by step, and Apte goes on to poke gentle fun at his own hero, at his own sentiments expressed to Kashibai and the out-and-out reformist views now associated with Agarkar. Is this the novelist's capacity to see and portray all sides of every question or would he have been less circumspect if he had still been writing anonymously? At all events although *Ganapatarava* consistently propagandizes reform in the treatment of women, Apte always intervenes at some point to counsel moderation. In one of his famous asides he writes, after telling how a mother-in-law of an earlier generation had put a stop to her daughter-in-law's education:

It is a thing to be borne in mind that when, at the beginnings of English rule people became blinded by the dazzle of western reform, their wives restrained them; but for this there is no telling how far the ship of reform would have been carried away and when and on to what rocks it would have run—yes indeed one must call them rocks for there is a great doubt that the ship would ever have reached harbour. As when they put a weight in a boat so that it will not roll too much, or sand in a balloon so that it will not rise too suddenly and fatally, so these women of ours filled the role of that weight and that sand. Only in some matters they overdid it.[37]

Two characters in the novel, Krishna and Ramabai, are a united couple who have educated their daughter and let her reach the age of thirteen unmarried but they are then content to accept the conventions of society and arrange her marriage so long as it is to an educated and forward-looking young man. They represent a kind of ideal middle way, a slightly older version of the Kanitkars perhaps, for Krishnarav, too, is a *munsif* operating in provincial towns and returning to Pune in the May holidays, like Govind Vasudev. There is no moderation though in the depiction of the awful life of Godavari, Nana's sister, cursed and starved by her mother-in-law, beaten by her oafish husband in the respectable Brahman household in Sadashiv Peth, and the novel ends with Ganpat and Nana planning to rescue her, with all that this implies for the future life of a Brahman wife. The harrowing scenes in Godavari's life which forshadow the more celebrated sufferings of Yamu in Apte's first major novel, *Pana lakshanta kona gheto,* were probably the more effective as levers of reform because they were set among more moderately expressed views.

Was Apte moderate through conviction, through cowardice or by artistic choice? Mostly the last, I believe, mixed with a little of the second. In his letters to Govind and Kashibai Kanitkar he is much bolder, but still with reservations. There is the interesting letter, written in English, undated but ascribable to June-July 1888, in which he reacts to the pre-publicity of Agarkar's *Sudharaka.* Note that this seems to be the first that he has heard of Agarkar's leaving the *Kesari* team, which bears out Kelkar's opinion that the divisions between the Tilak and Agarkar camps were scarcely realized by the general public until long after they had become entrenched.[38] Apte writes:

What do you think of this act of Mr Agarkar? Did you know of it before? Is it not an act worthy of a great man? In these days of servile obedience to customs and public opinion are not those men great who unflinchingly come forward, try to break the fetters, and advise others to do the same? I was so very glad to read the prospectus that my first thought was to go and give my respects to the worthy professor with these words, 'Well done, Professor Agarkar, you are a great man. Expose those jackdaws under the garb of peacocks, and if you allow me I shall very gladly and enthusiastically assist you in plucking off their feathers.' But unfortunately I am no one, since I am not a graduate. Day will soon dawn when I shall have a paper of my own. It is not distant. Till then, goodbye to you my thoughts of reform and civilisation.[39]

There is one more extraordinary letter of 19 August 1889, written just before the storm broke over Malabari's Age of Consent Bill, in which he criticizes Kashibai (his tone changes over the years from rather unctuous flattery to that of a kindly elder brother) for being nasty about the missionaries and Pundita Ramabai. Apte writes:

I am not saying that missionaries are pillars of virtue. They are human beings like us. They have their faults like us. But those who teach the Mahars and Mangs whom all Hindus call vile and will not even give the blessing of a sight of God, whose shadows even they will not let fall upon their bodies, are they all bad and you so good? . . . Anyway it's all the same to me if all Hindus are Hindus or if they become Christians, for you know very well my views about religion. . . . And so, Taisaheb, it is simply not true to say that missionaries do good works just because they have government support. Whether it's for Hindus or for Christians government will pay heed only in those matters in which it wants to pay heed. It is not the missionaries but many of our own people who say that the government should lend a hand in destroying our evil customs. But it does nothing. Where there are political and financial reasons the prolonged efforts of the missionaries are of no use.[40]

These were not the sentiments appropriate for the editor of a monthly magazine to which he hoped to attract 2000 subscribers or which, as he would claim, could be left lying around anywhere in the house without endangering the morals of women and children. We hear no more of them.

NOTES

1. For example, Wolpert, 1962: 19-21, 28-39; Tucker, 1972: 256-63, 268-9, 326; Johnson, 1973: 68-75; Cashman, 1975: 49-52. Johnson's account is the fullest.
2. To be fair, Cashman (1975: 89) does once refer to Hari Narayan Apte, but this is for 1910, when he was acting as a friend and informant of Gokhale.
3. Altekar, 1930: 42. Wolpert (1962: 19) calls him a 'superintending dakshina fellow'. The Senior Fellow acted as superintendent of resident students. See Nelson Fraser, 1902. Agarkar appears in a group photograph of 1879, looking quite grand in a gown in the front row.
4. The first number appeared on 15 October 1888.
5. Tucker (1972: 320) says: 'The vogue of Mill and Spencer was popularised in Poona by Professor Selby, the agnostic champion of the younger teachers who were replacing Wedderburn's generation.'

6. Nanda (1977: 26-38) probably does most injustice to Agarkar in English.
7. Joshi 1978, a slim volume in the Sahitya Academy's *Makers of Indian Literature* series is the only one known to me. The standard biography is by N.M. Kelkar (1964).
8. Except the beginning of his historical romance, *Usahkhala*, trans. Lt Col H. Harrison as *Dawn, Chapters I-XII*, Sangli, 1932.
9. In March 1881, according to N.M. Kelkar, 1964: 23.
10. Ibid., 27-8.
11. Vaidya, 1980 consists mainly of Kashibai's previously unpublished autobiography, supplemented by a lengthy postscript giving the life of the Kanitkars after 1909 in greater detail.
12. N.C. Kelkar, 1923: 36.
13. At the time called Part One of *Ajakalacya gosti* ('Stories of Today'), a title which subsequently became a series title for all of Apte's social novels.
14. V.N. Deshpande (ed.), *Haribhauncim patrem*, Satara, 1929 (hereafter *Patrem*).
15. The first number appearing on 26 July (Deshpande, 1929: 16).
16. Ibid., 6th edn. (1935): 161-3, 168-9. The identification is made by N.C. Kelkar, 1923: 307-8.
17. N.C. Kelkar, 1923: 307-8.
18. Raeside, 1970: 91.
19. Gidumal, 1892: 211-16.
20. Kelkar (1923: 186-9) gives a beautifully concise and vivid account of the affair. It is ironic that his biography of Tilak, invariably and rightly called the best, seems to be known outside Maharashtra only in the ludicrously awful translation of Divekar (1928). Heimsath, Johnson and Nanda all quote his flatulent idiocies without, apparently, the slightest awareness that Kelkar is not to be blamed for them—except, perhaps, in countenancing the translation.
21. Deshpande, 1984: 7. Unfortunately, there are no copies in England of Agarkar's collected articles from *Kesari*, first published by himself as *Kesarintila nivadaka nibandha*, 2 parts, Pune, 1887-8. (2nd edn., Pune, 1937-40.)
22. Ibid., 9. 'Vivahanirakarana', 78-81. Note that according to the editors of *Agarakara-vanmaya* there are only a few random copies of *Sudharaka* to be found in any of the major libraries of India (none in the U.K.), so that these selected essays, which are merely reprinted from earlier editions, can only be dated from internal evidence—a task that the editors have not undertaken.
23. Presumably the first chapter, or most of it, came out in the first number of *Manoranjana*. We have a vague idea of the contents of the early numbers from Apte's letters but the chances of finding a complete run of *Manoranjana* are even less than in the case of *Sudharaka*.
24. *Ganapatarava*, 3rd edn., Pune: Aryabhusana Press, 1965, 1.
25. Ibid., 3.
26. J.S. Mill, 1960, *The Subjection of Women* (World's Classics edn.), London, Oxford University Press, 541.
27. *Striyanci paravasata* was published in book form in Bombay in 1902. There are, of course, no copies, in England, nor would I be confident of finding one in India.
28. Ramabai Ranade, 1935: 28-32, 43-5.
29. *Patrem*, 26.
30. *Patrem*, 30-1.
31. *Patrem*, 44.
32. N.M. Kelkar, 58.
33. *Patrem*, 41.

34. Mahadev Apte founded this institutions, well-known to Sanskritists, in 1888 and put Hari Narayan in charge.
35. *Patrem*, 19.
36. *Ganapatarava*, 3rd edn, Pune: Aryabhusana Press, 1965, 58.
37. Ibid., 41.
38. N.C. Kelkar, 251.
39. *Patrem*, 100-1.
40. *Patrem*, 87-9.

REFERENCES

Agarkar, G.G., 1937-40, *Kesarintila nivadaka nibandha*, 2 Pts., Pune (2nd edn.; 1st pub. in 1887-8).

———, 1895-1918, *Nibandha-sangraha* (essays from *Sudharaka*), 3 vols, Pune: rpt. in Natu and Deshpande, 1984.

Altekar, M.D., 1930, *Gopala Ganesa Agarkara caritramaka nibandha*, Mumbai.

Apte, H.N., 1888, *Madhali-sthiti* (serially published in 1885-6).

———, 1919, *Ganapatarava* (serially published in 1886-92—unfinished).

———, 1893, *Pana laksanta kona gheto?* (serially published in 1890-3).

———, 1893, *Usahkala* (serially published in 1895-7).

Cashman, R.I., 1975. *The Myth of the Lokamanya: Tilak and Mass Politics in Maharashtra*, Berkeley.

Deshpande, V.N. (ed.), 1929, *Haribhauncim patrem*, Satara.

Deshpande, D.Y. (ed.), 1984, *Agaraka-vanmaya*, Pt. 1, Mumbai.

Divekar, D.V. (trans.), 1928, *Lokamanya Tilak*, Chennai.

Gidumal, D., 1892, *Behramji M. Malabari: a Biographical Sketch*, London.

Heimsath, C.H., 1964, *Indian Nationalism and Social Reform*, Princeton.

Johnson, G., 1973, *Provincial Politics and Indian Nationalism: Bombay and the Indian National Congress 1880-1915*, Cambridge.

Joshi, R.B., 1978, *Hari Narayan Apte*, New Delhi.

Kanitkar, G.V., 1902, *Striyanchi paravasata*, Mumbai.

Kanitkar, K., 1888, *Kai. Sau. Anandibai Josi yancem caritra*, Pune.

———, 1903, *Rangarava kadambari*, Pune.

Kelkar, N.C., 1923, *Lokamanya Tilaka yancem caritra*, 3 vols., Pune (1st vol. tr. by Divekar, 1928).

Kelkar, N.M., 1964, *Alaukida vidvana samajasevaka Hari Narayana Apte*, Mumbai.

Mill, J.S., 1960, *The Subjection of Women*, London.

Nanda, B.R., 1977, *Gokhale: the Indian Moderates and the British Raj*, New Delhi.

Nelson Fraser, J., 1902, *Deccan College: A Retrospect, 1851-1901*, Pune.

Raeside, I., 1970, 'Early prose fiction in Marathi', in *The Novel in India: its Birth and Development*, T.W. Grant (ed.), London.

Ranade, R., 1910, *Amacya ayusyantila kamhim athavani*, Pune.

Tucker, R.P., 1972, *Ranade and the Roots of Indian Nationalism*, unpublished thesis submitted to the University of Chicago.

Vaidya, S., 1980, *Srimati Kasibai Kanitakara: atmacaritra ani caritra (1861-1948)*, Mumbai.

Wolpert, S.A., 1962, *Tilak and Gokhale: Revolution and Reform in the Making of Modern India*, Berkeley.

An Overview of the Reformist Movement in Maharashtra with Special Reference to Lokahitvadi and Gopal G. Agarkar

PRATIBHA BHATTACHARYA

This paper is presented in two parts: the first deals with the concept of reform and the second with two personalities. It is true that the space devoted to Lokahitvadi is much greater than that given to Gopal G. Agarkar, and that he is dealt with rather more harshly. Also, it may seem one-sided that only his earlier writings are taken into consideration; however, by the time his later writings appeared, which are almost 'second thoughts' in any case, Lokahitvadi had lost his preeminence as the first social reformer, as others of greater stature—Ranade, Telang and so on—appeared on the scene. As Lokahitvadi predates Agarkar by almost 25 years, a comparison between them is only made on the basis of their motives behind advocating reforms.

With respect to Agarkar, he had often been accused by scholars of plagiarizing, especially in his views on religion, though whomever he is accused of plagiarizing (Macaulay, Mill or others), his life was certainly not a slavish imitation of these great figures. Also, two people can share views, and one can be converted to revolutionary thoughts and carry them further in advocacy, without being accused of plagiarism. In any case, Agarkar always wrote in Marathi and even if he was merely translating the thoughts of Englishmen, he could be said to have introduced a new vein of ideas into a hitherto closed community and thus be called creative. Certainly, without him his community could never have had access to the new vision provided by education. In him, English education and Eastern thought found a true synthesis within the native idiom, making him a revolutionary figure. In spite of this, he is maligned, though he would not have cared as he never did during his life, and his course of action remains unique to himself.

Justice Ranade believed that a

> true Reformer has not a clean slate to write upon—his work is rather like the completion of a half-written sentence. We cannot break with the past altogether, for it is a rich inheritance which we have no reason to be ashamed of. However, while respecting the past we must ever seek to correct the practical growths that have encrusted it.[1]

We will focus on a very specific period, spearheaded by different individuals in the context of nineteenth-century Maharashtra. Before we launch into our analysis, however, it would be significant to fit it into the classificatory order of the socio-political processes of transformation. Rao,[2] Damle,[3] Malik,[4] Misra[5] and others have gone to the heart of these processes and feel that reform belongs to the general sphere of social change, albeit in an explicit sense of the term. A large body of theoretical literature on the sociology of movements is available, along with a body of concepts, enabling the scholar to interpret the genesis, ideology, source of identity, organization and leadership of these movements. Sociologically, the structure of the event would be as meaningful as its internal dynamics and social consequences. The idea here is to emphasize the structure of a movement against the socio-political background of a given period in history, since it is a unique blend of the social conditions giving birth to it on the one hand, and the empirical relations of change on the other.

Rao[6] has brilliantly delineated these areas of involvement, and identifies three patterns, collective mobilization, ideology formation and orientation to change. These operate through the three processes of reform, transformation and revolution. The first aims at modifying the belief structure and lifestyle of the members of a group, the last is a total change in all aspects of society, while the middle position is ambivalent. Reform, then, is the introductory phase and is intimately connected with the belief system, world-view, outlook, rituals and lifestyle of the affected group. 'Religion-wise,' the realm of the ideal and its getting tied to a prescribed manner of practices is achieved through the media of symbols. The interpreter class of these was normally legitimized as the agent of privilege and power. Their created miasma of 'ritualism' (which is as far from 'ritual' as 'sentimentality' is from 'sentiment') through vested interests is always at variance with their original formulation, adulterating the content and leading the gullible into error, while perpetuating an unjust level of social and religious equilibrium. As a movement of reform against this, one can cite the early devotional movement of the mediaeval period as being extremely significant for encouraging opposition to the monopoly of a certain section of society over the various paths of salvation, by maintaining that Divine Grace could be achieved through devotion regardless of social position. This movement thus abrogated the principle of birth determining access to salvation with the aid of knowledge and ritual, and brought about a structural change in the sphere of religion.

The reform movement that emerged in British India, however, in addition to doctrinal changes, also led to structural alterations in social relations. In Maharashtra, a chain of scholars came forward to make the benefits of the new education known to ordinary persons, spreading a new social consciousness and providing a broader world-view from a different perspective. Since ideas can be transferred between groups, it was possible to spread a unified social consciousness over a wide population. Misra[7] calls a reformer a 'neo-prophet' in this light, who, with reason, rationality and personal experience, is able to evaluate 'malpractices' (dysfunctions), rather than wrecking the system he tries to nurture it back to health. Synthesis of the new antidote with the experience already gathered, from the knowledge of the actual to the thought of the possible, is visualized by him. He brings about change by creating an awareness in the mind of society about its crippling ills, be they political, social or religious in nature.

This is exactly what the English-educated elite of Maharashtra, and any other part of India, did. The psychological soil of Maharashtra was ready for a new crop of thought. It had gone through the trials of military defeat at the hands of the British; it faced, on the one hand, the indignity of having lost their independence and, on the other, the trauma of an uncertain future at the hands of their new, vengeful masters. It is in this context that the contributions of Lokahitvadi and Agarkar will have to be contrasted, as the false and true prophets, respectively, of a newly emerging social order.

One wonders why Lokahitvadi is considered the first Reformist. Mere urge to write about the ills of society, without the desire to remedy them, in fact perpetuating them in one's own life, hardly makes a reformer. Gopal Hari Deshmukh was a clear product of the days when the curtain finally dropped on the *Peshwai*; and Agarkar of the times when it rose again on an independence movement born in the abortive struggle of 1857. It is important, therefore, to examine the world-view of these two individuals against their historical background.

We are told repeatedly that people rejoiced at the fall of Bajirao II, when he failed to evade in the face of grave odds, the greedy hand of the British. It was the disloyalty of his liegemen and the vacillation of the Satara court that sealed his fate. At his fall, the mammoth bureaucracy associated with the sovereign was left in a vacuum before collapsing completely, unlike traditional peasant societies. By the same logic, the latter is less affected by a change in the seat of power and one must look for the inevitable discontent in the urbanized sphere of society. Due to the relative decentralization of power in the court of the last Peshwa, the 'middlemen' in his court were largely responsible for the chasms between people and ministers, and people and Peshwa. The presence of British lackeys like Balasaheb Natu further spread poison in the minds of the betrayed urban population, seething with indignation against their erstwhile ruler.

English education opened a new window onto the world, especially onto an England coming out of the Industrial Revolution. Such education for Indians undoubtedly had its altruistic side, though it also created a fertile soil for missionary activities (no intervention in native religion was officially acknowledged, but the difference between law and actual practice was, as always, that of 'four fingers'). Also, English education was the one means whereby the rulers and the ruled could communicate and understand each other. As a result, a new category of urban, educated Indians emerged quickly, and to this Lokahitvadi himself belonged; they regarded English rule as a blessing, a Divine decree to teach the corrupt, despicable weaklings of India the advantages of Western knowledge. The Maharashtrian community was thus going through an identity crisis, a social and political confusion, so if an ordinary man like Lokahitvadi was elevated to the status of a reformer, it is hardly astonishing.

True to his status, Lokahitvadi repeatedly blamed the debauchery of the ruler and the unjustified importance of the Brahman caste for the downfall of Maratheshahi, and most of his ilk accepted this diagnosis. He himself had a humble beginning and owed everything to the charity of Bajirao, who interceded for him with the British so that he may have his chance in life equal to those of the more fortunate. If after all this he still blamed the Peshwa for everything, it is a sad comment on human nature. This is not to defend the last Peshwa in any way, merely to point out that he is more sinned against than sinner, more maligned than he deserved to be: born into chaotic times and inheriting a declining *Peshwai* there was little he could do, and in this respect Lokahitvadi's criticism of him is ill deserved.

As for Lokahitvadi himself, he showed a strange psychological duality. On the one hand, he displayed obvious concern for social causes, especially the exploitation and degradation of women; on the other hand, he had an inexplicable partiality for all things British. Though in a different sense and context, he is what Goethe makes Faust say:

> Zwei Seelen wohnen ach! in meiner Brust,
> die eine will sich von der anderen trennen. . . .[8]

Most of his *Shatapatre*[9] appear to be from 1848 to 1850, seven to nine years prior to the Mutiny. The 'reasonable' Lokahitvadi is that of letters 90, 105 and an unnumbered letter of 30 October 1848. In these, he strongly expresses his disgust at the treatment of women, especially child-widows who did not even know the meaning of marriage before they became blighted. He condemns the manner in which society tortured its women through false precedents and quotations from religious texts. He feels that interpreters afflicted with vested interests—the Brahmans he already railed against for corrupting the *Peshwai*—deliberately misinterpreted the sacred texts for their own ends. His letter of March 1848 (No. 53) is an excellent example of his exposition of the ruling religious minority, who cheated gullible laymen, and of his insistence that the *karmakanda* perpetuated through this distortion of the Shastras must go.

However, just as one sees a ray of hope in him, no sooner is the word 'British' uttered than there is a frightening transformation. His letters of 21 May, 15 August and 10 December 1848 as well as an undated one—No. 25—are, to quote only a few, the very epitome of his servile Anglophilia. In his letter of 15 August, for example, he compares Sanskrit knowledge with English scholarship and maintains—much in the manner of Macaulay[10]—that a single English scholar is worth one hundred Sanskrit pundits, and a single room is sufficient to contain all of Sanskrit literature to his time, while English literature is comprised of millions of volumes (*kotyavadhi*). Although a historian, he undoubtedly neglected to make an objective study—the literary output of England prior to 1848, with a few accidental exceptions like Shakespeare, is rather doubtful. Indeed, a semi-barbaric nation which conferred knighthood on pirates like Sir Francis Drake and was only redeemed by the Industrial Revolution and its dubiously acquired colonies, cannot compare with an ancient civilization which projected a highly sophisticated political, literary and cultural reality. When Aryabhatta I (AD 476-550) was using algebra, having already computed the value of π, to study the earth's rotation, England was fighting Scandinavian invaders. So just who wrote those millions of volumes? It is sad to see Lokahitvadi so dazzled by the British rulers that he makes being an Indian sound like an offence; in his letter of 21 May 1848, for example, he maintains that foreign rule over India was a Divine Plan, as God wanted British wisdom to come to the Hindus. In his letter of 10 December (No. 38), he openly sides against the nationalists, and their dream of *Swarajya dharma*. While freely criticizing Scinde and Holkar for overtaxation, he does not breathe a word against the famous 'British methods' of extortion, against Warren Hastings or the expansionism of Wellesley. Indeed, he justifies the British takeover, saying that the latter only wanted trade, and had the Empire foisted on them by the Hindus, which they only accepted willy-nilly. But his most ridiculous letter is about 'that fool Nana Phadnavis', whose only greatness was that he was born in such bad times that he could actually appear to be a 'wise one'.

Lokahitvadi showed the same schizophrenia in his behaviour, as his preachings and practice were diametrically opposed. The louder he decried idol-worship, for example, the more he practised it, as shown by his sojourn in Gujarat. While he abused 'fools' who refused to cross the oceans, he also declined several opportunities to go abroad and even kept his son out of the house on his return from abroad until he performed the necessary purificatory rites. While exhorting his countrymen to recognise widow-remarriage he hid himself when personally asked to acknowledge one through normal social intercourse. One of his friends, Krishnabhat Puranik, even ventured the opinion that to call him a Reformist was a stupid joke. Indeed he was one who liked to run with the hare and hunt with the hound, as his writings have shown here. Worse, instead of succouring the crushed ego of his already disgruntled community, by offering the strong arm of an elder brother, he chose to trample on it some more, and in the false name of shock therapy he sought to send it into an abyss of degradation and inferiority. Instead of using English education positively, to eradicate social evils, he clubbed traditional lore on the head with it, seeking to snuff out all light with the cloud of self-doubt. True liberty would have had to be sought from within, though with the aid of a correctly understood Western education, and this Lokahitvadi—in addition to cowering away from positive action—failed to do. Averse to dealing squarely with personal precept, he is the kind of coward who throws dirt on the passerby through his language and from the security of his locked home.

Agarkar, by contrast, is famous for being true to his preaching even unto death, never bending even in the face of severe adversity. His message was that only when a society is free of its mental bondage to things—right or wrong—just because they are what is done, it is able to understand the concept of liberty. This brought him the title of Samaj Sudharak, his weapon in the freedom struggle. Agarkar's dignity was that of a rock, standing amidst swirling waters of opposition, even though it brought him more foes than friends, as well as slander, misunderstanding and frequent parting of ways with fellow-reformers. No scholar of this movement appears to be adequately aware of his physical and moral courage, and his commitment to reform. Plagued by ill-health, deserted by friends whom he idolized, he carried on his battle alone, and lived as he preached. He even spurned a possibly lucrative job, preferring to remain a poorly-paid schoolteacher. We know him mostly from his brilliant tirades against the exploitation of women, his fight for their upliftment and in particular his advocacy of widow-remarriage. Yet, his English education also made him think about religion and the mire of superstitious beliefs and practices emanating from it, and it would be as well to concentrate on this issue, rather than on his better known crusade for women's upliftment. In particular, one must mention some of his essays on religion: *Dharmakalpana ali kothun*?; *Atma ani pisacca*; *Thadgi ani devle*; *Mrityatmyanci dinacharya*; *Murti pujeche udbhava*; *Murti pujeche prakar*.[11] These deal with the origin, manifestation and perpetuation of religious ideas. Agarkar has introduced different groups of people so as to stress their distinctiveness of rituals, beliefs and modes of worship. He discusses how cenotaphs became temples and how the dead within became vested with divine powers, leading to idol-worship. In his *Devotapattivishayin shevatche char sabda*,[12] he propounds the idea that the all-powerful, invisible God of our belief has emerged from our world of dreams. This offers an individual free spiritual access to any of the areas of desire, nearly a divine power. The living and the dead both have, hence, this power of existing separately from the body. This is how all human qualities, good and bad, have been ascribed to a man-made God. He feels that with all the manifestations of the natural and the supernatural, religion finally boils down to *aham brahmasmi*.

Whether he was here voicing Western thought is immaterial; Agarkar was convinced of the truth of his sayings and was preaching in the native idiom, Marathi. This is no mean achievement. He was a confirmed agnostic and the rationality inculcated into him by English education made him an advanced courier of the times. While suggesting that rationality was the ultimate rung in the ladder of belief, he also stressed that its acceptance should be in the manner of a climber who must relinquish hold of the lower rung before he can fully advance to the next; thus old beliefs must likewise be abandoned in favour of the new. In contrast to Lokahitvadi, Agarkar's English education did not make him ashamed of his heritage, but provided him with a gauge of what must be retained and what eradicated, with a vision that enabled him to pinpoint areas of necessary change. Here, then, is an ideology of change, pre-determined and put into operation rationally. It fits well into the sociological premise of reformism (or reformation) discussed above. Agarkar's ideas of liberty, education and nationalism show profound wisdom and foresight which became the inspiration of not a few. For Agarkar true liberty came from within and unless one earned it oneself by extrication from erroneous beliefs and superstition, one would not be ready to become a truly free member of a truly free society.

At Agarkar's funeral Gokhale quoted from *Julisu Caesar:*

> the elements so mixed in him that nature might stand up, and say to all the world: 'This was a man.'

NOTES

1. S. Natarajan, 1959, *A Century of Social Reform in India*, Mumbai: Asia Publishing House.
2. M.S.A. Rao, 1978, *Social Movements in India*, vol. 1, Delhi: Manohar.
3. Y.B. Damle, 1977, 'Protest, Dissent and Social Reform', in *Dissent Protest and Social Reform in Indian Civilization*, S.C. Malik, (ed.), Shimla: Indian Institute of Advanced Study.
4. S.C. Malik, 1977, 'Problems of Social Change', in *Dissent, Protest and Social Reform in Indian Civilization*, S.C. Malik (ed.), Shimla: Indian Institute of Advanced Study, 19-29.
5. S.C. Misra, 1977, 'Dissent, Protest and Reform: A Note on Definition', in *Dissent, Protest and Social Reform in Indian Civilization*, S.C. Malik (ed.), Shimla: Indian Institute of Advanced Study.
6. Rao, *Social Movements in India*.
7. Misra, op. cit.
8. J.W. Goethe, 1971, *Faust*, Stuttgart: Reclam, 34: ll. 1112-13.
9. P.G. Sahasrabudhe (ed.), 1985, *Lokahitvadinchi shatapatre*, Pune: Continental Prakashan.
10. 'I have never found one among them [Orientalists] who would deny that a single shelf of a good European library was worth the whole native literature of India and Arabia'. Macaulay's Minute on Education, quoted in *Sources of Indian Tradition*, T. du Bary (ed.)., 1958.
11. M.G. Natu, and D.Y. Deshpande, 1985, *Agarkar vangmay*, vol. II, Mumbai: Maharashtra Rajya Sahitya ani Sanskriti Mandal, 176-201.
12. Ibid.

REFERENCES

Damle, Y.B., 1977, 'Protest, Dissent and Social Reform', in Malik, 1977b.

Deshmukh, G.H., 1985, *Lokahitvadinchi shatapatre*, ed. by P.G. Sahasrabudhe, Pune: Continental Prakashan.

Gajendragadkar, P.B., 1959, Introduction, in Natarajan 1959.

Inamdar, N.S., 1984, *Mantravegla*, Pune: Continental Prakashan.

Malik, S.C., 1977a, 'Problems of Social Change', in Malik, 1977b: 19-29.

Malik, S.C. (ed.), 1977b, *Dissent, Protest and Social Reform in Indian Civilization*, Shimla: Indian Institute of Advanced Study, 19-29.

Misra, S.C., 1977, 'Dissent, Protest and Reform: A Note on Definition', in Malik, 1977b.

Natarajan, S., 1959, *A Century of Social Reform in India*, Mumbai: Asia Publishing House.

Natu, M.G. and D.Y. Deshpande (eds.), 1985, *Agarkar vangmay*, Mumbai: Maharashtra Rajya Sahitya ani Sanskriti Mandal.

Rao, M.S.A., 1978, *Social Movements in India*, vol. 1, Delhi: Manohar.

The Passage from Hinduism to Christianity: The Case of Baba Padmanji

H. KOTANI

INTRODUCTION

Facing the cultural challenge of the West, young intellectuals of nineteenth-century Asia tried hard to find a response, and India was no exception. There were many alternatives, ranging from traditionalism to Westernization, and the choice depended on many factors, of which upbringing was one of the most crucial. Another important factor was inherent personal character or mental inclination, and we may also count some others such as education, including the personality of one's teachers. My interest, at present, is to sound the range of responses by young Asian intellectuals of the nineteenth century to Christianity, which had been the spearhead of Western modernity. Specifically, how and why some of them embraced Christianity is the question to which I seek an answer through the example of Baba Padmanji's inner trip to Christianity from Hinduism. He embraced Christianity after trying several alternatives, and thus by tracing his passage, the options open to Asian intellectuals can be appropriately examined.

BOYHOOD TO AUGUST 1849

I divide Baba Padmanji's passage to Christianity into three stages, the first beginning with his boyhood up to the time of his 'Repentance' on 25 August 1849. He was born in Belgaum in May 1831, though the exact date is not known. His father was of the Kasar caste, from Surat, educated in a Gujarati engineering school, and became a government engineer, to be transferred many times in the course of his career. His was a family of orthodox Hindus, with a firm faith in popular, folkloric Hinduism. Baba Padmanji's mother was a devout woman, and he learned various rites from her. After *munji*, Baba Padmanji began to perform almost all household rites by himself, and showed a premature inclination towards religion. However, his father was not so devoted, and as his mother and grandfather were inclined to *shakti* worship, he experienced the indecency of the latter while still a boy.

In 1843, Padmanji was admitted to the Mission School at Belgaum, which was run by the London Missionary Society. However, at that time he showed no interest in Christianity. In 1847, he came to Mumbai for further education and was admitted to the Elphinstone Institution. He soon left the Institution because the Principal of the school did not grant him leave for his wedding. Married in the traditional Hindu fashion in 1848, he moved to Aden on his father's transfer there the same year. In February 1849 he returned to Mumbai alone and stayed with a relative. He was admitted to the Free Church Institution (Mission School of the Free Church of Scotland), School Division, First Class. His teacher was Narayan Seshadri, the famous convert and later a minister of the Church of Scotland. Even at that time, Baba Padmanji remained immersed in the world of Hindu folkloric belief, and felt that it was not good to study under the 'polluted' (*batlele*) Brahman, Narayan Seshadri.[1]

But mission school education began to influence Baba Padmanji's mind. It gave him the first opportunity to reflect on his early life as a wayward Hindu. As long as he was deeply engrossed in the world of popular or folkloric Hinduism, he could not think of an alternative. But in the mission school he came across missionaries and Hindu converts, whose way of life seemed new and attractive to him. Thus, Baba Padmanji now found an opportunity to reassess his life and repent his past. He recalled the many bad habits he had indulged in his early life. For example, in Belgaum, he had committed several thefts during the Holi festival and used to gamble during Divali. In the Elphinstone Institution he had once concealed the money which a Parsi student had lost. He took to drinking in Bombay. And in Aden he committed another 'dirty sin' (*malin pap*),[2] perhaps adultery. All these remembrances now began to torture his mind. On 25 August 1849, he took the following oath:

> The Creator of the World, Shri Jagadguru, Sarvottama Narayana, recalling his holy feet (*yachya pavitra charananten smarun*), I take the following oath: From now on, I shall never do the under mentioned deeds even if my life (breath) goes out. Ishwara, do not give me the will to do such deeds. If I ever do such deeds, let the sin (*pataka*) of killing a hundred cows fall upon my head; Yamaraja, do cause me to fall into Hell (*narak*).
>
> (1) To tell untruths (*asatya*)
>
> (2) Theft
>
> (3) Procuring prostitutes; adultery and things associated with these activities, namely, vulgar songs, dancing, *tamasha* and idle talks.
>
> If I indulge in even one of these activities, then, Parameshvara, I will beg for your forgiveness. I will do repentance. Without your mercy no man can accomplish a good deed.
>
> 25 August 1849[3]

This self-proclaimed oath might appear as simply an ethical or moral declaration, but I think it reveals the real state of his mind at that point in time. By this oath, Baba Padmanji intended to bid farewell to the popular or folkloric Hindu world in which he was brought up. Even though we can find a reflection of Christian ethics in it, the framework and style are those of Hinduism, especially the reference to the 'sin of killing a hundred cows'. Clearly, while he lost faith in popular or folkloric Hinduism, he did not altogether give up hopes of redemption through Hinduism. In other words, he was still searching for the correct path, that is, the path of truth (*satya*).

THE SEARCH FOR TRUTH, AUGUST 1849-DECEMBER 1852

In 1850, probably in June, Baba Padmanji moved up to the College Division of the Free Church Institution, where he began to study under the instruction of J. Wilson, the Reverend R. Nesbit, and other missionaries. This made his inclinations toward Christianity stronger. At the same time, he found numerous friends of varying minds, some of them very keen on Hindu social reform. Baba Padmanji was himself aware of the defects of Hindu society. The bad habits he had indulged in his boyhood were, in a sense, the inevitable products of that society. His new self-consciousness and heightened sense of repentance now led him to criticize his society. His mind was now being pulled in two directions, namely Christianity and Hindu social reform.

During the latter half of 1850, Baba Padmanji seemed to be trying hard to grasp the essence of the Christian faith, but this was no easy task. Even in early 1851, he lacked full confidence in Christianity. In a contribution dated 1 February in *Dnyanprakash* he wrote:

> Some one says that we, [the members] of the sect of the City of Light (*divya nagaracha panth*—i.e. Christians) walk to the end guided by the light of knowledge of the Creator (*shristhtijanya ishvari dnyan*). Then I want to ask him [these questions]: How did you get the description of that city of light? Who gave you its information? What sort of certificate do you have to show there?. . . . And then another question occurs: What is the state of man after death? It cannot be known by way of the knowledge of the Creator. . . . It is my humble plea to any learned man of the above-mentioned sect to publicise the way by which he saves his soul. It will be beneficial to many.[4]

This document shows that he was agitated, eager to learn about the next world, but no explanation satisfied his mind. Even Christianity, or the Christian interpretation of salvation, could not convince him at this time.

In 1851, when he moved up to the higher class in the College Division, Baba Padmanji was given the task of teaching pupils in the School Division. This entailed teaching Bible classes even though he had not become a Christian. He seems to have been absorbed in this task, as he wrote in his autobiography:

> Sometimes I showed so much zeal in disclosing and explaining the matters in the Bible that my students, sensing it, used to ask me: If you believe these stories to be true, then why not become a Christian? On a few occasions, while explaining the Bible, God gave me light that pierced my heart and filled my eyes with tears.[5]

Thus we can infer with certainty that, in the latter part of 1851, Baba Padmanji's dispositions towards Christianity deepened enough to make him confident of matters written in the Bible. However, the decisive factor in this mental change is yet to be investigated.

HINDU SOCIAL REFORM

As mentioned before, the Christian education of the Free Church Institution made Baba Padmanji aware of his moral shortcomings, acquired as an impassive Hindu, and opened his eyes to Hindu social problems. In western India of the nineteenth century the critical attitude to the Hindu way of life, in other words social reform, was known as *sudharna* or *sudharnuk*. Baba Padmanji's attempts to root out his personal vices now brought him close to reform. With his widened horizon, he now sought to expose broader social problems like caste distinctions and discrimination toward women.

On the occasion of the annual examination of the Free Church Institution in April 1851, Baba Padmanji received the Nesbitt Prize for his essay on Hindu domestic reform,[6] which was subsequently published by the Bombay Tract and Book Society. In the same year, he won another prize for his essay *Strividyabhas Nibandh* ('Female Education'), which was also published by the Bombay Tract and Book Society, in 1852. We can observe in these two essays his views on the Hindu family; in the latter he particularly attributed domestic vices to the ignorance of uneducated women:

> In Hindu family, there is neither quietude nor satisfaction of the mind. Mutual affection, sympathy, harmony and good wishes are difficult to detect in Hindu family. Instead we find everywhere mutual ill will, hostility, envy and selfishness; the wish to take revenge; and deceit. If we were to enquire into the causes [of these disaffections], we find that they arise primarily from the stupidity and ignorance of women.[7]

He then urged female education as the first and most urgent step in Hindu domestic reform. In this approach we can see some reflection of his personally bitter—or at least uneasy—feeling about the women in his family. Yet he defended them from the accusation that they were different from men and hence unfit for education.[8] His reasoning owes its arguments to the statement of the Book of Genesis that God created woman from Adam's rib.

Baba Padmanji's outlook on Hindu social reforms was not confined to domestic problems; it included wider issues. In April or May of 1851 he joined the secret society for *sudharna*, Paramahansa Mandali, which was formed in Mumbai around 1849 with Dadoba Pandurang as its spiritual guide. The leading objectives of the Paramahansa Mandali were the abolition of idol-worship and caste discrimination, and the emancipation of women through, for example, widow remarriage. By joining it, Baba Padmanji showed his sincere desire for reform, but it appears that he never really felt at home. The main cause of uneasiness seems to have been the difference in outlook between himself and the leaders of the Paramahansa Mandali. The latter were quite worldly and rational, as exemplified by Dadoba Pandurang's *Dharmavivechan*, written in 1843 or 1844 and distributed in manuscript form.[9] Baba Padmanji, on the other hand was deeply religious and, in the end, his personal, spiritual *sudharna* through Christianity came into conflict with Hindu social *sudharna* as advocated by the Paramahansa Mandali. He was thus forced to choose one and forsake the other.

The decisive moment came on 10 December 1852, when Baba Padmanji read a paper at a meeting of the Paramahansa Mandali. He wrote about it in *Arunodaya*:

> When my turn came, I read a paper prepared on the lecture given by Akrur to cowherd women. On that occasion learned people from Poona were present and some of them

expressed atheistic views while discussing my paper. Their views appeared appalling to me and to some of my friends. There was another strange happening. Our wise and highly respected Chairman, Ravbahadur Ramachandra Balkrishna also participated in the discussion [and appeared to agree with the atheistic views] which made me feel particularly bad. Later, we asked him to explain his disposition. He replied that he only took part in the discussion to enliven it and that, as we should know, he was not an atheist. Even if this explanation be correct, I and some of my friends became so disgusted at the Paramahansa Mandali that we resolved to leave it. In fact, there was nothing in the thinking of the Paramahansa Mandali to quench our thirst; it was only a temporary resting place for men fed up with old ways of understanding. How to gain pardon for sin? Who is the saviour who gives peace of mind? These questions, and others of similar kind, never ever occurred to the members of the Paramahansa Mandali. It seemed to me that they never felt the necessity to ask them.

A person had prepared a book for this Mandali a long time ago,[10] but it was not in print. Seeing my inclination towards Christianity, my friends gave me its copy to read. After refuting caste discrimination, idol worship, and so on, the author tries to show in that book that there is neither religion given by God nor scripture revealed by God. By reading this book, all my respect for the Paramahansa Mandali was destroyed. I could never tolerate the view that denied God's giving man a scripture.[11]

This account makes it clear that a fundamental difference of outlook existed between the leaders of the Paramahansa Mandali and himself. The rational and worldly outlook of the former, which he considered 'atheistic' (*nastik*), estranged him from the society and caused him to leave it by the end of 1852. He thus showed his preference for a personal and spiritual *sudharna* through Christianity, over Hindu social *sudharna* along the lines of the Paramahansa Mandali. By doing so he was abandoning one popular alternative open to young Hindu intellectuals of nineteenth-century India, particularly of Mumbai, who were the products of Western modernity, and who were trying to accommodate it to Indian tradition.

CONVERSION, 3 SEPTEMBER 1854

When Baba Padmanji left the Paramahansa Mandali, he was already quite close to the Church, but he did not rush to embrace Christianity. On the one hand, though he repented his former way of life, he still had confidence in the Veda which he felt to be the scripture revealed by God. On the other, he felt some hesitation in conversion to Christianity because of the difficulties he anticipated would befall him and his family. Thus, after leaving the Paramahansa Mandali, he formed a small society named Satyashodhak, along with some friends. Simultaneously, he read the English translation of the *Rigveda* (by H.H. Wilson) and discussed it with Hindu scholars. Of this he writes:

On severing relations with Paramahansa Mandali, I and some friends of mine formed a society called Satyashodhak. In this, there were some like-minded young men who were of the opinion that God gave man a scripture which must be inquired into. We met on Sundays to pray and discuss religion. We read parts of the Bible and studied other religions.

> About this time, I obtained the first volume of eight of the English translation of the Rigveda by the learned Professor Wilson. My opinion of the Veda changed completely after reading it. There was no sign of divine scripture in it. Far from it. I was convinced that the prayers dedicated to Agni, Surya, Indra and others were mere forms of idol-worship. . . .
>
> After losing confidence in the Veda, I read other books on it and studied them with greater care. I discussed the proofs against Anaditva of Veda with learned Shastris and Pandits. However, their replies did not satisfy me. With this, the last indication of Hinduism as an asylum of mind[12] broke down.[13]

Thus Baba Padmanji lost confidence in the Veda, thereby abandoning yet another path, that of returning to the supposedly pure Hinduism of the Vedas, usually seen as a sign of Hindu fundamentalism. However, this abandonment appears hasty; he did not study the Sanskrit originals, and even of the English translation he read only the first two volumes. It appears that by now he was strongly inclined towards Christianity.

Indeed, for him Christianity remained the only alternative open. He still vacillated about conversion, anticipating difficulties for himself and his family. These feelings are expressed in his letter written to one of his Christian friends in 1852:

> I am convinced that idol worship is bad. Yet I am in the clutches of an idol-worshipping religion. I know that this is my fault. I am ashamed to admit the reasons why I still live in a state like this. I am not prepared for the trials, persecution, hostility and difficulties which we have to endure when we openly accept Christ in India. . . .
>
> I have to acknowledge that I have overlooked my determination to be converted, because of my affection toward my mother, my father, and other members of my family. . .
>
> In my mind, conflict between worldly desires and other-worldly hopes is continuing. I have despaired of my own merits (*svapunya*). . . . I need the saviour. . . .
>
> This is the present state of my mind. I am not overstating the case. I put nothing new in it to please you.[14]

Baba Padmanji finally overcame all hesitation and resolved to be converted publicly. His former teacher, Reverend Taylor of the London Missionary Society, baptized him in Belgaum on 3 September 1854. It was the end of his search for truth (*satya*).

CONCLUSION

Influenced by Western ideas, especially by Christianity, Baba Padmanji began to doubt popular or folkloric Hinduism. This might have led him to a simple modernist outlook, totally committed to Western values. It could also have led him to atheism, in the manner of Dadoba Pandurang and other young intellectuals of Mumbai. Yet another way open to him would have been to reform Hinduism through Western ideas, which could have enabled him to remain a pious Hindu, even if one accepting Western values. Last, he could also have joined the ranks of Hindu fundamentalists, through an attempt to return to Vedic practices even though this would also have been the result of Western influence. However, none of these alternatives satisfied him, and he eventually opted for Christianity. The Report of the Annual Meeting of the Bombay Auxiliary Missionary Society of the Free Church of Scotland, dated 19 December 1854, accurately illustrates Baba Padmanji's intellectual journey:[15]

The fourth addition to the Church is Mr Baba Padmanji, one of the most distinguished and successful students and monitors who have entered the educational Institution since its first formation. This young, native gentleman now in the 23rd year of his age, after obtaining considerable instruction at the Government Marathi School at Belgaum, entered the English School at that place under the instruction of the Reverend Messrs. Taylor and Beynon of the London Missionary Society, at which he remained for about 4 years, acquiring the elements of English reading and of Christian and general knowledge, and during which, at his own house, he perused various tracts and portions of the scriptures, though not infrequently with marked hostility to their contents. In 1847, he came to Bombay for the completion and perfection of his education, according to the views of his father, employed in the higher native department of engineer service of Government. In the first instance he entered the Elphinstone Institution, at which he remained for about a year, when, after residing about 8 months with his father at Aden, he joined the Free General Assembly's Institution in August 1849. At this time, he was, as he states, a firm believer in the Hindu Religion. From the higher classes of the School Division he soon passed into the College Division of the Institution, where he attended the classes of Biblical and Theological Instruction, Logic and Mental Philosophy, English Composition and Vernacular Translation, General and Ecclesiastical History, and other branches there taught. He prosecuted his studies with great zeal and interest and attracted the attention of all his teachers, both European and native, by his attention, candour and success in the acquisition of knowledge. The lectures and meetings of the Mission and services of the Church he also regularly attended. His respect for the Bible increased with his knowledge of its contents and his study of the Christian Evidences and Doctrines. He began in the first instance to doubt the stability and afterwards clearly to perceive the instability of the foundations of popular Hinduism, with the literature of which he was well acquainted. When drawn by the force of conscience from this system of belief, he was hopeful that a refuge might still be left for him in the ancient Vedas or philosophical Vedanta, but expositions of their contents in periodicals and lectures and classrooms, and the perusal of translations of some of their most important portions convinced him that these remarkable writings, instead having God as their author and salvation as their end, bear the most unequivocal marks of fallible paternity and are only the embodiment of the grossest religious error. The writings of the European infidels were put into his hands by an acquaintance aware of his religious anxiety, but a perusal of them gave him no satisfaction. His intimate knowledge of the Bible enabled him to see that these works deal most unfairly with the contents of the sacred writings; and his study of the Evidences of Christianity enabled him, through the spirit of truth and holiness, to repeal their arguments and insinuations. Three Marathi pamphlets of great excellence were published by him—two of which appeared through the Bombay Tract and Book Society—evidently written on principles congenial with the Bible. He became anxious about his relations to God as a sinner needing the pardon of his transgressions and the renewal and satisfaction of his soul. The Gospel offer, with his trust in that Saviour whom it reveals, imparted to him the Gospel hope. He became a Christian in conviction and feeling and the habits of his life. His duty of confessing Christ before men was gradually perceived by him in its imperative form. Yet, desirous of bringing his relatives with himself into the Christian Church, he paused at its portal, calling them both by word and letter to follow him. Last hot season, he left Bombay with his father and joined his family in Belgaum. His feelings in regards to its members ranged between hope and fear. He had long disused heathenish ceremonies and a call by those around him to resort to them on a particular occasion, showed him the danger of his position as stopping short of his full profession of faith in the only living and true God and Jesus Christ whom he had sent. He enjoyed kindest advice and sympathy of the missionaries at Belgaum. He found an endeared home in the family of the venerable Mr. Taylor. He opened a correspondence with us, his teachers, in Bombay. We advised his immediate entrance into the visible Church, and after listening to an excellent discourse by Mr. Beynon, and witnessing a good confession before many witnesses by deed and word, he was baptised by Mr. Taylor on the 3rd September last. He has since returned to Bombay, where he has resumed his duties at the Institution, to our great delight and satisfaction. We cherish the hope that, by his rare literary attainments and devotedness to the service of God, he may be an eminent instrument of showing forth the praise of God in this benighted land.

NOTES

1. Baba Padmanji, *Arunodaya* (Mumbai: Bombay Book Tract and Book Society), 64, 1st pub. 1879; 2nd edn. 1905. In this paper page references are from a 1955 reprint of the 2nd edn. In Padmanji's days Christian converts were called *batya* or 'the polluted'.
2. Ibid., 71-4.
3. Ibid., 80.
4. Ibid., Appendix I, 194-5.
5. Ibid., 82.
6. *Oriental Christian Spectator*, vol. XXII.4 (April 1851): 159.
7. Baba Padmanji, 1852, *Strividyabhas nibandh*, Mumbai: Bombay Tract and Book Society, 44.
8. Ibid., 16.
9. It was first published in 1868 and is reproduced in A.K. Priyolkar, 1966, *Paramahansa sabha va tiche adhyaksh Ramachandra Balkrishna*, Mumbai, 63-122.
10. That is, Dadoba Pandurang's *Dharmavivechan.*
11. *Arunodaya*, 105-6.
12. Meaning the *Rigveda*.
13. *Arunodaya*, 106-7.
14. Ibid., 121-2.
15. *Oriental Christian Spectator*, vol. XXV.1 (January 1855): 17-19.

Pundita Ramabai and Social Reform in Maharashtra

MEERA KOSAMBI

In the remarkable array of public personalities of the late nineteenth and early twentieth centuries involved in the social awakening of Maharashtra, the place of Pundita Ramabai Saraswati (1858-1922) remains ambiguous. Contemporary response to her life and work was marked by several swings, as the public adulation of her Sanskrit learning gave way to shock and outrage at her conversion to Christianity, and as the enthusiastic support of social reformers to her widows' home in Bombay, and later Pune, was withdrawn in the aftermath of allegations of proselytization. Ramabai's final shift to Kedgaon near Pune marked her retreat into virtual oblivion: although the new missionary institution flourished, it remained peripheral to Maharashtrian society. The ambiguity which coloured the contemporary response to Ramabai continues, in some measure, to tinge the current assessment of her contribution.

The time has now come for a reassessment, as the passage of time has served to underline Pundita Ramabai's unique position. Strange as it may seem, she was the only woman leader of the women's cause in Maharashtra, in a cluster of male leaders.[1] She was one of only two public figures who devoted themselves solely to the cause of women's emancipation, the other being Maharshi D.K. Karve who derived inspiration from her example.[2] She was also one of the only two social leaders in Maharashtra who resorted to conversion as a form of protest against the iniquities of Hindu society, the other being Dr B.R. Ambedkar half a century later.[3]

From the vantage point of the late twentieth century, one can explore certain basic themes related to Ramabai's role as a woman and as a social reformer: her own life, the social problems addressed by her and by other reformers, and the distinctiveness of her reform activities. This essay attempts to assess Ramabai's position and contribution in terms of her own temporal and social context, on the implicit assumption of its relevance to contemporary Maharashtrian society—a society not entirely free from the problems of a hundred years ago.

I. THE SOCIAL CONTEXT

The social context of Ramabai's activities was the traditional, caste-bound Maharashtrian society, and especially the numerically small Brahman elite which wielded hegemony over it. Consciousness of caste pervaded the entire society, and the rules prohibiting interdining and intermarriage were strictly observed.[4]

The Brahman preoccupation with caste observances was especially great and any violation had to be atoned for by corresponding measures, ranging from a simple cleansing bath to purificatory rites; while a severe violation or a failure to undergo atonement resulted in total excommunication.

The Life of High-Caste Women

The Brahman women who were the target group of Ramabai's initial activity, were subject to severe social constraints, judging by contemporary accounts (Athavale 1928; Kanitkar 1912; A. Karve 1944; D.K. Karve 1928; R. Ranade 1910; L. Tilak 1973). These women were totally confined to the home and to the extended family which was hierarchically graded along age and gender lines and premised upon the superiority of elders and men. The segregation of the sexes was such that men and women led their lives in separate spheres, to the extent of spending their daytime in separate parts of the house. Thus the women, mostly confined to the house and under constant supervision by older women or by those of higher status, were subjected to strong pressures to conform (R. Ranade 1910).

A woman's life pivoted on the concept of *saubhagya* or the married state. From the time of marriage, usually at the age of eight to ten, she was to devote herself completely to the husband's wishes and well-being; this was also internalized as a 'sacred commitment' (R. Ranade 1910: 303). Marriages were consummated soon after puberty and this led to an extended period of child-bearing, sometimes starting as early as the age of twelve or thirteen (Kanitkar 1912: 28-9). It was not unusual for a woman to deliver up to twenty infants, of which barely half survived (A. Karve 1944: 1-2, 12). The birth of sons enhanced the mother's status, while the birth of too many daughters lowered it. But childlessness was the worst fate, and constituted grounds for desertion.

Physical violence against women (and children, especially girls) was routine (L. Tilak 1973), and could take such extreme forms as whipping or burning with charcoal (Kanitkar 1912: 12-13). There was also the threat of assault from males within the family or from family friends, to which all women, especially widows, were vulnerable (A. Karve 1944: 63-9).

Within the household, the worst lot was unquestionably that of widows, especially child-widows and childless widows. Branded with the stigma of having 'killed' her husband (through sins in past lives), the widow was considered inauspicious even to look at, was disfigured by the shaving off of her hair, and compelled to wear drab clothes, eat only once a day, and generally to spend her time in household chores and religious rituals (Athavale 1928: 27-34).

Remarriage was out of the question for widows, while it was common for widowers of any age. Since the bride was always a pre-pubertal girl, the age difference between the partners, usually about ten years, could increase to thirty or forty years. Polygamy, though not common, was sanctioned by custom. The problem of widows was all the more acute because of their wide prevalence due to early and universal marriages, high mortality rates, and a ban on their remarriage. It was compounded by the inhuman treatment meted out to them.

Temptations of the flesh, combined with seduction or assault, led to several cases of suicide, infanticide or refuge in temples (D.K. Karve 1928: 148-53).

Education was a rarity for women, training in household tasks, given in early childhood, being regarded sufficient for their needs (Athavale 1928: 1-2). Although some families taught the rudiments of literacy to their daughters or daughters-in-law so as to enable them to keep household accounts or read simple religious works, this was by and large disapproved of. An effective measure preventing women's education was the common belief causally linking literacy with widowhood (R. Ranade 1910: 35)

A woman's life was, in brief, confined to the home and the family, while the family structure rested on the institutionalized subservience of, and frequent verbal and physical violence against, women.

Social Change and Reform

The late nineteenth century found this society in a state of turbulence due to the impact of the British Government (established on Bombay Island in the 1660s and in the rest of western India in 1818), which was channelled mainly through three agencies: legislation, Western education and Christian proselytization.

The legislation pertaining to women included the Abolition of Suttee Act of 1829 aimed at ameliorating the lot of widows, and the Widow Remarriage Act of 1858 which legalized the remarriage of upper caste widows, hitherto unlawful. A few decades later, the Age of Consent Act of 1891 raised the age at marriage to twelve for girls and sixteen for boys.

Western education in western India was introduced not by the government, but by Christian missionaries whose activities were allowed after 1813, when the English East India Company's monopoly of Indian trade was abolished. The Bombay Government followed suit, and opened schools and later colleges throughout the Bombay Presidency (Kosambi 1980: 82-4). The influence of Christianity permeated the educational system, whether run by government or the missionaries, and was reinforced by the proselytizing activity of the missionaries, which ranged from street-corner preaching and distribution of free Christian literature in regional languages, to religious debates and actual conversions to Christianity (Hewat 1953).

The three-pronged attack of British legislation, Western education, and Christianity, buttressed by the obvious superiority and achievements of the British Government, caused a general feeling of insecurity and inferiority. It also resulted in hard soul-searching on the part of the social leaders, which was reflected in the social reform activity of a series of prominent figures, most of whom were Brahmans, as, for example, 'Lokahitvadi' Gopal Hari Desmukh, Sir Ramakrishna G. Bhandarkar, Justice Mahadeo Govind Ranade, Principal Gopal Ganesh Agarkar, and 'Lokamanya' Bal Gangadhar Tilak, with a sprinkling of non-Brahmans such as Jyotiba Phule. Social reform was also coupled with religious reform, especially in the establishment of the Prarthana Samaj, a theistic religious movement which drew upon Christianity as well as the Bhakti tradition of

Maharashtra and espoused social causes, and which counted Ranade and Bhandarkar among its members (Masselos 1974: 81-5).

From the early days, the major institutions in urgent need of reform were identified as the injustices against lower castes and women. The issue of caste inequality was promoted vehemently by Brahman reformers, such as the pioneer Lokahitvadi (LS: 251-4), but found a militant champion in Jyotiba Phule, who (although a Mali or 'gardener' of intermediate caste) spoke in the name of all the oppressed castes against Brahman hegemony (especially in his booklet, *Slavery*; see Phule 1969: 67-176.) Women's issues had an urgency mainly for the Brahmans and the areas of reform were the age at marriage for girls, widow remarriage and education for women.

These women's issues were dealt with by all the major social figures. Lokahitvadi passionately protested against the plight of widows and stressed the need for their remarriage. He also advocated the postponement of marriage until maturity, allowing for the free choice of both partners, and education for women in order to encourage them to flout unjust customs. At the same time, he cautiously introduced the theme of gender equality (LS: 221, 234-5). The theme of the equality, or even superiority of women was further elaborated by Phule (1969: 358-61). Bhandarkar actively supported the Age of Consent Bill and Ranade supported women's education and widow remarriage (Phadke 1975). Agarkar emphasized gender equality in terms of intellectual and other capability and advocated freedom for women to decide whether, when, and whom to marry (Agarkar 1984: 193-208, 408-29).

However, the connection between preaching and practice was tenuous, and the reformers' performance varied greatly. Some largely confined their activities to raising public awareness and moulding public opinion through journalistic writings and speeches, and fell short of decisive action on the issues they strongly advocated. Lokahitvadi, for example, refused to attend a widow's wedding due to family pressure (LS: 41), and Ranade, as a widower of thirty-two, married not a widow but a girl of eleven at the insistence of his father (R. Ranade 1910: 25-33). Among the active reformers were Bhandarkar who arranged the remarriage of his widowed daughter, for which he was unsuccessfully threatened with excommunication by his caste-fellows (*Sudharak*, 22 June 1891: 2, 3; 12 October 1891: 3), and Phule, who opened the first girls' school in 1851 with the help of his wife whom he himself had educated, and later a rescue home for pregnant Brahman widows and their children (Keer 1974: 28-31, 86-7). Some champions of widow remarriage, such as Vishnushastri Pundit and later D.K. Karve, themselves married widows in the face of massive opposition and social boycott (Phadke 1975: 27-8; D.K. Karve 1928: 54-73). But pioneering large-scale effort for the rehabilitation of needy women, starting with high-caste widows, had to await the advent of Pundita Ramabai.

II. RAMABAI'S LIFE AND WORK

Against the backdrop of conventional society, Pundita Ramabai's life stands out in sharp contrast, as seen from the available autobiographical material (which include *A Testimony*; recollections reproduced in Adhav 1979; and *Letters and Correspondence*) as well as several biographical works (Adhav 1979; Bodley 1981; Fuller 1922; Macnicol 1926; Sathe 1975; Sengupta 1970; Shah 1977; Thakre 1950; D.N. Tilak 1960 and Vaidya 1985).[5]

The Formative Phase, 1858-78

Ramabai's father, Anant Shastri Dongre, was a Chitpavan Brahman from Karnataka who had studied at Pune during the last years of Peshwa rule, and been deeply impressed by the sound of the Peshwa's wife reciting Sanskrit verses. This inspired his own ambition to teach his wife Sanskrit, which was fulfilled in his second marriage at the age of about forty-four to the nine-year-old Laxmibai.

Having earlier enjoyed royal patronage in the state of Mysore for many years, Anant Shastri now settled down with his new wife at the sacred forest site of Gangamul where he ran a small educational institution, and cultivated rice and fruits to support it and his family. Six children were born to the couple of whom three survived, Ramabai being the youngest.

Anant Shastri was an orthodox Brahman except in the matter of women's education, which he had to publicly defend in a large assembly of Shastris, and in deferring Ramabai's marriage due to the shock of her elder sister's conventionally early and unhappy marriage. In all other matters the children were raised according to orthodox Brahman ways. Ramabai's childhood and early youth were spent in an endless family pilgrimage across the length and breadth of the country. The family supported itself by narrating the Puranas and spent the residue on honouring holy men. Secular education and employment for earning a livelihood were strictly prohibited as incompatible with the way of life of superior Brahmans.

The life of poverty and hardship took a toll of both Ramabai's parents and her sister in 1876. This was a period of emotional trauma and practical difficulties. Being among strangers who questioned their Brahman credentials, the family had to manage the last rites for Anant Shastri themselves. After Laxmibai's death, two kind Brahmans offered help to carry the body, with Srinivas and Ramabai making up the four pall-bearers. Ramabai and Srinivas then continued the pilgrimage in the old style, suffering the same poverty. In one extreme incident, on a visit to Kashmir the pair had to bury themselves up to the neck in sand on the river bank, as the only protection against the bitter cold. Finally, in 1878, they reached Calcutta.

Entry into Public Life, 1878-82

In Calcutta the twenty-year-old Ramabai was much lionized and publicly honoured for her Sanskrit learning and extempore verse compositions with the titles of 'Pundita' and 'Saraswati'. Accompanied by Srinivas, Ramabai travelled extensively in eastern India lecturing on the status and emancipation of women on the strength of the Hindu sacred books. In Calcutta she also came into contact with the leaders of the Brahmo Samaj and the philosophy of Theism.

Two years later, on the sudden death of her brother, Ramabai married his friend and her persevering suitor, Bipin Behari Das Medhavi, a Bengali lawyer. The inter-communal and inter-caste marriage (he being considered a Shudra) was registered in a civil court, and drew much criticism from the orthodox and the ostracism of the couple by some relatives. It was a happy marriage which produced a daughter, Manorama, but ended abruptly with Bipin Behari's death in 1882.

Left a widow with an infant daughter, at the age of twenty-four, Ramabai decided to visit Maharashtra on the invitation of well-wishers. It says much for the strength of caste-bonds in contemporary society that, in spite of having had no roots in Maharashtra, she was immediately claimed by Justice Ranade and his friends as 'one of us Konkanastha Brahmans' (R. Ranade 1910: 10). Her fame had preceded her, and with the support of social reformers such as Ranade she immersed herself in social work. Building on an earlier women's organization in Pune she started the Arya Mahila Samaj, adding branches later at Mumbai and other parts of Maharashtra. The aims of the Arya Mahila Samaj were to work for the deliverance of women from the traditional evil practices of child marriage, and for their uplift in terms of religion and morality.

About this time Ramabai appeared before the Hunter Commission on Education to outline her programme for women's education and to stress the need for educating women as physicians, so as to treat women in need of medical care, since male doctors had no access to them.[6] While her proposals were receiving the attention of the Empress and were being implemented as Lady Dufferin's reforms, Ramabai herself developed a plan to study medicine. The ground was prepared by taking lessons from a missionary teacher, and by making arrangements for accommodation with the Community of St. Mary the Virgin at Wantage, England, where she proposed to support herself by teaching Marathi to the Sisters leaving for western India. The passage was raised by writing a Marathi book, *Stree Dharma Neeti* (Morals for Women). In late 1882 Ramabai sailed for England with her infant daughter and a woman companion.

Travels in England and America, 1883–8

The trip to England was quite an adventure for a single woman in that day and age, and Ramabai received much opposition even from friends and well-wishers. Although this did not daunt her, what proved to be a real obstacle was the realization that her increasing deafness ruled out medical studies.

Ramabai's religious life had been in some turbulence during the previous years. Her originally staunch belief in the tenets of Hinduism had been shaken by the way her parents' lives had ended, and acquaintance with the ideas of the Brahmo and Prarthana Samaj had offered alternatives, as had the Christian doctrine introduced by missionaries. In late 1883, after a period of uncertainty and contrary to her earlier declaration, she and her daughter embraced Christianity.

After the disruption of her planned medical studies, Ramabai registered as a teacher-student at Cheltenham Ladies' College, to study natural sciences and English, teaching Sanskrit in return when interested students were available. Her three years as a boarder at Cheltenham were sponsored by the Wantage Community.

In 1886 Ramabai travelled to the USA to attend the graduation of a distant cousin, Anandibai Joshi, the first Indian woman to receive a medical degree in that country. In the USA Ramabai travelled widely, giving public lectures on the emancipation of high caste Indian women. Support for her cause was provided by the Ramabai Association of Boston, which was established in 1887 and which pledged material assistance for a secular women's school in India for a period of ten years. The Ramabai Association of the Pacific Coast, an auxiliary, was founded in 1888. Ramabai made a special study of kindergarten schools and women's vocational training centres, prepared illustrated Marathi textbooks (paying for the costly illustration plates from the sales of *The High Caste Hindu Woman* written for the purpose), and generally equipped herself with the necessary knowledge and experience to start a women's educational institution. In late 1888 Ramabai returned, via Japan (where she gave a few public lectures during a brief stay), to India where her daughter Manorama awaited her, having spent most of her time at Wantage.

Return to India and the Widow's Home, 1889-93

Ramabai met with a warm welcome in Mumbai and Pune from social reformers and supporters, in spite of their earlier misgivings about her conversion, since religious conversions on intellectual grounds were not unknown in those days. Favourable publicity also attended the opening of her Home for high caste women,[7] mainly widows, in the presence of an impressive gathering of public personalities. It was named Sharada Sadan or 'Home of Learning' (which was also the name of the first pupil, though not a widow, to join) and was located in Chowpatty in Mumbai. The Sadan was supported by the Ramabai Association of the USA, and the local Advisory Board included Bhandarkar and Ranade. Strict religious neutrality was to be maintained in the running of the Home, no religious propaganda being allowed.

At this time, Ramabai also remained active in public life, appearing as one of the handful of women delegates at the National Social Conference held in Mumbai in 1889, to oppose the practice of disfiguring widows. In early 1891 she participated in a women's convention to discuss, and support, the proposed Age of Consent Bill.

In 1891 Sharada Sadan was shifted to Pune, the heart of Maharashtrian orthodoxy, so as to be accessible to more high caste widows in need of help, and also in the interests of economy. Ramabai's policy of religious neutrality, at this time, seems to have amounted to a kind of tight-rope walking: while open persuasion was not used, various inducements were offered to encourage the girls to attend her private prayers and to take an interest in Christian literature.

Later that year, a storm broke out over allegations that the inmates were encouraged to follow Christianity. Many of the girls were promptly withdrawn by their guardians and the members of the Board tendered their resignations directly to the Ramabai Association in Boston; the Association issued a reprimand to Ramabai for her violation of the rules of secularity and sent a commission to investigate the matter. Its enquiry established that no effort had been made to proselytize, and that it was Ramabai's good example and kind behaviour which had inspired some of the girls. The Association decided to continue its support.

Missions and Proselytization, 1894–1922

Ramabai's confidence in American support had, by now, weakened and she resolved to make the Sadan self-supporting. To this end she bought a 100-acre site at Kedgaon, about 40 miles south of Pune, with the intention of cultivating it. Here the Sadan was reorganized in 1898. The bare and rocky plot was gradually converted into a green expanse by digging a well, planting an orchard, and through the incessant efforts of the inmates.

To the original Sharada Sadan, intended as a home for high caste Hindu widows, were gradually added new sections: Mukti Sadan (Home of Salvation) for Christian women, and Kripa Sadan (Home of Mercy) for victimized women, attached to which was the Mothers' Home for unmarried pregnant women. Separate sections were gradually added for blind girls (where braille was taught by a specially trained foreign teacher) and for orphans. Dormitories, school rooms, work rooms for different skills taught and practised there, and the Mukti Church made up the large complex. Formal schooling at Kedgaon included a kindergarten and several school sections, while vocational education encompassed a very wide spectrum, including tailoring, embroidery, knitting, laundering, weaving of saris and carpets, cooking, teaching, nursing, gardening, oil-pressing and operating a printing press.

In 1898 Ramabai revisited the USA after the completion of the ten-year period of American support, and a new Ramabai Association was formed whose rules allowed conversion but only if voluntary. Hindu inmates were allowed to practise their own faith, although idol-worship was not allowed. The new establishment at Kedgaon, especially the Mukti Sadan and Church, changed the complexion of Ramabai's activities. Proselytization was a matter of policy and mass conversions took place regularly.

In the meantime, Ramabai's active efforts to reach widows in distress took her on an adventurous though not very successful trip, disguised as a pilgrim, to holy places in north India, where temple priests routinely exploited homeless widows. From 1896 to 1900 Ramabai was actively engaged in famine relief in the Central Provinces and Gujarat, and hundreds of famine victims, mainly women and girls saved from starvation and moral degradation, were accommodated at Kedgaon. By 1900 the population of the Kedgaon Mission was close to 2,000.

The turn of the twentieth century witnessed intense religious activity at

Mukti Mission, including the introduction of religious revivals where the women were visited by the Holy Ghost and affirmed their Christian faith. These revivals culminated in mass conversions. Prayer bands were also organized and dispatched to different areas to preach the gospel. Ramabai's proneness to fanaticism and dictatorial tendencies increased with the years, with greater emphasis on discipline and set forms of worship.

Towards the end of her life, in 1919, the King Emperor honoured Ramabai with the Kaiser-i-Hind Gold Medal. In 1921 Manorama, an able and devoted assistant in all her mother's work, died in Miraj after a few years of hectic activity in establishing and supervising a mission and school at Gulbarga in the Nizam's dominions. The following year Ramabai herself passed away at Kedgaon at the age of sixty-four.

Ramabai's Writings

In the midst of a life packed with public lectures, establishment and maintenance of organizations, uplift of the oppressed, and travel, Ramabai found the time for a prolific literary output both in Marathi and in English.[8]

Ramabai's earliest works had a social critical orientation. Her first book *Stree Dharma Neeti* (Morals for Women) written in 1882, was a guidebook for the welfare of the 'helpless and ignorant' Indian woman, by educating her and making her capable of self-improvement (1967: 5-6). Reflecting the major preoccupations of the day, it dealt with the qualities necessary in a woman for a meaningful life, the need for female education and self-reliance, the duties of married life, the upbringing and education of children, and the nature of cooperation between men and women.[9] It received much congratulatory attention as a pioneering effort by an educated woman to extend the benefits of her knowledge and experience to other women, a task previously only performed by men (*Kesari*, 1 August 1882: 3). While the tone of this book was that of moral and practical instruction, the tone of *The High Caste Hindu Woman* was generally militant. It was written in 1887 for Western readers and described the position of contemporary Brahman women against the background of Hindu sacred law, especially the Code of Manu. It emphasized the discrimination and injustice against women in childhood, youth, married life and widowhood, and outlined measures for improving their lot. The book ended with an appeal to Western men and women to help free 'my countrywomen . . . from life-long slavery and infernal misery' (1981: 59).

These were paralleled by two travelogues. The booklet *Maza Englandcha Pravas* (Travels in England) written in 1883 was found to be 'informative and amusing', while testifying to Ramabai's 'intelligence and courage' (*Kesari*, 16 October 1883: 4-5). *United Stateschi Lokasthiti ani Pravas-vritta* (The Peoples of the United States) was a frank appraisal of social, political, economic, religious and educational conditions in the USA. It was written largely in that country and completed and published in Bombay in 1889, and is consciously positive in its approach (1889, Preface: 1-2). *A Pamphlet on Famine Relief* described the devastating famine in the Central Provinces and Gujarat in the closing years of the nineteenth century.

There was also a group of religious works. *A Testimony*, written in 1907, is an autobiographical account which traced her spiritual evolution before and after her conversion to Christianity. It was 'a testimony of the Lord's goodness to me', intended to bring 'the light and life' of Christianity to 'the people of this land [who] are steeped in sin and are sitting in a terrible darkness' (1977: 46). A four-page pamphlet, *The Word-Seed* was written in 1908 in order to 'bear my testimony to the wonderful power of the blessed name of Jesus Christ to save sinners' (Adhav 1979: 104). Ramabai's scholarly Marathi translation of the Bible from the original Hebrew and Greek was a massive enterprise which took many years to complete, and was published posthumously at the Kedgaon Press in 1924. Her object in revising the old translation (written in 'high Marathi language') was to make it simpler and understandable to 'the common men, women and children, especially those living in villages' and also to 'rid the Bible, and the Christian language in general, of certain words [i.e. Sanskrit words] which express idolatrous ideas' (Adhav 1979: 201-2).

Ramabai's substantial correspondence from 1883 onward has also been published as *Letters and Correspondence* (1977), with notes from her spiritual godmother, Sister Geraldine.

Ramabai's Personality

Contemporary accounts testify to Ramabai's charisma. Her physical appearance was attractive, with a petite figure and the fair skin and greyish green eyes often found among Chitpavan Brahmans. It had an immediate appeal, which led Rabindranath Tagore to poetize her as 'a white lotus' (Sengupta 1970: 205). She always wore a simple white sari and wore her hair close-cropped as a token of her widowhood. But it was her personality which made a lasting impact; it was a curious blend of self-confidence, courage, vast learning, immense capability and forthrightness on the one hand, and modesty, gentleness and compassion on the other.

From all that has been written by and about her, it appears that the basic traits which formed the motive force of her personality were her individualism, devotion and compassion. Of these, her individualism is the most surprising in the context of a society which has always rested on collectivity. The answer perhaps lies in her imperfect socialization into traditional Hindu society. Ramabai's formative years were spent on the periphery of society, as endless pilgrimages took the family across the subcontinent without a permanent resting place. The support and constraints of community life were unknown to her. Coupled with this fact were the physical hardships which toughened her body and taught her self-reliance and the capacity to make decisions for herself. This was another surprising phenomenon in a society of ascribed roles and collective decision-making. Ramabai's religiosity, it may be assumed, stemmed from Anant Shastri's rigorous, orthodox Brahman way of life, and was probably buttressed by Hindu society's insistence on religious anchorage as a precondition for social existence. The need for religion as the sustaining force of life was strong enough for Ramabai to discard a religion which could no longer fulfil this function, and to accept another. Her inner compulsion to proselytize probably also stemmed from this need, even in face of the realization that it would lose her the only support she had within Hindu society: the liberal reformers might accept her conversion, but they would certainly condemn her proselytization. Compassion for the oppressed which provided the goal for Ramabai's life was a counter-balance to her individualism. It was also closely linked with her acceptance of Christianity as a religion which promised forgiveness and mercy, rather than dire punishment for human errors.

III. RAMABAI AND CHRISTAINITY

Conversion to Christianity was probably the single most important event in Ramabai's life: it provided the impulse and guiding force for her work on women's emancipation, and it shaped contemporary perspectives on her work.

Scattered through Ramabai's writings are a few prominent issues related to her disillusionment with the Hindu doctrine and way of life, and to the contrast between Hinduism and Christianity. They stem basically from Ramabai's strong need for religion as a personal belief system and as sustenance for her social work, and form an indictment of the philosophy (*vichara-dharma*) and practice (*achara-dharma*) of Hinduism, which failed to satisfy her on those counts, and a defence of Christianity which did.

The issues related to her personal belief system focused on the two doctrines. Ramabai saw in Christianity a revelation of spiritual truths of a higher order than Hinduism [*Dnyanodaya*, 48 (1889): 133–4]. More importantly, in Hinduism, spiritual salvation is contingent upon an individual's sex and position in the caste hierarchy; while Christianity treats all as equal in the sight of God (*Testimony*: 13–14). The denial of salvation to women in Hinduism was a source of great spiritual distress to Ramabai. This aspect of her conversion has been consistently played down by her critics and followers alike. Further, Hinduism stresses conformance to duty in following one's *dharma* or appropriate way of life, and links the fruits of one's *karma* to future rebirths and the possibility of salvation, while Christianity offers salvation to all believers, here and now. The Hindu has to earn his salvation, the Christian receives it as a free gift from God (ibid.: 25–7). The Hindu doctrine is metaphysical and impersonal, while Christianity is a direct contract between God and each individual. 'The Hindoo religion brings the Supreme Being, the Holy God to the level of a creature like myself, but Christianity lifts man up to God' (*Lectures and Correspondence*: 151).

The social work issues related to the practice of the two religions. Ramabai felt keenly that the Hindu social order is preserved through emphasis on sin and punishment, while the strength of Christianity lies in its offer of forgiveness and compassion. This was sharply brought home to Ramabai during her visit to the Rescue Home at Fulham run by the Wantage Sisters, which impressed her deeply. Whereas the Hindu scriptures advised dire punishment for 'fallen' women, such as being driven out of town and left to be eaten by wild animals, Christianity enjoined compassion and efforts for their rehabilitation. It was after this visit that Ramabai 'began to think that there was a real difference between Hinduism and Christianity' (*Testimony*: 19-20).

An additional factor related to Ramabai's own social needs, although she herself has not explicitly mentioned this, was probably the need for a supportive social structure. She was 'greatly impressed by the holy life of the Sisters and their sublime unselfishness', although this was not the cause of her accepting the Christian faith (cited in Adhav 1979: 136). The need to belong to a community was, however, strong, as recorded by Max Muller who had met Ramabai several times at Oxford: 'as she told me, she could no longer stand quite alone, she wanted to belong to somebody, and particularly to be able to worship together with those she loved and who had long been so kind to her' (cited in Sengupta 1970: 136). Here we perhaps find another manifestation of Ramabai's social isolation due to her peculiar circumstances, which had deprived her of her entire family and which had never provided her with a stable community to belong to.

A vital issue regarding Ramabai's conversion, much debated even during her lifetime, has been whether it was a spiritual or practical necessity enabling her to carry on her work for women. The *Kesari*, in its brief obituary of Ramabai, cited Professor Karve's institution and the Seva Sadan under Ramabai Ranade's guidance as proof that 'deeds for the uplift of women, such as their education, could be performed while remaining within Hindu society' (11 April 1922).[10] The same argument has been advanced more recently, with the addition that if Ramabai had followed the Prarthana Samaj a while longer, its strong emphasis on the Bhakti tradition could have provided her the emotional and spiritual comfort lacking in mainstream Hinduism (Ghate 1973). Both these claims, however, seem doubtful in view of the fact that the inherent discrimination against women in Hinduism was pivotal in Ramabai's conversion, and that her position in society was far from identical with that of a Brahman man or of the widow of a much honoured social leader. Again, Ramabai's rejection of the Prarthana Samaj was based on her perception of its unsatisfactory nature on philosophical and metaphysical grounds, which she herself has outlined (*Testimony*: 17-18; Adhav 1979: 136). In this connection it is important to note that the compulsion for conversion following religious conviction was itself a necessity in the traditional and pre-secular Indian society of the time. This society mandated formal adherence to a religion, and its insistence on the observance of daily ritual was too inflexible to allow belief in the tenets of another religion (Rege 1973: 25).

Ramabai and Her Contemporaries

Contemporary reaction to Ramabai was a complex fabric woven out of many strands. It was a reaction mainly to three related but conceptually separable aspects of Ramabai's personality and work: as a woman, as a social reformer championing the women's cause, and as a Christian. It would appear that the reaction of her contemporaries to her as a social reformer was heavily biased by their negative opinion of her as an unconventional, and Christian, woman.

The perception of Ramabai as a woman was inevitably coloured by the contrast she presented to the prevalent ideal of womanhood. This ideal was embodied in the life and thoughts of Ramabai Ranade, who maintained that the true commitment of a woman was to serve the interests of her husband, and that education should not lead women to cross the limits laid down by convention but make them more obedient to their husbands and elders (R. Ranade 1910: 126-7, 303). It was fully endorsed by a progressive leader such as Gopal Krishna Gokhale in preference to the Western equality of the sexes (Gokhale in R. Ranade 1910: 5), and by one of the few educated women of the day, Kashibai Kanitkar, who applauded Justice Ranade for having married a young girl whom he could mould according to his ideas and for having presented his countrymen with the ideal woman (Kanitkar in Umakant 1925: 12-15).[11]

Pundita Ramabai clearly deviated from this ideal, being first an educated and independent woman who had married late and outside the community out of choice, then a widow who was prominent in public life. It was an extraordinary combination, difficult for many of her contemporaries to comprehend and even more to tolerate.

Nor was it tolerated by convention-bound women who were themselves subject to all the constraints and pressures which Ramabai disregarded. Their outrage was hardly suppressed: here was a Brahman woman whose father had married her to a god in her childhood (which was the popular explanation for her remaining long unmarried), but who had committed the sacrilege of marrying a man, that too a Bengali, had then destroyed him and destroyed her marriage—on top of all this she had now come to contaminate the rest of the world (R. Ranade 1910: 102-3)! The outrage was unabated by Ramabai's orthodox Hindu lifestyle, including her regular recital of the Puranas, prior to her conversion, and she was treated like an outcaste.

Ramabai's impressive and independent personality, and the publicity she received, were also to arouse to hostility of conventional men like Tilak, who set great store by modesty (interpreted as self-effacement) in a woman's behaviour (Kelkar 1923: 331). Also, the very fact of a woman giving public speeches was considered unpalatable, and occasioned much vulgarity among male audiences (Agarkar 1984: 267-9).

Even so, as a social reformer Ramabai was initially lionized by most public personalities of the day. Even the largely orthodox *Kesari* eulogized her enterprise on behalf of women:

> It is a wondrous deed to collect a few thousand rupees in a foreign land by begging for the sake of people of an alien religion, and alien tradition and customs. The fact that this was accomplished by an unsupported weak woman through her firm resolve, courtesy, and other laudable traits makes us pity our menfolk and also makes us feel proud that such an extraordinary woman was born in our midst. By our misfortune she became somewhat alienated through her religious conversion which is a sad event indeed. (12 February 1889: 3)

And again:

> Today our society greatly needs women like Pundita Ramabai. The beneficial effects of good education will be more firmly imprinted on people's minds through her mature thinking and zeal for her countrymen's uplift than through any other institution or through other efforts. It is our misfortune that the Pundita changed her religion. However, it would not be proper to abandon her only for this reason. It is to her credit that she has not given up her national pride together with her religion. (28 May 1889: 2)

The *Kesari's* tone underwent a complete change, however, when suspicions of proselytization in the Sharada Sadan were aroused in 1891, and the paper accused her of deceit, mischief, and even wickedness, turning into her bitterest enemy. Beginning with an editorial on 14 July 1891, the *Kesari* referred to the Sharada Sadan not as the 'Widows' Home' but as the 'Widows' Mission House', and later described Pundita Ramabai's famine relief activities as the 'incarceration' of 2,500 girls and women at Kedgaon under her 'jailership' (28 January 1902: 5; 27 January 1903: 4-5).. Tilak himself reacted negatively to all of her social reform activities, viewing them as a disguise for proselytization, and talked of the inmates at Kedgaon as 'widows caught in Ramabai's net during the unique opportunity of the famine years' and voiced a general alarm about her nationwide missionary designs [*Kesari,* 12 January 1904: 5, reproduced in Tilak 1976 (V): 492-4]. Also, the *Mahratta* confessed that 'Female education is dear to us, but certainly not at the expense of our religious beliefs' [cited in *Dnyanodaya* 52 (1893): 274].

The progressive *Sudharak* initially defended her staunchly against the *Kesari's* attacks (6 July 1891: editorial). The liberal Hindu social reformers retained their support of Ramabai's activities for a few years and later diverted it to the widows' home opened by Karve in 1896, on his 'being convinced that our people will not benefit from the Sharada Sadan here' (*Sudharak*, 25 May 1896: editorial).

IV. AN ASSESSMENT OF RAMABAI'S CONTRIBUTION

The social reform climate of late nineteenth-century Maharashtra was shaped by certain basic issues related to women's emancipation: raising the age at marriage, allowing widow remarriage, and the need for providing education to women. In concurrence with these issues Ramabai was active in educating women for self-improvement and in forming a favourable public opinion. This message was spread through writings, speeches, and even Purana recitations, demonstrating the use of appropriate media. She actively campaigned for the Age of Consent Bill, partially through the Arya Mahila Samaj, and also publicly advocated late marriages for girls. She also accepted, though did not try to promote, widow remarriage. In fact, the most publicized widow remarriage of the day was that of Ramabai's pupil Godubai to Professor D.K. Karve, which was celebrated at Sharada Sadan in 1891 and at which Ramabai herself played the role of mother. She strongly advocated education for women, including medical and vocational education, the latter being provided at her own institutions for women.

But Ramabai was much in advance of her contemporary reformers in several ways. The first was her emphasis on the need to reinstate the woman to her rightful position in the family and in society. While other social reformers, practically all men, emphasized the need for redressing the worst social injustices against women yet keeping them in an essentially subordinate position, Ramabai's activities were predicated upon the woman's inherent equality with men, and in her capacity to do what men did. Her educational home for Hindu widows and girls was a radical departure from tradition in many ways: it provided the first real alternative for women who were earlier confined to the home and its restrictive atmosphere, by giving them shelter, education, and also the means to earn a livelihood. This leads to her second distinction: even while other reformers were largely fighting on issues and principles, Ramabai showed concrete achievement. Her organizational capacity in transforming the message into reality was truly awesome. Her Arya Mahila Samaj, Sharada Sadan and Mukti Mission were institutions which pioneered shelter and education of women, and her greatest contribution to the women's cause.

Ramabai's third distinction was her vision of women as a force in public life. Even while others were content to limit women's participation in public life to occasional speeches at social gatherings, Ramabai envisioned a role for Indian women in political life as well. At a time when a leader like Ranade did not approve of such a role, Ramabai headed a small delegation of women at the Fifth National Congress at Mumbai in 1889 (Kanitkar in Umakant 1925: 6; *Sudharak*, 24 February 1890: 1). Her own nationalist commitment was strong and she was openly critical of the British colonial regime:

> the British Government is sucking Indian blood and wealth while per force despatching Indian armies to march and fight the British battle in Egypt and ultimately die over there. This very Government has swallowed our Indian States wherever they found no legitimate heir to the throne! Not to speak of other atrocities enforced by treatment of the Press Act; Act that reduced the age of Indian Civil servants; Act of disarmament, and worst of all, our poor Indian citizens have to pay so many taxes to Government, whether we afford them or not. We may as well sell our houses and properties but we must pay the taxes levied by the Government!' (cited in Adhav 1979: 37)

Perhaps Ramabai's best known anti-government position was during the plague of the closing years of the nineteenth century. The measures rather high-handedly implemented by British soldiers under the instructions of the Plague Commissioner had aroused widespread anger and resentment, especially at Pune. G.K. Gokhale, then in England in connection with a Finance Commission, was notified of this discontent by several friends, and at their behest he lodged a complaint before the Parliament. When this resulted in an enquiry instituted in Mumbai, all these friends retracted their earlier statements, begging their names to be kept secret, so that Gokhale had to withdraw the charge and tender an unconditional apology. Only Ramabai was willing to openly support him and testify; she also took up the matter with the Plague Commissioner. For this show of courage she was honoured in a Marathi ballad (Kelkar 1923: 331).

Ramabai was the only woman leader of the movement for women's emancipation, at a time when public opinion was not ready for female leadership. The *Kesari* strongly criticized her discussions of women's issues at the Arya Mahila Samaj on the grounds that 'it is the men's task to uproot the evil practices [related to women], women will not be able to handle it for many years to come. . . . Our women will have to remain subservient to men for a long time' (18 August 1892: 5), although it welcomed her Sharada Sadan a few years later. Supporters like Dr Bhandarkar, in complimenting her achievement which had outshone those of most men, cited her as an example of what an educated woman might accomplish if her potential were allowed to develop, concluding that it was obvious whether her sex should be described as the weaker or the stronger (*Sudharak*, 1 August 1892: 3).

In juxtaposing Ramabai with other social reformers, one is struck by the contrast in their impulses to reform. Lokahitvadi, Phule, Bhandarkar, Ranade, Agarkar and Karve were products of Western education (Phadke 1975), and its all-pervasive criticism of Indian society. Ramabai had received no Western education at all until well after her entry into public life, and what propelled her were her own observations of women's sufferings during her family's extensive travels, which 'made us think much of how much it was possible to improve the conditions of women and raise them out of their degradation' (cited in Adhav 1979: 59), and her intensive study of the Hindu sacred books, especially when she was requested by the learned pundits of Calcutta 'to lecture to the Purdah women on the duties of women according to the Shastras', with the resultant realization of the spiritually inferior status of women in Hinduism and their inability to attain salvation (*Testimony*: 18–19). Thus her awareness of the need for the uplift of women predated her exposure to Western ideas and resulted from the internal dynamics of Hindu society.[12] This exemplifies 'orthogenetic' social change, or change from within (Redfield and Singer 1954), in contrast to 'heterogenetic' change arising through contact with alien cultural influences, as in the case of other social reformers.

Paradoxically, Ramabai was the only social reformer to leave the Hindu fold, and the effects of her conversion on social reform is a central question in assessing her contribution. Theoretically it may be argued that the potential of Ramabai's conversion in initiating social reform (on the grounds of discrimination against women in Hindu society) was lost since she never tried to transform her personal protest into a social protest; significantly, neither her supporters nor her adversaries took notice of this issue.[13] On a more practical plane, the religious philosophy of Christianity, conducive to the rehabilitation of victimized women, undoubtedly played a supportive role in her activities, and her entry into the Christian fold brought moral and material support from women in Christian countries to whom she could appeal as a coreligionist.[14] That this support, especially the funding, was crucial to the running of her organization was emphasized by all her contemporaries. Against this has to be set her consequent alienation from mainstream Hindu society and its reformers. Through her proselytization she lost touch with the upper stratum of society, whose women she strove hardest to help, and in the process also lost potentially capable helpers to her cause, such as the likes of her own favourite pupil Anandibai Karve, who was to become an asset to D.K. Karve at Hingne. Access to such assistance would have spread Ramabai's work for women's education and self-reliance widely through the upper castes which she had primarily tried to reach.. As it happened, she had to contend mostly with lower caste women and underfed famine victims, whose problems were more of survival and basic socialization than of education and achievement. This is not to deny that their need was as great as that of upper caste women, merely to submit that their impact on society could not be as great as the latter's.

Another far-reaching consequence of this alienation was the distorted perception of all her actions by Hindu orthodoxy. The general image of Pundita Ramabai as a deceitful woman, who used social reform as a guise for her Christian missionary designs still lingers in the popular Maharashtrian mind, almost a hundred years after the real storm blew over. Hence the need for a reassessment.

In the ultimate analysis, it would appear that Ramabai's contribution was as much through her work as through her personality, both of which show the usual tension between the reformer and her society, and the imperative of the reformer to carry at least some sections of society with her. Here was a woman, entirely alone, a widow too and thus socially unacceptable, who, in the face of massive opposition, struggled for the causes she believed in. Here was a devout Hindu who turned Christian as a matter of spiritual conviction, again in the face of opposition. Here was a social reformer who pioneered several aspects of women's emancipation. In her sixty-four-year-long life Ramabai spanned the cultural distance of several centuries: with her roots in traditional Hindu society, her vision was focused on a modern egalitarian society of the future—a society which still remains a vision.

NOTES

1. Other women connected with social reform, such as Savitribai Phule and Ramabai Ranade, were drawn into public life mainly through the activities of their husbands.
2. In the case of other reformers, all men, women's issues were only one component in a series of educational, economic and political issues that engaged their attention.
3. Both Ramabai and Ambedkar reacted intensely to the inbuilt discrimination against women and Shudras in both Hindu philosophy (as reflected in the very denial of salvation to them) and in the functioning of Hindu society. However, basic differences in their conversions exist: for the former it was a personal statement, for the latter a political and social one. Also, while the former embraced the religion of the colonial rulers, the latter adopted a native, albeit forgotten, one which was more appropriate in an independent India (Keer 1962). A detailed discussion of Ramabai's conversion has to be omitted here due to lack of space and will appear elsewhere.
4. The ritual *jati* or caste hierarchy of Maharashtra has the numerically small 'literate' castes of Brahmans and Prabhus at the top, followed by a large middle layer of Marathas (of whom a small elite claims Kshatriya descent, and the bulk, also known as Kunbi Marathas, are peasants), several artisan and service castes of a status equal to the peasant

Marathas, and finally the 'untouchable' *jatis*. Caste segregation was strictly observed. Intermarriage was rare even among Brahman subcastes, and was actually advocated as a desirable reform by many, starting with Lokahitvadi in 1848 (LS: 259).

5. The major events in Ramabai's life, recounted here, have been replicated in most of these works; separate references are therefore not provided.
6. The need for training women in the medical profession was also being actively propagated by people such as Dr Sakharam Arjun of Bombay (Varde 1982: 188–9).
7. The preoccupation with caste is understandable in a society that had to guard carefully against polluting contact with lower castes. A revealing case in point is that of D.K. Karve's Home for Women, where he refused to admit the sister of Vitthal Ramji Shinde, a well-known Maratha reformer, since he considered the time not yet ripe for the mixing of castes (cited in Shah 1977: xxvi).
8. Only Ramabai's best known books, which also had a social impact, are listed here. For a complete list see Adhav 1979: 237–8.
9. As an example of this preoccupation may be mentioned the *Vividha Jnana Vistara*, a Marathi monthly, which ran several articles advising women on proper conduct, e.g. Book 3 (1871): No. 9; Book 20 (1888): Nos. 1-2.
10. All English translations from Marathi are by the author.
11. The issues regarding the women's role and the positions of social reformers or women's emancipation and equality have been further explored in Kosambi 1988.
12. This was not an entirely unknown phenomenon. Some reformers themselves based their arguments on the authority of the Shastras (e.g. M.G. Ranade 1889). More interesting is the fact that the first known attempts at widow remarriage in Maharashtra predated British rule (Malshe 1977).
13. Tilak, her persistent adversary, for example, chose to ignore her arguments regarding the treatment of women in Hinduism, and in a famous editorial note in the *Kesari* [12 January 1904; reprinted in B.G. Tilak 1976 (V): 492–4] parodied her conversion mercilessly, without once refuting her statements. He even suggested that she exchange her title of Pundita for that of Reveranda, wherein many have detected a play upon the Marathi word *rand*, a vulgar epithet applied to a widow.
14. A report in the *Bombay Guardian* of Ramabai's address in Philadelphia in 1886 on the occasion of the graduation of Anandibai Joshi substantiates the point: 'The simple manner in which she pressed the teaching of the New Testament upon her audience was irresistible. And when the earnest little lady suddenly closed her address by asking an American company of educated and refined men and women to join with her in a moment's silent prayer "to the Great Father of all the nations of the earth" on behalf of the millions of her Hindu sisters to whose cause she has given her life, there was something almost startling in the strangeness of the unique situation' [cited in *Dnyanodaya* 5 (1886): 274–5].

REFERENCES

Abbreviations

HCHW: *The High Caste Hindu Woman* by Pundita Ramabai.
L&C: *The Letters and Correspondence of Pundita Ramabai.*
LS: *Lokahitavadinchi shatapatre.*

Adhav, S.M., 1979, *Pundita Ramabai*, Chennai: The Christian Literature Society.

Agarkar, G.G., 1985, *Agarkar Vangmaya* of Gopal G. Agarkar, ed. by M.G. Natu and D.Y. Deshpande, vol. 1, Mumbai: Maharashtra State Board of Literature and Culture.

Athavale, P., 1928, *Mazi Kahani*, Hingne.

Bodley, R., 1887, 'Introduction', *The High Caste Hindu Woman* by Pundita Ramabai.

Dnyanodaya, An Anglo-Marathi weekly published by the American Marathi Mission at Mumbai.

Deshmukh, G.H., 1985, *Lokahitavadinchi shatapatre*, ed. by P.G. Sahasrabuddhe, Pune: Continental Prakashan.

Fuller, L.B., 1922, 'Pundita Ramabai: Scholar, Saint and Servant', *Dnyanodaya* 81: 122-3, 162-3, 178-9.

Ghate, V.D., 1973, 'Dharmantare', *Vicharavilasite*, Mumbai: Mauj Prakashan.

Hewat, E.G.K., 1953. *Christ and Western India* (2nd edn.), Mumbai.

Kanitkar, K., 1912, *Anandibai Joshi yanche charitra ya patre*, Mumbai: Manoranjak Granthaprasarak Mandali.

Karve, A., n.d., *Maze Puran*, ed. by K. Karve, Mumbai: Keshav Bhikaji Dhavale.

Karve, D.K., 1928, *Atmavritta*, Hingne.

Keer, D., 1962, *Dr Ambedkar: Life and Mission*, Mumbai: Popular Prakashan (2nd edn.).

———, 1974, *Mahatma Jotirao Phooley*, Mumbai: Popular Prakashan (2nd edn.).

Kelkar, N.C., 1923, *Lokamanya Tilak yanche charitra*, vol. 1, Pune.

Kesari, Marathi weekly published in Pune.

Kosambi, M., 1980, 'Bombay and Poona', Stockholm (unpublished doctoral dissertation in sociology, Stockholm University).

———, 1988, 'Women, Emancipation and Equality: Pundita Ramabai's Contribution to Women's Cause', *Economic and Political Weekly—Review of Women's Studies* (29 Oct. 1988): WS 38-49.

Macnicol, N., 1926, *Pundita Ramabai*, Calcutta: Association Press.

Malshe, S.G., 1977, *Don punarvivaha prakarane*, Mumbai: Mumbai Marathi Grantha Sangrahalaya.

Masselos, J.C., 1974, *Towards Nationalism*, Mumbai: Popular Prakashan.

Pundita Ramabai, 1887. *The High Caste Hindu Woman,* Mumbai: Maharashtra State Board of Literature and Culture (rpt. 1981).

———, 1977, *The Letters and Correspondence of Pundita Ramabai*, Compiled by Sister Geraldine, ed. by A.B. Shah, Mumbai: Maharashtra State Board of Literature and Culture.

———, 1882, *Stree dharma neeti*, Kedgaon: Ramabai Mukti Mission (rpt. 1967).

———, 1907, *A Testimony*, Kedgaon: Ramabai Mukti Mission (rpt. 1977).

———, 1889, *United Stateschi lokasthiti ani pravasvritta*, Mumbai.

———, 1908, *Word Seed* (rpt. 1979).

Phule, J. *Mahatma Phule samagra vangmaya*, ed. by D. Keer and S.G. Malshe, 1969, Mumbai: Maharashtra State Board of Literature and Culture.

Ranade, M.G., 1889, 'Shastric Texts on the Subject of Infant Marriage and Vedic Authorities for Widow Remarriage', in *The Status of Women in India* by D. Gidumal, Mumbai: Fort Printing Press, 299-336.

Ranade, R., 1910, *Amchya ayushyatil kahi athavani*, Pune: Dnyanprakash Press.

Redfield, R. and M. Singer, 1954, 'The Cultural Role of Cities', *Economic Development and Cultural Change* 3.1: 53-73.

Sudharak or The Reformer, Anglo-Marathi weekly published at Pune.

Rege, M.P., 1973, 'Prabodhanache Swarup', *Bharatiya prabodhan*, Pune: Samaj Prabodhan Sanstha.

Thakre, K.C., 1950, *Pundita Ramabai Saraswati*, Mumbai: Ramakrishna Book Depot.

Tilak, B.G., 1976, *Samagra Lokamanya Tilak*, 5 vols., Pune.

Tilak, D.N., 1960, *Maharashtrachi tejaswini Pundita Ramabai*, Nasik: Nagarik Prakashan.
Tilak, L., 1934–5, *Smriti chitre,* ed. by A.D. Tilak, 4 vols., Nasik: Nagarik Prakashan.
Umakant, 1925, *Kai, Shri Ramabai Ranade*, Mumbai.
Vaidya, S., 1985, *Eka samajik shokantikechi nayika, Sankraman*, Pune: Shrividya Prakashan.
Varde, M., 1982, *Dr. Rakhmabai: ek artha*, Mumbai: Popular Prakashan.

Three Letters of Govind Babaji Joshi on Inter-*jati* Marriage in Nineteenth-Century Maharashtra

N. K. WAGLE

Govind Babaji Joshi (1826-1901) belonged to the middle and late nineteenth century group of Maharashtrian social thinkers and activists who were pioneers in challenging Maharashtrian *jati* and family mores and practices. Bal Shastri Jambhekar,[1] Mahadev Govind Ranade,[2] Gopal Hari Deshmukh,[3] Gopal Agarkar,[4] Bhau Mahajan,[5] and Vishnushastri Pandit[6] are a few of the Maharashtrian Brahman intellectuals who are regarded as the leading critics of Maharashtrian society and the innovators of social change in Maharashtra. Despite Govind Babaji's writings and public lecturing—his published works include sixteen books and tracts and he served as Public Preacher in Baroda state from 1873 to 1893—his contributions to Maharashtrian thought remain largely unknown. Arun Joshi's biography of Govind Babaji in Marathi is the only book which surveys his achievements in the economic, social and political arena.[7] Arun Joshi credits Babaji with the founding of the first cooperative bank (1863 to 1869) in Vasai, Govind Babaji's native place. As a political activist, he was a founding member of the Vasai and Thane Jilha Association.[8] As a nationalist, Govind Babaji intermittently attended the annual Indian National Congress sessions from 1887 to 1894 as a delegate from Baroda state.[9]

Govind Babaji was a pragmatist, whose efforts focused on the clearly attainable. This paper deals with his convictions that Indians should begin their efforts in a small way, by allowing their daughters to intermarry with other close sub-castes with whom they did not mind eating. More importantly, at the time of marriage the girl should have passed the age of puberty. True to his convictions, he had his daughters married when they were thirteen and fourteen respectively. Although a Konkanastha Brahman, Govind Babaji married his elder daughter to a Karhade Brahman and the younger one to a Deshastha, transcending barriers among the three Brahman castes of Maharashtra.

CHILD MARRIAGE

By arranging his daughters marriages at the ages of thirteen and fourteen in 1881 and 1884 respectively, Govind Babaji was clearly acting against the shastric injunction that a girl should be married before reaching the age of puberty. It was considered a matter of great shame to keep the daughter unmarried thereafter, especially in the Brahman milieu of Govind Babaji.[10] But as early as the 1840s, we witness a growing concern among Maharashtrian Brahman intellectuals about widow-remarriage and child-marriage. The issues were debated in a liberal, and rather charged, Marathi journal, *Prabhakar,* edited by Bhau Mahajan.[11] In the 9 February 1842 issue a person signing off as *Dharmabhimani* (proud of *dharma*) writes,

The man should be married after the age of sixteen and the woman after the age of ten. If one goes by this recommendation, then there would be very few instances of child widows and the *dharma* will be secured (*dharma rakshana hoil*).[12]

In the 17 May 1847 issue of the *Prabhakar,* a 'Hindu' proposes later dates for marriageable couples, and tries to explain the shortcomings of marrying very young.

A girl should be married at the age of sixteen instead of eight, and the boy at twenty. Due to the child marriages, the differences surface in ways of thinking between husband and wife, and become sharper in the later years. Lack of mutual love results from this situation, and sometimes it may lead to adulterous behaviour.[13]

Gopal Hari Deshmukh's (Lokahitvadi) *Thoughts On Marriage,* written in the late 1840s, appears to be the most liberal view of the subject.

There should not be a rule (*niyam*) stipulating that a girl should be married at a specific age. When the girl reaches the ages of eight to nine, the parents became anxious to marry their daughters as early as feasible. "Otherwise [the parents think] the people will scoff (*lok hastil*) at us, saying, 'How can these people let their daughter grow so big and keep her unmarried?" This mode of thinking is absurd (*vedepanaci samjut ahe*). Why should one be so preoccupied with this subject? Childhood [of a girl] should be spent receiving education. When she is under twenty years of age, and is mature enough, with her and her parent's consents, she should be married (*tice va aibapace sammatane lagna karave*). This is a profitable course of action to take. In these days the parents forcibly arrange marriages of their daughters. Their self-interest motivates them to sell off their daughters. Can this not be construed as a great oppression (*julum*)?[14]

Thus in the middle of the nineteenth century, the issue of child-marriage was on the agenda of Maharashtra's progressive thinkers. By 1870, we find concrete organizational efforts to implement post-puberty marriage among girls. A committee to oppose child marriage was established in 1873 in Ahmedabad under the leadership of Gopal Hari Deshmukh (Lokahitvadi) who became its president with Bholanath Sarabhai as vice-president. At a meeting convened in Ahmedabad as many as 125 people took an oath that they would not get their daughters married before they reached puberty.[15]

Govind Babaji, besides marrying his daughters in their post-puberty period, used to deliver public speeches on the bad effects of child marriage.[16] He had identified that subject as one of the key topics for a public preacher.[17] For instance, in 1887 in his sojourn in Madras, he lectured to the Gujarati Khedwal caste resident in Madras, on the 'Disadvantages of Childhood Marriage'.[18] Govind

Babaji's mettle is commendable in the light of the inaction of leading opponents of child marriage like Lokahitvadi, who was unable to exercise his influence over such matters within his immediate family. His granddaughters were married, for instance, at the ages of four and five![19] Much to the chagrin of many progressive Maharashtrians, Mahadev Ranade, a leader who advocated a ban on child marriage, at the behest of his parents, married his second wife when she was eleven years old.[20] The subject of child-marriage drew public attention in 1885, when preliminary discussions began on the issue. These appear in the subsequent Age of Consent Bill which became a reality in 1891. The actual debates on the Act now became acrimonious, and split Indian public opinion.[21]

That Govind Babaji should enter the initial phase of the controversy concerning the Age of Consent Bill is not surprising. Citing passages from *Samsara Kaustubha* and *Prayogaratna* (*Narayana Bhatti*), Govind Babaji wrote that these books did not advocate child marriage.[22] Significantly, Govind Babaji backed his statement with verifiable contemporary data which showed that, because of the child marriage, women suffered from diseases associated with birth, tuberculosis and stomach disorders, and died young. Instead of creating widows out of the child-brides, according to Govind Babaji, it was better that they remain unmarried. Girls suffered additionally when their husbands died young. He quoted the Bombay Presidency census data of 1881 to prove his point. Of 1, 653,475 girls below the age of ten, 171, 852 or one in sixteen was a widow.[23] Govind Babaji was unequivocally critical of double standards.[24] He presents an example of a Prarthana Samaj leader—a vocal critic of child marriage—who married his ten-year-old daughter to a 19-year-old son of another Prarthana Samaj leader. Govind Babaji cites this story to make a point that despite the public protest, the leaders had failed to follow their own advice in action. Govind Babaji wanted government intervention in banning child marriage. He therefore endorsed the Age of Consent Bill.[25] Remaining consistent with his progressive views, Govind Babaji was in favour of widow-remarriage. He did not care if people ostracized him for his views. He was responsible for arranging a marriage for his widowed sister.[26]

CASTE AND MARRIAGE

With the inception of *Darpan*, the Marathi and English weekly (1832-40), run by Bal Shastri Jambhekar, intensive dialogue took place on the issue of caste. In issues of the *Darpan*,[27] 30 March to 27 April 1832 a bold view was advocated that human beings are of one species, and all human beings originated from one seed. The dialogue was intended to prove that varna was an unnatural institution created by human beings, and not nature's work. The Marathi journals like the *Prabhakar* (and the Christian missionary voice in Marathi as expressed in *Jnanodaya*) sustained the dialogue started by the *Darpan*, and soon it became a major plank for the Marathi writers who began to criticize the value of the caste system. The ubiquitous Lokahitvadi was also engaged in attacking the system. His

Marathi penmanship concerning marriage and caste appeared in the *Prabhakar's* 17 December 1848 issue.[28]

The Brahmans [of Maharashtra] are split into *jatis*: Deshastha, Konkanastha, Palashe, Kudale, Jaula, Khristi, Tirgul, Karhade, Kirvant, Shenvi and others. The differences among them are many. They do not intermarry. But this custom is bad. Brahmans should freely establish matrimonial alliances (*soyarik*) with other Brahmans; there should not be any hindrance in this respect (*brahmanamashi Brahmanani khushal soyarik karavi tyams tyavishayi atkav asu naye*). If a Konkanastha finds another Konkanastha as a suitable match, then there should be a matrimonial alliance between them. But there should not be any prohibition imposed on a Konkanastha if he were to engage in matrimonial alliance with a Deshasthas; whichever is more convenient to the party should be practiced.

Govind Babaji was against the *jati* system, and, in the letter translated below, holds it responsible for dividing the country. He looks back nostalgically at the ancient period, when the *jati*s freely married, which led to the unprecedented prosperity of India. He wanted the ruling political and intellectual elites to help incapacitate the *jati* system. On his part, he would undermine the *potvibhaga* (subdivision) of a Brahman *jati*, that is, he would violate the existing inter-*jati* barrier. He would make his daughters marry outside their Konkanastha *jati* into the Karhades and Deshasthas. He would bring to fruition the idea of inter-caste marriage which Lokahitvadi had germinated three decades earlier.

Govind Babaji's musings on the subject of inter-caste Brahman marriage, his views on the varna system, his advice to the ruling elite to correct unsavory social customs, and his personal trauma in coping with the concerns of his family, are all embedded in his three open letters in Marathi which I translate below.

LETTER 1[29]

On Girls' Marriages

All over the world, at all times, health (*arogya*) is an essential component of the survival of mankind and nature. A person may possess pots full of *ghee*, sacks full of sugar, a five-story palace to live in, and a bed made of sandalwood, but what good is that bed for a person ridden with bronchial tuberculosis (*kaph kshayaci vyatha*)? All his possessions conducive to pleasure cause him pain. It is truly said that a healthy body is the greatest asset of wealth. In order to ensure the presence of worthy offspring, one needs a healthy body; without it one cannot expect to have healthy progeny. In the absence of healthy progeny no nation (*rashtra*) can prosper. Those desirous of raising the nation to the heights (*deshas cadhtya kalevar ananyaci icha*) must take every measure (*ilaj*) possible to ensure the healthy growth of their progeny. There are many ruinous restrictions, imposed in our Dharmashastras, and endorsed by our false customs, which cause malfunctioning of our state of health. One such rule is 'girls should be given in marriage within the caste.' In bygone days, inter-caste marriages were practised by the four varnas. As a result, this *arya bhumi* saw the likes of the great warriors and truth seekers such as Bhishma and Drona. As long as the practice of inter-caste marriage was in vogue,

Hindustan's glory reverberated all over. The day when Hindustan became afflicted by the terrible disease (*maharoga*) of caste differentiation (*varna bheda*), like roosting chickens, we took refuge in our little nests. The country was ruined to cinders. We gave up going abroad. We became obsessed by the notion of pollution at every stride. Within Hindustan thousands of castes emerged. And girls' marriages took place within their *jatis*. Inter-dining between the *jatis* ceased. Every *jati* turned itself into a nation (*partook jat eke rashtrac banli*). In such an anomalous state of affairs, we find an abundance of unmarried daughters in many *jatis*, without spouses to wed. Like a troublesome contraption to be removed from the neck (*galyamtil lachanda kadhun takave*), beautiful and accomplished daughters are discarded in gutters by getting them wed to fools or disease ridden men by offering them money out of one's pocket. It is known that the Kulin Brahmans of Bengal, each one of them, have ten to fifteen wives. Similarly in our neighbouring Gujarat, we find such [polygamous] examples in the Audica and Sahasra jatis. When I was at Siddhapur [Gujarat], upon inquiry I discovered that, out of fifty odd men, only two will have one wife. In the *jat* living next to those, we find drought of girls (*mulica itka dushkal*). Witness the Nagars. In Charotar [district], with the exception of the group of twelve villages, in other villages only one among two to three brothers ever get married. On the other hand, in the twelve villages men have two to three wives each.[30] The girls [in those *jatis*] despite being unhealthy and dirty (*khebad lebad*), and even if one were prepared to pay a thousand to two thousand rupees [to wed them] are not [easily] available [for marriage]. Pity those many men [in such communities], who, unable to contract marriage, die in that unmarried state (*avivahitace avivahit marun jatata*). Although our [country's] population on paper stands at 250 millions (*pancavis koti*), in reality we are a nation formed of many units [of *jatis*], each unit incorporating a membership of five to ten thousand, and those, when counted, reach the figure of 250 millions. According to Milton's statement the unity of a nation (*rashtrace aikya*) comprise: community of religion, community of games, community of language, and community of dress. This caste differentiation (*jati bheda*) is the contributing cause of a great loss of health among the citizens [of this country]. It is not my intention to ponder over these difficult issues. The usefulness of such thoughts would amount to something, if great personages and power-holders, among you, were to be convinced of the above comments [and to remedy the situation]. At this point in time I would merely comment on a tertiary matter of subdivisions (*pota behda*). The subdivisions I am referring to relate to a *jati* in which there already exists interdining (*annodaka vyavahara*); in the same *jati*, inter-marriages (*kanya vyavahara*) should take place without fear (*bindhok*). I am determined to pursue this matter.

If a routine is established to exchange daughters within only one restricted group (*ekac niyamit samudayamta*), the group's health gets adversely affected and ruined. Future generations in progression become weak and small. You will comprehend the matter with clarity when I explain with examples.

When the girl is escorted to the husband's home and on their way back home, the parents become despondent. They experience the same feelings during the marriage ceremony of *kanyadana* (giving of daughter), when the priest conveys the intentions of the patron (*yajamana*, the girl's father) and says to him, 'Sir, from this day onwards your daughter belongs to them.' Those who have experienced those [feelings] will know. Concluding from these examples, one may feel that by following the practice of giving daughters within a restricted group and within the family might be a good custom. Muslims allow marriage within the family [that is, marriage with first cousin]. However, the learned among Muslims these days feel that it is not a good custom to follow. But the writers of the Shastras have regarded such a marriage within family as a great sin. Seriously deliberating on marriage, within the patrilineal family (*sagotra*), they prohibited them. They did so in order to preserve the health of the future generations. For the same reason, sages like Yajnyavalkya and others have clearly stated that marriages within the *sagotra* and *sapinda* are totally prohibited.

The above point can be explicated. by resorting to examples from the vegetable world (*vanaspativarun*). If the seeds of the grain grown from the same soil are replanted two to four times in that soil, the quality of the grain produced is inferior and remains without nutrients (*nisatva*). When that grain is compared with grain produced from a soil which has experienced rotating grain seeds, the difference in quality between the two becomes all the more clear.

This differential quality is also noticed in the animal world. In places like Ahmedabad, the English government have farms to produce excellent breeds of horses for use in their military. The horses selected for cross-breeding are from Australia and Arabia and their brood is stronger and disease free as compared to the cross-breed horses originating from this country. Unhealthy progeny is burden on a country. In our land of the Bharat (*bharat bhumi*) the sages imposed restrictions [on marriages]. They would not allow progeny to be born unless a person was healthy. The Pandava raja suffered from tuberculosis, hence his wife was allowed to have children by *niyoga*. It is a well known fact in the Mahabharata that the progeny born of this union became brave warriors.

Compared to the Deshasthas and Karhades, the Konkanasthas are weak and of small stature. Among several reasons for this phenomenon is the fact that they do not receive and give their daughters [in marriage] outside their restricted group (*niyamit samudaya*). Our famous Balaji Bajirav Peshwa alias Nanasaheb [a Konkanastha] must have pondered over this matter, and appropriately married the daughter of a Deshastha Brahman named Vakhare of Paithan, whose *wada* in Shanivarpeth, Pune, is well-known even today.

A good example of how progeny becomes frail and small by reproducing within the same bloodline is exemplified by the case of a lapdog. These dogs are kept by wives of the English and are seen occasionally when the latter go for outings in their carriages. The dogs are as delicate as flowers; like a folded handkerchief they could be inserted in one's pocket! Their physical state is so frail that they become sick instantly at the slightest shift in the weather. These are carefully bred. The litter of a bitch are bred repeatedly without cross-breeding with other species of dogs, and after a few generations a new breed emerges (*kahi pidhyamni hi jat banate*). If this new breed were to be compared in stamina and strength with other dogs, then the gap between them becomes evidently clear.

The effect of this bad practice is well known in England. Many years past, the widespread convention of its aristocrats (*lard lokant*) was not to marry with the members of other classes. The giving and receiving of the girls was restricted within this class. As a result there was a considerable increase of congenital and inherited diseases within this class, such as wickedness, imbecility, and epilepsy. These afflictions became the traits of the aristocrats. If it became known that someone was down with epilepsy, people assumed that person to be an aristocrat. The unhappy consequence of inter-marriages, limited to the group, was realized by the intelligent among [the aristocrats] and they started the convention of marrying out of their class. Since then, the progeny of the aristocrats have grown to be strong, without illness. The glory and the heroism of the British royalty rests considerably on their aristocracy. This is the lesson of history.

OBSERVATIONS

Quite appropriately, the title of Govind Babaji's leaflet, written in the 1880s, is 'On Girls' Marriages' (*kanyavivaha sambandhi*). Govind Babaji lashes out at the caste system and its adverse effect in dividing Indians into several thousand nations. Calling caste a great disease, *maharoga*, he makes caste divisions responsible for the regression of Indian society from its glorious past. As long as there were unrestricted intermarriages among the four varnas, Indian society produced heroes, warriors, and truth seekers. Each caste became a nation in its own right when people began to marry within their restricted group and stopped interdining with other castes. Govind Babaji then describes situations in which, in one community there would be an excess of marriageable girls, and in others, a dearth.

Govind Babaji turns next to the science of eugenics. Marrying within a restricted group is positively harmful to the next generation. The offspring become weak. Govind Babaji cites the wisdom of the *shastrakaras* who disallowed *sagotra* and *sapinda* marriages. He does not want a diseased person to marry, because the next generation may inherit the disease and be a liability to the nation. He applauds the efforts of the ancient sages of India who would not allow children to be born of a diseased person. He cites the example of Pandu raja whose wife was allowed to have children by *niyoga*, because her husband was suffering from tuberculosis.

In order to illustrate the point how marrying within a narrow group is harmful to people, Govind Babaji presents examples from the animal and vegetable kingdom. Better breeds of horses result from cross-breeding; crops give a better yield if the same seed is not repeated. His 'lapdog' example demonstrates how a weak breed of dog is created without cross-breeding with other species. He ends his discussion by looking at the English class system. He says imbecility and other congenital diseases which were found within the English aristocracy were due to the custom of marrying within a limited circle of families to maintain the purity of the class. According to Govind Babaji, the English relented when they discovered the adverse effects of this practice. Once the aristocracy started marrying outside their class, its vigour, the mainstay of British royalty, has increased, according to Govind Babaji.

In order to legitimize his point concerning the opening of *jati* gates to neighbourhood Brahmans, Govind Babaji juxtaposes examples from the Western history with those from India's past without bias. He praises the *shastrakaras* for their rational and scientific thinking on heath and healthy progeny. However, he ought to have noticed that the same *shastrakaras* were responsible for consolidating the rigid *jati* society.

The leaflet is important for an understanding of Govind Babaji's overlapping ideas of nationalism and a barrier-free caste society. But Govind Babaji will pursue only a limited goal: to break existing marriage barriers among the Deshasthas, Konkanasthas and Karhades, the three Brahman, *potvibhag*, subdivisions, of Maharashtra. As stated in his 1982 letter, he would leave the task of demolishing varna barriers to future generations.

LETTER 2[31]

To
Rajmanya Rajashri, Nagpur
27 August 1882

I had informed you earlier that I shall be communicating with you on matters of public interest (*sarvajanik kamat*). I shall now do so.

I have two daughters. Although I had initially thought of reviving the ancient custom of intermarriages between the four varnas, I am convinced that it is not the right time for reintroducing the old practice—one should leave this work to the next generation (*he kam pudhil samtativar takle pahije*). But it is an extremely bad situation in which there are no intra-marriages (*kanyavyavahar*) allowed among Brahmans who otherwise practice interdining (*annodaka vyavahara*). Reflecting on this situation, I was determined to arrange my daughters' marriages [to spouses from other Brahman castes of Maharashtra]. Accordingly, last year I got my elder daughter married. I shall now narrate the difficulties I encountered in pursuing my goal.

I inserted an advertisement, signed 'one Konkanastha', stating, 'I am willing to give my daughter in marriage to a Karhade or Deshastha Brahman'(*mi apli kanya deshastha kimva karhade brahamanas denyas tayar ahe*) [See the issue of *Induprakash*, 17 September 1879]. In response to my advertisement, I received ten to twelve letters from the gentlemen who expressed their desire to enter into matrimony. But most of the letters turned out to be useless (*nirupyogasarakhi hoti*); for instance, one suitor had passed his forties (*calisi ultun gelela*), one had a wife and desired a second. One letter, however, was found worth pondering over, but that gentleman was living far way on the borders of Mysore state. Although he was a Karhade Brahman, he was surely a Karnataka man (*nival kanada*). There was none, upholding this worthy public cause, coming forth from Maharashtra country *desh* (region). Quite obviously, it is not a false dictum that in a nation (*rashtra*), which is under foreign rule, the people loose their intrepidity (*dhirya*) with the loss of their sovereign power (*satta*). After corresponding with the [Karhade Brahman] it was decided to give him my daughter in marriage. At that time my family members were at Vasai my town (*majhe gavi vasait*). When they came to know of this [marriage arrangement], all of a sudden they turned against it. From time to time I used to discuss with my wife my intentions [about my daughters' intra-caste weddings], and because of our immutable camaraderie (*satatce sahavasamule*) I had her tacit approval (*garbhit sammati*). But when my wife and my elder sister realized that the [prospective groom] was living in a far away place like Malabar, where grows *veldoda* (cardamom), and in a land with totally different crop and harvest (*pikpani*), their eyes became red with crying (*radun dole lala kele*). The women from the neighbourhood (*shejari pajarni*), when they came to visit, had no other subject to discuss. My son-in-law's name is Huccarav Anant Dongare. As this name is not found among Brahmans of Maharashtra, the household priest had his doubts about the kind of Brahman my son-in-law might turn out to be. Similarly, my affinal relations, friends and acquaintances (*soyaredhayre*) became suspicious, and they collectively wrote me a letter stating that they were not pleased with my choice of the groom (*varyojana*). When I received this letter, I took leave of absence and immediately came home [to Vasai], and discovered that all were behaving towards me as if stuffed with anger (*dhuspusleli*), and no one was willing to talk to me.

One day, at noon, as I was sitting in my house facing the street, my daughter came to me with crying eyes and pleaded with me. She said, 'Baba, mother and my aunt (*atya*) are constantly reading your letters from Baroda. Yesterday they told me about [the news] my . . . [lines missing] . . . they say that, like a prisoner with a life sentence, who is sent across the black water, you are sending me away. They are saying that you are sending me to a country across the seven seas where Marathi is not spoken. Father, if you won't get angry with me, may I ask you a question? Why are you giving me away to a distant land? What crime have I committed? Listening to her pathetic and anguished words, I cannot describe to you the state of my mind. Somehow or other, I comforted her by telling her sweetly the tale of the marriage of Draupadi. I think you may not be even familiar with this anecdote. From childhood, in the process of familiarizing ourselves with English books (*ingreji buke*), we tend to ignore many of our Puranic tales of morality (*nitibodhacya katha*). I shall, therefore, recount to you the core of the story.

The Pandavas on their wandering, arriving in the city of Drupad, reached the house of a potter. That very day was the *svayamvara* (a woman choosing her own spouse) of Draupadi. Drupad had vowed that he would offer the princess to any person who, looking down at the reflection of a fish in the oil in a cauldron, would pierce the right eye of the revolving fish. The [Pandav] boys routinely went begging in the marriage hall, and came to know that none had won the prize. One of the boys, in his garments made of bark, stretching the bow with an arrow pierced the right eye of the fish. The kings and the people assembled there became awestruck. But King Drupad abiding by his word gave Draupadi to that boy who lived on alms. The uproar generated by the women and the priests of [Drupad] is described in detail in the Mahabharata. I told her this anecdote and pacified her.

Considering the [uneasy] situation in my household, and the obstructions the townspeople might bring to bear on the [wedding ceremony], I got her married in Mumbai. The function was attended by: Ravbahadur Gopalrav Hari Deshmukh, the owner of Induprakash, Ravbahadur Balaji Pandurang, Ravbahadur Khanderav Chimanrav and others. This is how I ended this matter.

I am now obliged to arrange my younger daughter's marriage. I am determined to marry her to a Deshastha. But I have not yet found a suitable groom for her. I am, therefore, deeply concerned over this matter. [Please] inform me if you find a bright boy as a match [for my daughter]. The boy should not be older than twenty-five years. Our *gotra* is Shandilya. The girl is thirteen years old. We would give an affordable dowry of 150 rupees. Please respond [to this letter].

Your friend,
Govind Babaji Joshi, Vasaikar

OBSERVATIONS

This is a public letter, addressed to the citizens of Nagpur, justifying his daughter's inter-caste marriage: how it took place, and reaction it generated in his near circle of relatives and friends. Govind Babaji in his letter also wants the people of Nagpur to support his inter-caste marriage crusade by recommending a suitable Deshastha groom for his younger daughter. Govind Babaji ideally would like to go back to ancient times where there were, according to him, no restrictions on inter-caste marriages among the four varnas. But he is realistic enough, by his own admission, to assign the breaking of caste barriers to future generations. He is preoccupied with the unification, through inter-marriage, of the three main branches of Maharashtra Brahmans, who practice interdining, but not intermarriage. Govind Babaji would like to set things right by personal example. He would marry his daughters to a member of the other two Maharashtrian Brahman castes. His individual efforts to arrange such a marriage must have come to naught. He had to overcome double jeopardy; his daughters were past the age of puberty in a society where the pre-puberty marriages of the girls was a norm. Second, he had to find suitable spouses from outside his Chitpavan (Konkanastha) *jati*. He had to resort to a matrimonial advertisement in a newspaper which was, presumably, an innovative thing to do in 1879. Govind Babaji's choice of the *Induprakash* for his advertisement is significant. Its readership would be naturally socially progressive, for the journal was notable for spreading radical social ideas. For instance, Vishnushastri Pandit, the pro-widow remarriage advocate, was the editor of the Marathi section of *Induprakash*. Considering the poor response Govind Babaji received from the advertisement, the reality of inter-caste Brahman marriage was difficult to sell. Eventually, he settled on a respondent from the far south, who, except for his Maharashtrian Karhade origin, had domiciled long enough in Karnataka to assume a Kannada identity. Since no suitable match was found among Brahmans of Maharashtra proper, Govind Babaji, donning his nationalist cap, was quick to attribute this evident lack of enthusiasm for inter-caste marriages in Maharashtra to its dispirited males under foreign domination, who had apparently lost their grit along with their freedom. Govind Babaji's deductions appear clear; a free nation state, *rashtra*, will rejuvenate pride and confidence in Maharashtra, and will lead to a desired social change.

This public letter also exposes Govind Babaji's inner conflict arising out of his convictions and the resistance with which it was met by his close network of friends and relatives. He is deeply touched by the conversation with his daughter and had a hard time justifying his choice of groom to his daughter. Yet his reason for citation of the story of marriage of Draupadi in the *Mahabharata* to his daughter is hard to follow. He probably wanted to impress on his thirteen-year-old daughter that like Drupad her father was a man of determination and went by his word to choose the best qualified man for his daughter by arranging a difficult contest. Govind Babaji's newspaper advertisement was a sort of contest, the prize was Govind Babaji's daughter. Inadvertently, Drupad, not knowing the Pandavas, chose the right person for his daughter Draupadi. Govind Babaji, similarly, chose the previously unknown person as the best spouse among other candidates. By marrying her future husband she would be happy like Draupadi. The tantrum thrown by the women of Drupad's household and his priest, are like those of the women of his family and his priest, but it should be taken in stride in order to attain a higher goal of producing healthy progeny and thereby uplifting the nation—an idea he stressed in the first letter.

His friends and the members of his immediate family expressed doubts about his choice of groom, ostensibly because the latter came from the south, a cultural stranger, but in reality the matter was probably compounded by the fact that it was an inter-caste marriage—how dare a Chitpavan girl marry a Karhade boy? Sensing a real hindrance from the Vasai crowd, and from his loved and near ones, Govind Babaji chose to perform the wedding ceremony in Mumbai. The attendance of Gopal Hari Deshmukh (Lokahitvadi) and the owner of the

Induprakash, established Govind Babaji's fraternal-solidarity with the socially progressive group in Maharashtra.

LETTER 3[32]

To
Shrimant Sarkar Sayajirav Gaikwad Senakhaskhel Samsher Bahadur, Samsthan Badoda, Badoda, February 1883

Maharaj, currently, out of several very important areas of public interest ((*sarvatrik sambandhane*), the prohibition of marriages of girls and boys in their childhood is most worthy of consideration. A writer has stated in his book:

> Due to English education and due to interactions with Europeans, the natives might become great and powerful (*netiv lok thor va baladhya hotil*). But if they do not renounce the ways of their ancestors (*purvaja*) of practicing child marriages, and if their women are not given their rightful freedom (*yogya svatantrata*), the natives may talk like parrots as much as they could, but all their accomplishment will be judged as those of a small child.

I have two daughters. I am determined to arrange their marriages to conform, as much as feasible, to two of my goals. First, the daughters should not be married in their childhood. Second, the marriages of my two daughters should be so arranged that it should facilitate inter-marriages among the Konkanasthas, Deshastha and Karhade Maharashtrian Brahmans. In accordance with these resolutions, three years ago I got my elder daughter married. Following is the account of the event.

At the time of the marriage of my elder daughter I gave an advertisement in a newspaper that 'I am ready to give my daughter to either a Deshastha or a Karhade Brahman.' Out of the several responses I received pertaining to this advertisement, I was satisfied only with the letter of a Karhade Brahman living on the borders of Mysore state. I therefore started corresponding with this man, and subsequently I gave my daughter to him. This gentleman is assistant teacher in Karwar High school The kinds of difficulties (*adcani*) I experienced during the course of this marriage is stated in the attached letter [the letter of 1882 written to the Nagpur people].

I have recorded, in the attached letter, the questions my daughter had asked me at that time. I forthwith pacified her by giving her explanations. I was perturbed by her agonizing questions that had emerged spontaneously out of her deep anxiety, and I could not get over this trauma for several days. The saying of the sages that God never deserts the believer who follows a true path, became true. By God's grace, the day and night worry that I had about this marriage, dissipated. My daughter has found a good match. Her husband is a decent person. This is the story of the marriage of my first born daughter.

I am intent on getting my second daughter married in the month of *Margashirsha* (November-December). I am worried because I have not yet found a groom as expected. As I gave my elder daughter in marriage to a Karhade Brahman, I am determined to give the younger one to a Deshastha Brahman. I am repeating the same efforts (*yatna*) that I had put in to secure a husband for my elder daughter, but to this day I have yet to find a proper match for her.

History teaches by examples that, wherever the subjects are unwilling to take progressive measures due to ignorance, their protectors, the kings, or the learned ones of their country, lead them on to a true path (*satya marga*) by fiat.

The subjects are generally unwilling to accept innovative ideas, whatever might be their worth. In these situations the kings and the learned ones, by their noble deportment, guide the subjects to embrace the correct path (*yogya margas lavitat*). During the regime of the Russian emperor, Peter the Great, Russians valued the custom of keeping long beards and wearing flowing gowns as symbols of great honour, vied with each other in observing this dress code, especially the courtiers. The emperor had long thought of abolishing this custom, and from time to time recommended his people to give up the custom, but to no avail. In the end he himself shaved his beard and shortened his gown. The emperor also ordained that no one should spend more than a fixed amount for a dress. Within a short time a new custom (*navi rit*) [of shaven beard and shortened gown] came into vogue, and is maintained to this day.

The time when potatoes were first introduced into Europe, there was widespread belief in France that eating them resulted in disease. Therefore people did not consume them that much. The king of France, however, began cultivating potato patches in his palace garden, and he would visit the garden accompanied by his entourage. Sometimes he would send them food prepared with potatoes. With his efforts, the people lost their misgivings about potatoes, and potato eating started all over [France].

Until the time of the Bajirav Peshwa [1720-40] there was no interdining between the Konkanasthas and the Deshastha Brahmans. Because of this foolish division (*vedya bhedamule*), constant bickering between the two used to flare up during the north Indian campaigns of the Peshwa. This situation was like the adage 'eighteen hearths for seventeen foreigners'. On the occasion of a dinner given by the Panta Pratinidhi, Konkanasthas and Deshasthas sat and ate together in the same *pangat* (line), thereby breaking, once and for all, the taboo on interdining between the two.

With the rise in power of the great and famous Pilajirav Gaikwad [the founder of the Gaikwad dynasty of Baroda], his army grew in strength. Gujarat has hot summer months, has deep wells, and has settlements of Muslims spread all over the land, therefore, the Marathas from the south would not take appointments as grooms for horses and as water-carriers. It is obvious that this should be so. The [Marathas] who had the propensity to lord over all of Hindustan, why would they choose to work at these [lowly] jobs? (*ughadac ahe, sarva hindusthanvar saradari karnyaci jamci yogyata te ahi cakari kay mhanun patkartil?*). Hence the Gonds from the hills of the Satpuda range were brought into the kingdom and were employed as grooms. From that time to this day the same people work in the army as grooms, and are called, *vavchi*. Similarly, Muslims are employed in the army as water-carriers.

It is quite appropriate to surmise from the above examples that wherever there is patronage and support of the royalty (*rajashraya*), the goals are achievable without hindrance (*nirvighnapane*). For this reason I plead with you with great humility that should you lend a helping hand to my cause, the cause will have enhanced itself, and will successfully reach its fruition; and people will acquire courage to enact the practice [of intermarrying within the three Brahman castes of Maharashtra].

Fifteen years ago in Mumbai when the first [Brahman] widow remarriage took place, the High Court judges, and the members of government's law council, along with their families, attended the wedding ceremony. The gentleman who married the widow was given a lucrative job in the High Court, and to this day he enjoys (*upabhog*) that position.

The main reason for submitting this information at your feet is: I shall act out my resolution to give my daughter in marriage to a studious Deshastha Brahman boy; it does not matter if that boy lives on alms [to carry on with his studies]. In this land of the

Bharat, you are a sovereign of great fame. The bonds which unite us are our country (*desh*), our nation (*rashtra*), and our religion (*dharma*). I appeal to you to grace my daughter's marriage ceremony with your presence. My daughter should not spend her life in misery on account of my resolution. If you feel that what I resolve doing is for the good of the country, notwithstanding in minuscule form (*yatkincit*), then after the wedding, I hope you will provide for my daughter's husband a suitable job in your kingdom.

Your most humble servant,
Govind Babaji Joshi

OBSERVATIONS

Govind Babaji's letter to the Maharaja of Baroda continues the same topic of inter-caste Brahman marriage as that found in the February 1882 Nagpur letter. Govind Babaji was an employee of the Maharaja of Baroda, working as his Public Preacher (*sarvjanik vakhyata*), and the humble tone of his letter makes that clear. Govind Babaji reiterates his two resolutions that his children would not be married in their childhood, and that he would promote marriages between Konkanasthas, Deshasthas and Karhades, by his personal example of marrying his daughters out of the Konkanastha caste. He recounts the difficulties he encountered in marrying his daughter to a Karhade Brahman from the south. Govind Babaji explains to the Maharaja the anguish he underwent trying to pacify his daughter who was questioning his motive for giving her away to a strange man from a distant land.

According to Govind Babaji, political leverage is a requirement for changes in social habits of people. Govind Babaji argues, by citing historical precedents, that royal interventions are effective instruments to introduce and promote changes in the customs and habits of people. Therefore the ruling elite should, by setting personal examples, enforce change. In other words, social change is dependent on the political power of the land. Govind Babaji's repertory of examples from world history is impressive. He gives examples of the Russian Czar, Peter the Great, and how he ended the custom of courtiers wearing long flowing gowns and long beards, by trimming his own beard and wearing a short gown, and by fixing the amount one can spend on the formal dress. The introduction and popularization of potatoes by the king of France is another example to prove how the political elites could be harbingers of change in any society. To make the equation of political power and change relevant to India, Govind Babaji gives examples from Maratha history. Pant Pratinidhi, a powerful minister had promoted interdining between the Deshasthas and Konkanasthas, by inviting them to his house for a dinner. Govind Babaji then gives the example of Pilaji Gaikwad of Baroda. Pilaji started using Muslims as water carriers in his army because of the availability of a large number of Muslim hired hands in Gujarat, with its hot summers, and deep wells. Clearly, by initiating this move, Pilaji had broken a cardinal shastric rule not to accept water from *mlecchas*! But this was due also to the unwillingness of the proud Marathas to do such chores, adds Babaji. Babaji also comments on the employment of the tribal Gonds as grooms in the Baroda army. He thus impresses on the Maharaja that absolute power can transcend, and subvert, the established habits and customs of the people. Royalty and educated elites, as leaders of the community, have their special roles to play in the changing social norms. With their patronage, the new social customs could become a reality.

The pragmatic side of Govind Babaji surfaces in the last two paragraphs of the letter. He wants the Maharaja to attend the wedding of his second daughter and, what is more, to give his future son-in-law a job in his kingdom. He gives an analogy of the Mumbai government's patronage of the marriage of a Brahman widow, Venutai Bapat, to Vinayak Karmarkar that had taken place in Mumbai. The British officers who had attended the ceremony evidently gave a good job to the married man.[33]

CONCLUDING REMARKS

Govind Babaji was an Indian nationalist who was in favour of the democratic model of government. He would claim his trip to Madras in 1887, to attend the third session of Indian National Congress, a pilgrimage to a sacred complex. By listening to the 'ambrosia-like (*amrit tulya*) speeches' of the distinguished speakers there, he 'was filled with priceless (*amulya*) and sanctified notion of love for his country' (*svadesh pritici pavitrata*).[34] He talks about the Congress session as being instrumental in planting 'the seedling of love for the nation' (*rashtriya premace bijaropan*).[35] And he would spend time mixing with other delegates of the Congress 'happily in brotherly love' (*bandhu pritice sukhat*).[36] However, Govind Babaji did not lose his Maharashtrian pride and identity. He carried a picture of *param pratapi* Shivaji Maharaj in his pocket during his journey to Madras, and would show it to strangers and try to explain the greatness of Shivaji, if any one cared to listen.[37] Above all Govind Babaji believed in grassroots changes in Indian society, in making it more integrated and open. In his writings he links national interests with parochial interests like the eradication of caste barriers, more specifically, the inter-caste barriers found among the three Brahman *jatis* of Maharashtra.

In 1887, Govind Babaji Joshi called on Jotiba Phule on his death bed, and writes approvingly about him:

> I have known Jotiba for the past fifteen years. Jotiba's creed is that one should act according to one's conscience and convictions and ignore people's criticisms. One should do what one considers to be the right thing. If this quality were to be found among learned people, the country would have profited much.[38]

Like Phule, Govind Babaji lived up to his convictions.

NOTES

1. G.G. Jambhekar's three volume work (*Bal Gangadhar Shastri Jambhekar,* Pune: Lokashikshashan Karyalaya, 1950) is a primary source for the study of Bal Shastri Jambhekar's life and early nineteenth-century Mumbai society.

2. Richard Tucker's article ('From Dharmashastra to Politics', *Indian Social and Economic History Review*, 1970) succinctly analyses Ranade's writings on topics such as child marriage and widow remarriage, and his public embarrassment when he took an eleven year old girl as his second wife.
3. See S.R. Tikekar (ed.), *Lokahitvadinci shatpatre*: Pune: Vidyamandir Prakashan, 1963; See also Arun Joshi (ed.), *Lokahitvadi nave samshodhan*, Mumbai: Maharashtra Rajya Granthalaya Sangh, 1977. Joshi produces little known Gujarati letters of Lokahitvadi, written in his mature period in early 1880s. For a stinging critique of Lokahitvadi, see Pratibha Bhattacharya's chapter in this book.
4. For bibliographical information, see Ian Raeside and Pratibha Bhattacharya's chapters in this book. V.S. Khandekar's (*Agarkar caritra*, Pune: Ganesh Mahadev ani Campani, 1932), sketch of Agarkar's life and work is still a required reading.
5. J.V. Naik's chapter in this book is probably the best concise account of this little known, yet progressive thinker and journalist of early nineteenth-century Maharashtra. Naik gives a multidimensional analysis of Bhau Mahajan's nationalistic journalism, and his role as a social critic.
6. Vishnushastri Pandit's widow-remarriage crusade in nineteenth-century Maharashtra remains the topic of analysis in most Marathi books dealing with the widow-remarriage movement. See S.G. Malshe and Nanda Apte, *Vidhava vivaha calval* (1800-1900), Mumbai: Stri Samshodhan Kendra, Shri Nathibai Damodar Thakarsi Mahila Vidyapith (S.N.D.T. Women's University), 1978: 28-68. For an analytical bakground of the widow-remarriage movement, and to place Vishnushastri Pandit's contributions to this field, see Pratibha Ranade, *Stri prashnaci carca: ekonisave shatak*, Mumbai: Popular Prakashan, 1991, 168-292. A short but useful biographical information is found in S.S. Pandit's, *Vishnu Parashuram Shastri Pandit yance caritra*, Pune: Vidhva Mandal, 1936.
7. Arun Joshi, *Govind Babaji Joshi Vasaikar: ek upekshit samaj sudharak*, Thane: Marathi Grantha Sangrahalaya, 1981. His appendices, 104-44, deal with the reports and the open letters Govind Babaji distributed to the public. I have translated Govind Babaji's three letters from his Appendix DI, 121-8.
8. See Arun Joshi, *Upekshit sudharak*, 28-47.
9. See N.K. Wagle, 'Govindrav Babaji Joshi Goes to Madras: A "Diary" of the Third Indian National Congress', *The Congress and Indian Nationalism*, John L. Hill (ed.), London: Curzon Press, 1991: 114-32. This article was based on Govind Babaji's "Diary" (in Marathi), Vadodara: Government Printing Press, 1888. I had managed to purchase the diary in 1973 in Pune. Arun Joshi (*Upekshit sudharak*, 97) claims that he did not have access to Govind Babaji's diary, since it had been discarded by the Baroda Public Library. For Govind Babaji's other nationalist activities, see Arun Joshi, *Upekshit sudharak*, 92-3.
10. See Pratibha Ranade, *Stri pashnaci carca*, 75-7.
11. See J.V. Naik's chapter in this book.
12. *Prabhakar*, 9 February 1842. Mumbai: Sahitya Sahakar Sangh Prakashan, reprinted the 1841-2 issues in 1975.
13. *Prabhakar*, 17 May 1847.
14. S.R. Tikekar (ed.), *Lokahitvadi*, 315. The date of the letter is not given, but from the internal evidence it appears to have been written in the late 1840s.
15. *Native Opinion*, October 1973, quoted in Arun Joshi, *Upekshit sudharak*, 59.
16. Arun Joshi, *Upekshit sudharak*, 72.
17. Ibid.
18. Wagle, *Madras Diary*, 115.
19. *Induprakash*, 31 March 1884.
20. Pratibha Ranade, *Stri Prashnaci Carca*, 79; see also Richard Tucker, 'From Dharmashastra to Politics', 333-8.

21. See Pratibha Ranade's analysis of the debates between the orthodox and liberal parties on this issue, *Stri Pashnaci Carca*, 92-160.
22. Govind Babaji Joshi, *Hindu lokas vinanti*, Vadodara: Central Gujarat Press, 1885: 7, 8.
23. Govind Babaji, *Hindu lokas vinanti*, 14-20.
24. Ibid.
25. Arun Joshi, *Upekshit sudharak*, 62.
26. Ibid., 64.
27. *Darpan*, 30 March to 27 April 1832.
28. *Prabhakar*, 17 December 1848; Tikekar, *Lokahitvadi*, 361.
29. Arun Joshi, *Upekshit sudharak*, Appendix DI, 120-4.
30. I have incorporated Govind Babaji's asides and further explanations in the main body of the text. Arun Joshi reproduces them as footnotes in the appendix.
31. Arun Joshi, *Upekshit sudharak*, Appendix DI, 126-8.
32. Ibid., DI, 123-5.
33. See Pratibha Ranade, *Stri Prashnaci Carca*, 255-6. The date of the marriage mentioned there is 15 April 1869. She has taken the information from S.S. Pandit's, *Visnushastri Pandit*, 30-4. However, in my personal collection I have a copy that the author, S.S. Pandit, presented to one Nanasaheb. In the copy, Pandit corrects the date in his own handwriting as 15 June 1869.
34. Wagle, *Madras Diary*, 121. Govind Babaji emerges in the diary as an Indian nationalist who refers to India as *Bharat* and *Arya Bhumi*, the model for the future Indian nationalist government. That he was a Maharashtrian proud of his Maharashtrian heritage is clearly established in his diary. In fact, like many Maharashtrian nationalists of his generation, he would reconcile Indian nationalism with his Maharashtrian identity. Govind Babaji's major work is his book, *Gelya tis varshapurvice lok va tyanya samjuti athava majhe pravasaci hakikat*, published by him privately.
35. *Madras Diary*, 121.
36. Ibid., 123.
37. Ibid., 119.
38. Ibid., 115.

REFERENCES

Darpan, Marathi Journal (1832-40).

Joshi, Arun (ed.), 1977, *Lokahitvadi nave samshodhan*, Mumbai: Maharashtra Rajya Granthalaya Sangh.

———, 1981, *Govind Babaji Joshi Vasaikar: ek upekshit samaj sudharak*, Thane: Marathi Grantha Sangrahalaya.

Joshi, Govind Babaji, 1885, *Hindu lokas vinanati*, Vadodara: Central Gujarat Press.

———, 1896, *Gelya tis varshapurvice lok va tyancya samjuti athava majhe pravasaci hakikat*, Vadodara: Author.

Jambhekar, G.G., 1950, *Bal Gangadhar Shastri Jambhekar*, 3 vols, Pune: Lokashikshasan Karyalaya.

Khandekar, V.S., 1932, *Agarkar caritra*, Pune: Ganesh Mahadev ani Campani.

S.G. Malshe and Nanda Apte, *Vidhva vivaha calval (1800-1900)*, Mumbai: Stri Samshodhan Kendra, Shri Nathibai Damodar Thakarsi Mahila Vidyapith.

Pandit, S.S., 1936, *Parashuram Shastri Pandit yance caritra*, Pune: Vidhva Mandal.

Prabhakar, Marathi Journal (1841-52?).

Ranade, Pratibha, 1991, *Stri prashnaci carca: ekonisave shatak*, Mumbai: Popular Prakashan.

Tikekar, S.R. (ed.), 1963, *Lokahitvadinci shatapatre*, Pune: Vidya Mandir Prakashan.

Tucker, Richard, 1970, 'From Dharmashastra to Politics', *Indian Social and Economic Review*, VII, 3, 325–46.

Wagle, N.K., 1991, 'Govind Babaji Joshi Goes to Madras: A Diary of the Third Indian National Congress', in *The Congress and Indian Nationalism*, Johan L. Hill (ed.), London: Curzon Press.

Contributors

PRATIBHA BHATTACHARYA is Reader, University of Delhi, Delhi, India.

UTTAM BHOITE is Vice-Chancellor, Bharatiya Vidyapith, Pune, India.

R.N. DANDEKAR is Professor, Bhandarkar Research Institute, Pune, India.

PHILIP ENGBLOM, 2115 Cumberland, Rockford, Illinois 61103, USA.

E. FASANA is Professor in Tristane University, Milan, Italy.

MILTON ISRAEL is Professor of History, University of Tononto, Canada.

MEERA KOSAMBI is Professor and Director of the Research Centre for Women's Studies at S.N.D.T. Women's University, Mumbai, India.

H. KOTANI is Professor, Tokyo Metropolitan University, Tokyo, Japan.

K. JAYANT LELE is Professor in the Departments of Political Studies and Sociology at Queen's University, Kingston, Canada.

J. MASSELOS is Reader in History at the University of Sydney, Australia.

J.V. NAIK is Professor of History, University of Bombay, Mumbai, India.

I.M.P. RAESIDE is Reader, School of Oriental Studies, University of London, London, England.

AROON TIKEKAR is the Editor, *Lokasatta*, Mumbai, India.

RAJENDRA VORA is Professor of Political Science, University of Poona, Pune, India.

N.K. WAGLE is Professor of History and Director, Centre for South Asian Studies, University of Toronto, Canada.

Index